Lifestyle

English for work, socializing & travel

Pre-intermediate Coursebook

Vicki Hollett & Norman Whitby

Contents

1

A Present simple and continuous
B Present simple and adverbs of frequency
C **Communication strategies** Requests
D **Interaction** Networking

Building networks

Present simple and continuous

Listening: A chain of acquaintances

1 Shake hands with some other students in the class and introduce yourself. Make sure you know everyone's name.

2 Look at this chain of friends and acquaintances. How many countries do the people come from?

3 Work in pairs. Ask and answer these questions about each person in the chain.

1 Where does he/she live?

2 What does he/she do?

3 How does he/she know the other people in the chain?

4 1.1 Listen to three different people in the chain answering questions. For each person decide who is talking and which person they are talking about.

Six degrees of separation

Six degrees of separation is the theory that any two people in the world are connected to each other through a short chain of friends and acquaintances. If the theory is true, on average, it takes just six people to make a chain. Take Gudrun in Germany and Chuck in the USA, for example. Look at how they are connected.

Gudrun Hohner
Waldorf, Germany
Financial controller

Gudrun works for the same software company as Sameer

Sameer Advani
Bangalore, India
Trainer

Sameer's niece is studying Maths at a university in the UK

Prema Ghuptah
Edinburgh, Scotland
Student

Prema is training for a marathon. She goes running with Christine.

Christine Cowper
Edinburgh, Scotland
Medical researcher

Christine belongs to the same professional organization as Rob. They often meet at conferences.

Rob Shaw
Philadelphia, USA
Doctor

Rob takes his car for service to Chuck's service station.

Chuck Bridges
Cherry Hill, USA
Service station owner

4

5 🔊 Listen again. Are these statements true (T) or false (F)? Correct the ones that are wrong.

1 Christine and Prema go running on Thursdays and Saturdays.

2 Prema is training for the New York marathon.

3 Gudrun works closely with the offices in India.

4 Sameer is working in Delhi at the moment.

5 Rob's waiting for the service station to call him.

6 Rob pays Chuck by credit card.

Grammar: Present simple and present continuous

6 Look at the table below and answer the questions.

Present simple and present continuous	
Present simple	*She **lives** in Waldorf.* *They **run** on Tuesdays and Saturdays.*
Present continuous	*We**'re working** on a project together.* *Rob **is waiting** for his car.*

1 Which tense do we use to talk about:

   a short-term or temporary activities?

   b long-term situations or regular activities?

2 Which tense do we form with the verb *to be* and *-ing*?

3 When do present simple verbs end in *s*?

4 Find more examples of these two present tenses in the chain.

>> For more information on the present simple and present continuous, see pages 164 and 165.

7 Complete this text. Use the present simple or present continuous form of the verbs in brackets.

It's 4:30 p.m. in Edinburgh and Prema ¹ *is training* (train) for the London marathon. She ² ____*tries*____ (try) to run for three hours every day. Her friend Christine sometimes ³_____ (come) with her but Prema is alone today. Christine ⁴_____ (attend) a conference in the United States.

Christine ⁵_____ (go) to medical conferences five or six times a year. Today she's in Philadelphia, with Rob. It's 11:30 a.m., they ⁶_____ (have) brunch together and Rob ⁷_____ (ask) her questions about her research.

Meanwhile it's 10:00 p.m. in Bangalore and Sameer ⁸_____ (check) his emails. There's a message from Gudrun but it isn't urgent. It's 5:30 p.m. in Germany and Gudrun ⁹_____ (get) ready to go home. Sameer can answer her message in the morning. He ¹⁰_____ (want) to go to bed now.

8 Do you know people in other parts of the world? What time is it for them now? What do you think they are doing?

Speaking: Finding connections

9 Work in pairs. Find out more about each other and find connections.

1 Tell each other about where you live and your job.

2 Tell each other about a project you are working on now.

3 Find some things you have in common. For example, interests you share or organizations you both belong to.

10 Report back to the class. Which pairs have most in common?

TALKING POINT
- Do you think the 'six degrees of separation' theory is true?
- Are you connected to anyone famous?

Reading: Animal networks

1 Look at the photo in the article below. What do you think the article is about? Think of some words you expect to read in the article.

2 Read the article and find out if you are right.

How does an ant change jobs?

We all know the benefits of meeting new people and having contacts. When there's a problem, we often know someone who can help, and life is usually more interesting if we have lots of friends and acquaintances. But it's not just people who network. Ants network, too.

Ants always live in colonies* and they do different things. Some work on nest maintenance and some carry food. An ant rarely changes its job. But sometimes things happen – rain damages the nest or some ants find extra food. When the colony needs more maintenance workers or food carriers, some ants change jobs.

Ant colonies don't have managers. The queen ant is the biggest ant and she lays eggs. But she never gives orders and nobody is in charge. So how do ants know what job to do? They network. If an ant meets a lot

of food workers, then it becomes a food worker, too so it changes jobs. The colony doesn't need a leader because the ants network. The system is very successful. Colonies survive for many years and ants cover the Earth.

colonies: groups of animals or plants of the same type that live and grow together

3 Find words in the article that mean the same as these words and phrases.

1 good things, advantages

2 people you have met but do not know well

3 meet and communicate with new people, especially people who can be useful in your job

4 the place where ants live (birds live in these places, too)

5 affects something so it doesn't work properly

6 work we do to keep something in order and working properly

7 continue to live, don't die

4 Answer these questions about the article.

1 What two benefits of networking does the article mention?

2 In what situations do ants change jobs?

3 Does the queen ant tell the other ants what to do?

4 How do ants know when to change jobs?

5 Discuss with a partner.
How do organizations survive a long time in your industry? Do they need …

• leaders who give orders?

• employees who network?

• something else? (what?)

Grammar: Present simple and adverbs of frequency

6 Look at the article again and find examples of these things.

1 Two question forms

2 Two negative forms

3 Six frequency adverbs (words that tell you how often things happen)

7 Complete the rules.

Present simple

+	*Ants* **live** *in colonies.* *The queen ant* **lays** *eggs.*	Add ¹_____ to the verb with *he/she/it.*
–	*Ant colonies* **don't have** *managers.* *The colony* **doesn't need** *a leader.*	Use ²_____ or _____ to form negatives.
?	**How does** *an ant* **change** *jobs?* **How do** *ants* **know** *what to do?*	Use a question word and ³_____ or _____ to form questions.

8 Where do we generally place frequency adverbs: before or after the verb? Write these frequency adverbs in the correct spaces in the table below.

> sometimes   usually   rarely   often

Frequency adverbs

Ants **always** *live in colonies.*   *She* **never** *gives orders.*

always	_____	_____	_____	_____	never
100%					0%

>> For more information on the present simple and frequency adverbs, see pages 164 and 165.

Speaking: Questionnaire

9 Work in pairs. Complete the questionnaire below and find out if you are good networkers. Ask the questions and make a note of your partner's answers.

10 Turn to File 6, page 140. Add up your partner's score and read your results together. Do you agree with them? How important is networking in your job?

11 Tell the class two things your partner does that are good ways to connect with other people.

Are you a good netw rker?

1 Do you belong to any professional or social organizations?
 a No
 b Yes, but I don't have much time for them.
 c Yes and I take an active role.

2 When you go to a social event, how many people do you talk to?
 a I try to talk to everyone if possible.
 b I usually talk to a lot of people.
 c I don't talk to many people. It's difficult to end conversations.

3 Do you remember people's names?
 a Yes, I always try to learn them.
 b I can never remember names.
 c I remember faces but not names.

4 When people give you their business cards, what do you do with them?
 a I put them in a box so I can find them if I need them.
 b I usually put their information on my computer.
 c I don't keep them. I just throw them away or lose them.

5 What do you say when someone asks you: 'What do you do?'
 a I tell them my job title.
 b I say a sentence or two about my job.
 c I explain who I work for and what I do, and I ask them about their job.

6 When you leave a job, do you keep in touch with your colleagues?
 a I try to keep in touch with a lot of them.
 b I try to leave on good terms but I don't stay in contact.
 c If I don't like someone or something, I say so when I leave.

7 How often do you carry business cards?
 a Always. I have some with me now.
 b I don't use business cards.
 c I sometimes take them to business and social events.

8 What do you usually do on Friday night?
 a I go home and turn on the television.
 b I usually go out. There is often an event or a party somewhere.
 c I try to get home early and spend time with my family.

TALKING POINT   Describe how networking has helped you in your career or your life, for example, with finding a job or solving a problem.

Reading: Learning from children

1 Answer these questions.

What are some useful things that …

1 parents can teach their children?

2 parents can learn from their children?

2 Look at the article. What does the writer think parents can learn from their children? Do you agree?

How children get what they want

Children are very good at getting what they want. Take this example:

'Mum, can I go out and see Timmy for an hour?'

'Yes, of course.'

'I called Timmy and he's going swimming. Could I go with him?'

'Oh, OK then.'

'I don't have any money to get into the swimming pool. Could you give me some?'

'Well, all right then.'

'Would you give us *a lift* there?'

'I suppose so.'

'And could you possibly *pick* us *up* later?'

Hang on a minute! What's going on here? First they ask for something small and then they build on that to get big things. And it works because after we say 'yes', we want to think we did the right thing. We don't want to *contradict* ourselves, so we continue to say 'yes'.

So here's something we can learn from our children: how to *manipulate* people and make them do what we want.

3 Find words and phrases in italics in the article which mean the same as these phrases.

1 say something different from what you said before

2 go and collect someone or something

3 a ride in a car

4 make someone do what you want by influencing or deceiving them

5 wait

4 Discuss these questions.

1 Are children good at making their parents do what they want? How? Why?

2 Think of someone you know who is good at getting what they want. How do they do it?

Listening: *Please*

5))) **1.2** English and American parents teach their children to say 'please' to be polite. But when do English speakers actually say 'please'? Listen to four people asking for things and match the conversations to the pictures. Then answer these questions.

1 What do they ask for?

2 Do they say 'please'?

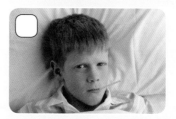 

6))) Listen again and complete these extracts from the conversations. Write in the missing words.

Conversation 1

1_____ _____ _____ your name, please?

Conversation 2

A: Sorry to 2_____ you, but I've got a 3_____ … I need to leave now. 4_____ _____ cover for me?

B: Yes, 5_____ _____ .

Conversation 3

A: OK, 6_____ _____ sign here, please?

B: 7_____ .

Conversation 4

A: I need to take some 8_____ up to the third floor … There's a trolley over there. 9_____ _____ _____ _____ I borrow it?

B: Not 10_____ _____ .

7 Do English speakers normally say 'please' if they make small requests or big requests?

8 Does your language have a word like 'please'? When do you use it?

9 When English speakers make big requests, they often explain or apologize first. Find examples of this in exercise 6.

10 Read the requests and responses and answer the questions.

Requests	
A	**B**
Can I go out for an hour? **Could I** go with him? **May I** have your name, please? **Do you mind if I** use it?	**Can you** sign here, please? **Could you** cover for me? **Would you** give us a lift? **Could you possibly** pick us up?
Saying 'yes'		**Saying 'no'**
Of course. Certainly. I suppose so.	Well, all right then. No problem.	I'm afraid I can't. I'm sorry but … (+ a reason)

1 Which request forms (A or B) do we use to …
  a ask people to do things?
  b ask if it's OK to do things?

2 Look at all the request forms. Which ones do we use to …
  a make big requests.
  b make small requests.

3 Look at the different ways to say 'yes'. Which ones sound most positive?

> **!** Notice the reply to this question.
> **Q:** Do you mind if I borrow it?
> **A:** No, not at all. = I'm happy for you to borrow it.
> If we **don't mind** something, we'll be happy with whatever happens.

Word focus: *lend* and *borrow*

11 Complete these definitions with *lend* or *borrow*.

1 If you _____ something <u>from</u> someone, you take something that belongs to them, use it for a short time and then give it back.

2 If you _____ something <u>to</u> someone, you give it to them so they can use it for a short time.

12 Complete these sentences with *lend* or *borrow*.

1 Do you mind if I _____ this pencil for a moment?

2 This book looks interesting. Can you _____ it to me?

3 May I _____ these headphones for a moment?

4 I didn't bring my hairdryer, would you _____ me yours?

5 Could you _____ me $20? I'll pay you back tomorrow.

6 Could I possibly _____ your car this afternoon?

Speaking: Asking for help

13 Work in pairs. Take turns to make and respond to requests in these situations.

1 You want to borrow your friend's English dictionary for a day or two. You also want them to lend you €50 so you can buy a new English textbook.

2 You want a friend to give you a lift to the gym. You also want them to stop at the post office and wait while you post a letter.

3 You want your assistant to work late tonight. You also want them to go to the dry cleaner's in their lunch hour and pick up your shirts.

4 You're going on holiday for a week. You want your neighbour to water your plants. You also want them to feed your cat.

5 You want a colleague to show some visitors around your workplace. You also want them to pick the visitors up from the airport, and take them back to the airport at the end of the day.

Communication strategies

9

Reminder

Grammar reference
pages 164 and 165

We use the present simple to talk about long-term situations and regular activities.
My friend works with computers.
We use the present continuous to talk about short-term or temporary activities.
I'm working on a new project.

Remember there are some verbs that we do not usually use in the continuous.
Examples: *want, like, need*

Listening: Perhaps I can help

1 Where do you sometimes meet new people? Add more places to this list.

* private parties
* conferences
* the gym or sports centre

2 🔊 1.3 Listen to three people meeting at a party. How are they connected? Answer these questions.
Who …

1 is Lucy's neighbour?
2 is Lucy's cousin?
3 is finishing an MBA course?
4 is looking for a job?
5 is a financial analyst?
6 thinks they need a holiday?
7 wants to go to France?
8 is trying to find a translator?
9 speaks Spanish?

Julia

Lucy

Paul

3 🔊 Complete the missing words. Then listen again and check your answers.

1
A: So you're an MBA student?
B: Yes, I ¹_____ this summer.
C: Paul's ²_____ _____ a job.

2
A: I think she's a ³_____ .
B: Oh, I'm not. But I think I ⁴_____ a holiday.
A: I ⁵_____ to go to Paris for a few days. Do you ⁶_____ to _____ with me?

3
A: I'm ⁷_____ _____ find someone who can translate for us. The person who speaks Spanish is ⁸_____ _____ .
B: Paul ⁹_____ Spanish.

4 Think about some things you want to do. Complete these phrases to make true sentences about your life.

1 I'm trying to …
2 I need …
3 I want to …
4 I'm looking for …

Speaking: Personal networks

5 Work in pairs. Follow these instructions and talk about some of the people you know.

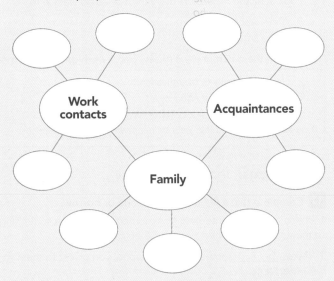

Work contacts

Acquaintances

Family

1 Write the names of three of your work contacts in the diagram. For example, the names of your boss, a colleague, a customer or supplier. Then explain to your partner what each person does.

Maria's my boss. She's responsible for …

2 Write the names of three family members in the diagram. For example, the names of your husband/wife, sister/brother or son/daughter. Then ask and answer questions about each person.

A: Is Johan your brother?
B: No, he's my son.
A: Really, how old is he?

3 Write the names of three other friends or acquaintances in the diagram. For example, the names of your friends or neighbours. Then explain how you know these people and how often you meet.

Tom's my neighbour. We sometimes play squash together at weekends.

6 Read some problems with your partner.

1 Choose three of the problems and think of someone you know who can help. For example, one of your colleagues, a friend, a neighbour or a relative.

2 Tell your partner who can help and why.

Nina needs to speak to Pete. Pete's my neighbour and he runs an import-export business. He often employs interns.

Nina

My 18-year-old nephew is trying to get some work experience. I'm looking for someone who can offer him an internship.

Sven

I want to find someone who works with computers. I have a problem with my internet connection and need help.

Keiko

I can't take my daughter to her piano lesson next week. I'm looking for someone who's free at 4 p.m. on Wednesday and can drive her there.

Edyta

I want to go to New York next summer. I'm looking for someone who knows the city and can tell me about hotels and things to do.

Zhi Peng

I need more exercise. I'm trying to find someone who wants to play tennis or go cycling with me.

Jean-Claude

I'm trying to find a native English speaker. I want to write an English version of my resumé and need some help.

7 Network with the class. Show your personal network diagram to some other students and look at theirs. Ask and answer questions about the people you know.

Try to find…

1 someone interesting – someone you'd like to meet.

2 someone useful – someone who can help you with one of your problems.

Writing: Keeping in touch

8 You received an email from a friend yesterday. She started a new job this week and says it is going well. Write a reply. Complete the message below with your own ideas.

Hi … .

Great to hear from you. It's good to know that … .

At the moment, I … . I want to … .

… is very well. He/She … . He/She is trying to … .

Hope to hear from you again soon. Take care and keep in touch.

…

Interaction

11

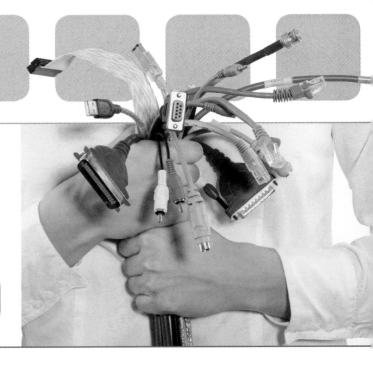

2

A *will* for offers and decisions
B Emails
C **Communication strategies** Apologies
D **Interaction** Solving travel problems

Trouble-shooting

will for offers and decisions

Listening: Calling tech support

1 Who do you ask for help when you have a computer problem?

2))) **1.4** Listen to someone asking for help and follow the conversation in the chart. What is the problem?

			Tech support. Can I have your employee number, please?			
Where are you?	Yes, a group of us have the same problem.	Are you sure it's the network and not your computer?	Yes, it's 240721 and my name's Chris Orth.	What's the problem?	The 's' key doesn't work.	Bring it to the lab and we'll take a look.
In a meeting room on the third floor.	OK, I'll look into it and get back to you.	The wireless network isn't working.	Thanks, Chris. How can I help you?	I'm having trouble with my computer.	Fine. See you soon.	OK, I'll come now.
You're welcome.	I'll wait to hear from you, then.	Ah, they're doing some maintenance work on the system.	I'm having trouble reaching the HR site.	With your laptop or desktop computer?	My desktop. It's running very slowly.	You're welcome.
Thanks very much.	Yes, I'll get back to you as soon as I can.	So is the site down?	Is your internet connection OK?	How soon can they be here?	OK. I'll send someone over to take a look.	That's great. Thanks a lot.
Yes, try again in 15 minutes and let us know if you still have problems.	OK. I just need to wait, then.	Yes, but it'll be back up and running soon.	Yes. Is the HR site down?	I'll find out and let you know.	Can you call me back on my mobile?	Yes, no problem.

12

3 Work in pairs. Take turns to be tech support and Chris Orth. Use the chart to make up more conversations.

4 Match the expressions with similar meanings.

1 I'm having trouble with it.
2 I'll look into it.
3 I'll find out what's wrong.
4 I'll get back to you.
5 I'll let you know as soon as possible.
6 It'll be back up and running soon.

a I'll work out what the problem is.
b I'll call you back with the information.
c I'll tell you as soon as I can.
d I'm having a problem with it.
e It'll work again soon.
f I'll investigate.

Grammar: *will* and *'ll*

5 Read the information about *will* and *'ll* in the table. Then find more examples of decisions, offers and promises in the chart in exercise 2.

will and 'll

The contracted form of *will* is *'ll*. We often use it when we're deciding what to do.
I'll wait to hear from you, then.
We also use it to offer and promise help.
OK. I'll look into it and get back to you.

>> For more information on *will*, see page 169.

6 Work in pairs. Take turns making some more tech support calls. Use the problems below.

1 You can't log on to the system.
2 You can't connect to the printer.
3 Your computer is running slowly and you think it has a virus.
4 Your German colleague changed your keyboard settings so now, when you type the letter 'Y', you get the letter 'Z'. You want to change the settings back.

Word focus: Verbs with *back*

7 We can use *back* after many verbs. Look at the examples below. Then complete the sentences with the verbs in the box.

Call me back on my mobile. (Return my call.)
I'll get back to you as soon as I can. (I'll reply soon.)
He'll be back in the office on Friday. (He'll be here again.)

send go phone put bring be write come

1 If it's not the right size, _____ it back here and we'll change it for you.
2 Mr Harris isn't here at the moment. Can I ask him to _____ you back?
3 The doctor says he'll _____ back and see me again tomorrow.
4 Some of these goods are damaged so we'll _____ them back to the supplier.
5 The system is down at the moment but it'll _____ back up soon.
6 The new system of processing orders isn't working. Do you think we should _____ back to the old system?
7 Please _____ the files back on the shelf when you finish with them.
8 I sent her a card last month but she didn't _____ back.

Speaking: Quick decisions

8 Work in pairs. Practise making decisions, offers and promises. Take it in turns to read a situation to your partner. They should respond and say what they will do.
Student A: Turn to File 18, page 142.
Student B: Read the situations below.

A: Your shirts are dirty.
B: I'll take them to the cleaners.

1 Your mother rang while you were out.
2 It's very hot in this room.
3 The wastepaper bin is full.
4 The gas company sent us another bill today (a red one).
5 I'd like to speak with your manager.
6 The sweater you bought is too big.
7 This light doesn't work.
8 There aren't any taxis.
9 I can't find my house keys.
10 Help! The building's on fire!

TALKING POINT
• How good are you at fixing computer problems?
• Do you ever help to solve other people's computer problems? If so, whose?

Reading: What's in your inbox?

1 Discuss these questions.

1 How often do you check your email? For example, every hour?

2 Approximately how many emails are in your inbox right now?

2 Terri Mahler has six messages in her inbox. Which ones need urgent action?

1 ⬜

> Just a quick message to say I'm working at home this afternoon. Tan Keung Yam is manning the office.

2 ⬜

> Hi all,
> FYI today is 'National Leave-The-Office-Early Day'.

3 ⬜

> Hi Terri,
> Re your visit next week, can you send me your flight details ASAP so I can organize transport from the airport?

4 ⬜

> Terri,
> I just got your voice message. I'm attaching the answers to some FAQs about uploading files to the website.

5 ⬜

> Dear Terri,
> I'm writing to confirm that we're expecting to ship your order for European plug adaptors Ref. No. 437281 on Friday. We're just waiting for one part to arrive.

6 ⬜

> Dear Ms Mahler,
> Thank you for your enquiry. Yes, we have a room available for the 30th. The rate is $150 per night and we will require your credit card details to make a reservation.

3 Look at the endings to the emails. Match them to the correct beginnings in exercise 2.

A

> We're looking forward to seeing you on the 15th.
> Thanks a lot and have a safe trip,
> Jan Svensson

B

> If you need to speak with me, feel free to call me here on 215 555 9436.
> Cheers,
> Elly

C

> See question 4 – I think it will solve your problem.
> I hope this helps,
> Aleksy

D

> We apologize for the delay and thank you for your patience.
> Best wishes,
> Enid

E

> If you have any further questions, please do not hesitate to ask.
> Kind regards,
> Emily Dickson

F

> Why are you still here reading this?
> Agostina
> P.S. Have a great weekend!

4 Answer these questions.

1 What's Jan Svensson looking forward to?

2 What's Elly doing today? And what about Tan Keung Yam?

3 What's Aleksy attaching to the email?

4 What's Enid expecting to do on Friday and what's she waiting for?

5 Where does Emily Dickson work?

6 According to Agostina, why is today a special day?

5 Find all the abbreviations in the emails. What do they mean? Then check your answers: Turn to File 8, page 141.

6 Match these two subject lines to the correct emails. Then suggest subject lines for the other four emails.

1 Request for flight information

2 Website upload problem

Word focus: *wait, expect, look forward to*

7 Match these phrases to the meanings below.

> We're looking forward to …
> We're waiting for …
> We're expecting to …

1 you think that something will happen

2 you're doing nothing until something happens

3 you think that something good will happen; you're excited and you're thinking about it a lot

8 Complete these sentences with one of the phrases from exercise 7.

1 _____ the bus. It's five minutes late.

2 _____ see a rise in inflation this year.

3 The exhibition starts July 19th. _____ meeting you at our stand.

4 _____ complete the project before the end of the month.

5 Have a good trip. _____ hearing all about it when you get back.

6 There's nobody at the ticket desk. _____ someone to come and serve us.

> **!** After *expect* we use an infinitive form (*to do*):
> *We're expecting **to see** you soon.*
> After *look forward to* we use an *-ing* form (*doing*):
> *We're looking forward to **seeing** you soon.*

Speaking: Starting and ending emails

9 Look at the emails in exercises 2 and 3 again. Which two are more formal? How do you know?

10 Discuss these questions about English emails.

1 When do we use the titles *Mr, Mrs, Ms* and *Dr* in English?

2 Look at the closings below. Which ones are suitable for an email to a …

   a professional contact you don't know well?

   b friend or colleague you know well?

(Some are suitable for both.)

> **Email closings**
>
> *Kind regards*
> *Thank you for your patience.*
> *Best wishes*
> *I hope this helps.*
> *If you have any further questions, please do not hesitate to ask.*
> *We're looking forward to seeing you on the 15th.*
> *Look forward to seeing you on Friday.*
> *Cheers*
> *Thanks a lot.*
> *Have a great weekend.*
> *Feel free to call me.*
> No closing – just sign off with your name or initials

11 Answer these questions. Then turn to File 9, page 141 to find out how British and American speakers start and end emails.

1 How do you normally start and end emails in your language?

2 Do you ever start an email without a greeting (like *Dear …, Hi* or *Hello*)?

3 Do you ever end an email with no closing?

12 Work in pairs or groups. Decide how to start and close English emails in these situations.

1 You're organizing a large meeting. You need to ask the guest speaker what equipment they need for their presentation.

2 You need one of your employee's expenses claims. The end of the month is approaching so it's urgent.

3 A customer wrote and asked if your products come with a guarantee. The answer is yes. Attach your warranty terms to your reply.

4 You're going to England next week. You need to email all your work contacts to tell them you will be out of the office.

   Dear Dr Davies … Kind regards, Jo Hall

Writing: Emails and responses

13 Work in pairs or groups. Write one of the emails in exercise 12 together. One person writes; the others check spelling and grammar.

14 Swap your email with another pair or group and write a reply.

TALKING POINT What will the next email you write be about?

Reading: Sorry!

1 Discuss these questions.

1 Think of some different situations where people might say 'sorry'.

2 Would you say 'sorry' to someone if you accidentally bumped into them in the street? How about if they bumped into you?

2 Read the article and find out about English customs. Do English people say 'sorry' in the same way as you?

Sorry, I'm English.

'Sorry' is a very common word in British English. In fact people probably apologize more in England than anywhere else on Earth. The anthropologist* Kate Fox did some experiments to find out just how automatically English people say 'sorry'. She bumped into passersby in busy, crowded places like train stations and shopping centres and counted how many people apologized. Even though the 'accident' was clearly her fault, about 80 per cent of English people said 'sorry'. Then she tried the same experiment on people from the USA, France, Belgium, Poland, the Lebanon, Scandinavia, Italy, Russia, Spain, Japan and Australia. Most people said 'Careful' or 'Watch out' and many were very nice about it and held out a hand to help her. Only people from Japan came close to saying 'sorry' so often. But she found it difficult to experiment on Japanese people because they were very good at jumping out of the way.

anthropologist: someone who studies people and their origins, customs and beliefs

3 Answer these questions.

1 Who did this experiment and what's her job?

2 Who caused the accidents: the passersby or Kate?

3 Do Americans say 'sorry' as often as English people?

4 Why was it difficult for Kate to experiment in Japan?

5 Why do you think English people say 'sorry' so much?

Listening: Sorry to interrupt

4 Answer these questions.

1 Do people ever interrupt you when you're working? Who interrupts you and what for?

2 What do you do when you don't want to be disturbed? Do you ever take your phone off the hook?

5))) **1.5** Here is one half of a telephone conversation. What do you think the other person is saying? Complete the conversation. Then listen and find out if you are right.

A: Jean Pierre Moreau.

B: ¹_____

A: Hi, Rosemary, Look, can I call you back?

B: ²_____

A: Yes, I'm in the middle of something.

B: ³_____

A: Thanks. Bye.

6 Look at these phrases. Then answer the questions.

a Is this a good time to call?

b Look, I'm really busy right now.

c Have you got a minute?

d I'm sorry, but I'm in a meeting.

e Can I call you back?

f Are you busy?

g Is it important?

h Sorry, but it's not a good time.

Which phrases can you use to …

1 stop people interrupting you?

2 check it's OK to interrupt people?

7))) **1.6** Listen to Jean Pierre and Rosemary's next call. How many times do they say 'sorry'?

8))) Listen again and complete examples 1–4 in the table. Then match each example to the correct reason a–d.

Saying 'sorry'

Examples:

1 A: Thanks for _____ _____ to me.
  B: Sorry I couldn't _____ _____.
2 I'm sorry _____ _____ you but I _____ an email address for Steve Parks.
3 A: Eight _____ four?
  B: No, _____ -four.
  A: Sorry, eighty-four?
4 A: That's right.
  B: Sorry?
  A: _____ _____ that's right.

Reasons:

English people apologize for many different reasons. For example, when they …

a interrupt someone's work.
b regret something they did.
c don't hear.
d need to correct something they said that was wrong.

Word focus: Emails and web addresses

9 Label the email and web address. Use the words and expressions in the box.

slash at dot colon hyphen underscore all one word

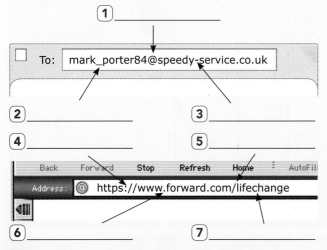

1 _____

To: mark_porter84@speedy-service.co.uk

2 _____   3 _____
4 _____   5 _____

Back Forward Stop Refresh Home AutoFill
Address @ https://www.forward.com/lifechange

6 _____   7 _____

10 How do we pronounce these parts of addresses?

com net uk us org ac co fr gov jp biz

Which do we say …

1 as one word?
2 as separate letters?

11 Write down three email addresses you know. Then work in pairs and take turns to dictate and write the addresses. Check you have the correct spelling.

12 When you are spelling words in English, which letters are difficult to remember or pronounce? Do you have any clever ways of remembering them? What are they?

double U

J rhymes with *say*

Speaking: Is this a good time?

13 Work in pairs. Make two telephone calls.
Student A: Look at the information below.
Student B: Turn to File 10, page 141.

Call one:
Student B promised to send you the email address of a potential client last week but they didn't. You know Student B is very busy so perhaps they forgot. Call them but make sure it's a good time to call before you ask for the address again.

Call two:
Student B calls you. Accept their apology and write down the email address.

Reminder

Grammar reference page 169

We use *will* to make offers and promise help.
I'll come and get you. I'll wait outside.

When someone apologizes, we can say:
It's all right.
It doesn't matter.
It's not a problem.

Listening: Help!

1 What problems do people often have when they are travelling by train? Make a list.

2 🔊 **1.7** Listen to a traveller making a telephone call. What problem do they have and what do they arrange to do?

3 Here is what Ana says but what about Bridget? Work in pairs. Write what you think Bridget says.

A: Bridget? It's Ana.

B: 1 _____

A: I'm at the airport, London Heathrow. But Bridget, I have a problem.

B: 2 _____

A: My bag didn't arrive.

B: 3 _____

A: They say it's in Miami. They'll send it on the next plane.

B: 4 _____

A: I'll get it tomorrow but my driving licence is in the bag. I can't hire a car to get to your house.

B: 5 _____

A: Oh, that's very kind of you. I'm so sorry to trouble you.

B: 6 _____

A: I'm at terminal 3. How long will it take you to get here?

B: 7 _____

A: OK. I'll wait outside in half an hour. Bridget, thank you so much.

B: 8 _____

A: I'm looking forward to seeing you, too. See you soon.

4 🔊 **1.8** Listen to the whole conversation and see if you are right.

5 Play a game in pairs. You are going to London to make a presentation at a conference. The first person to finish is the winner.

Rules

1 Toss a coin to move. Heads, move one square, tails move two.

2 Follow the instructions on each square. When necessary, act out conversations.

3 If you land on a square someone landed on before, move on to the next new square.

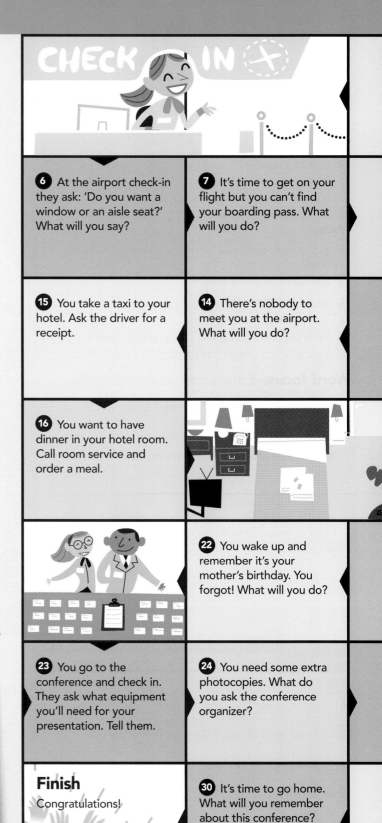

CHECK IN ✈

6 At the airport check-in they ask: 'Do you want a window or an aisle seat?' What will you say?

7 It's time to get on your flight but you can't find your boarding pass. What will you do?

15 You take a taxi to your hotel. Ask the driver for a receipt.

14 There's nobody to meet you at the airport. What will you do?

16 You want to have dinner in your hotel room. Call room service and order a meal.

22 You wake up and remember it's your mother's birthday. You forgot! What will you do?

23 You go to the conference and check in. They ask what equipment you'll need for your presentation. Tell them.

24 You need some extra photocopies. What do you ask the conference organizer?

Finish
Congratulations!

30 It's time to go home. What will you remember about this conference?

Start

1 What will you need to take to the conference? Say what you'll pack in your bag.

2 Call and book a taxi to the station.

3 Your taxi doesn't arrive. How will you get to the station?

5 You think the passenger next to you has finished with their newspaper. Ask if you can read it.

4 You spill some coffee over the passenger sitting next to you. What will you say?

8 It's windy when you're getting on the plane. Your hat blows away. What will you do?

9 You're vegetarian but the flight attendant asks: 'Chicken or beef?' What will you say?

10 You ate your meal but you're still hungry. Ask the flight attendant for another one.

13 Your luggage doesn't arrive. What will you do?

12 The British immigration officer asks: 'What's the purpose of your trip?' Explain.

11 Your headphones aren't working. The passenger next to you is not using theirs. What will you say?

17 The television in your room isn't working. Call and ask for help.

18 Your room is very cold. You don't know how to increase the temperature. What will you do?

19 You go for a walk, get lost and can't find your hotel. You stop a passer by. What will you say?

21 You think the restaurant bill is wrong. What will you say to the waiter?

20 You have dinner in the hotel restaurant. You don't understand something on the menu. Ask the waiter to explain.

25 You left your reading glasses at home and can't read your presentation notes. What will you do?

26 The person introducing you gets your name wrong. What will you do?

29 There's a mistake on your hotel bill. They're charging you £90 for phone calls but you didn't use the phone. What will you do?

28 You booked a sightseeing tour at your hotel but now you have no time for it. Ask if you can cancel and have your money back.

27 Half way through your presentation, the electricity goes off. You can't show your PowerPoint presentation! What will you do?

Interaction

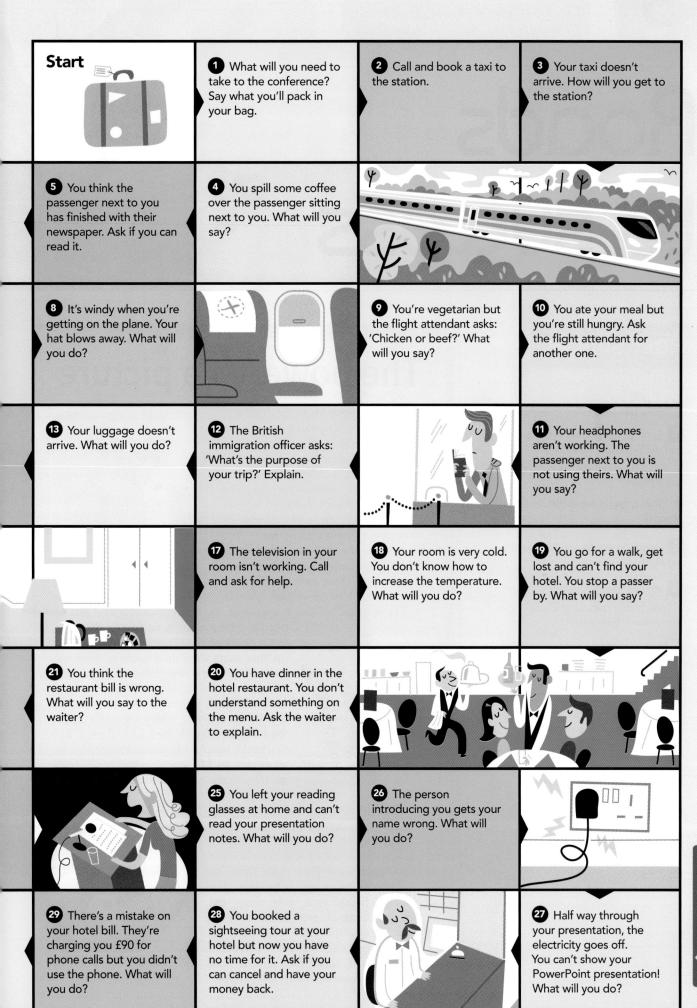

3

A Past simple
B Past simple questions
C **Communication strategies** Active listening
D **Interaction** Learning from experience

Roads to success

Past simple

Reading: Compliance

1 Look at the photos in the article and discuss these questions.

1 What do you think the picture of the hand shows?

2 What can you see in the other two photos?

2 Read the article and find out if you are right.

3 Answer these questions.

1 Why didn't doctors at Cedars-Sinai always wash their hands?

2 How did the hospital try to solve the problem? List the different things it did.

3 What things worked and motivated the doctors to wash their hands?

4 What does the story tell us about how we can motivate people?

The power of a picture

The Cedars-Sinai Medical Center was one of the top hospitals in the US, but it had a problem. Its doctors didn't always wash their hands before they examined the patients. There were a number of reasons for this. The doctors were very busy. Sometimes there weren't any *sinks* nearby or they were behind equipment. And sometimes the doctors didn't think it was important. They thought their hands were clean enough and only other people's hands carried *bacteria*.

The hospital administrators sent the doctors emails and put up *posters* telling doctors to follow the rules, but it didn't work. 35 per cent of the time the doctors didn't wash their hands so there was only 65 per cent *compliance*. The hospital planned a new *strategy*. They created a Hand Hygiene Safety Team who walked around the hospital. When they saw a doctor washing their hands they gave them a $10 Starbucks *voucher*. The doctors earned a lot of money so $10 wasn't a lot. But nobody said 'No thank you' and compliance went up to 85 per cent.

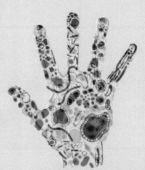

85 per cent was good but not good enough. So one day at a meeting of important doctors, a hospital administrator asked everyone to put their hands in a Petri dish. Then she sent the dishes to the laboratory. The doctors' hands were very dirty and lots of bacteria grew. The hospital took photographs and used them as *screensavers* on everyone's computer. The doctors saw the photos and compliance rose to nearly 100 per cent.

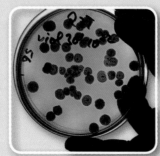

4 Find the words in italics in the article. Then match them to these definitions.

1 a software program that puts a picture on your computer screen

2 a ticket you can use instead of money

3 things you fill with water to wash your hands

4 a large notice or picture used to advertise something

5 small living things that can cause disease

6 a set of plans to get what you want

7 following rules

Grammar: Past simple

5 When do we use *was*, *were*, *wasn't* and *weren't*? Complete the table below. Look for examples in the article if you need help.

Past simple: be

+		–	
	I _____		I _____
	You/We/They _____		You/We/They _____
	He/She/It _____		He/She/It _____

6 Write the past simple forms of these regular verbs. Then complete the rule in the table below. Look for examples in the article if you need help.

examine _____   create _____   ask _____
carry _____   walk _____   use _____
plan _____   earn _____

Past simple: Regular verbs

Add _____ to the base form of the verb.

>> For a list of irregular verbs, see page 176.

7 Write the past simple forms of these irregular verbs. Look for examples in the article if you need help.

have _____   put _____   say _____   take _____
think _____   see _____   go up _____   rise _____
send _____   give _____   grow _____

8 How do we form negatives in the past simple? Complete the rule in the table below. Look for examples in the text if you need help.

Past simple: Negative forms

Use _____ + the base form of the verb.

>> For more information on the past simple, see page 166.

9 Complete this story. Use the past simple forms of the verbs in brackets.

The Phyllis Harman Medical Center (PHMC) [1] _wanted_ (want) to provide good quality health care. It [2]_____ (ask) its patients to complete satisfaction surveys and it [3]_____ (hold) regular meetings to discuss the results. The meetings [4]_____ (be) difficult because they [5]_____ (focus) on things that [6]_____ (go) wrong. The survey results [7]_____ (not change). Every month patient satisfaction [8]_____ (be) OK but it [9]_____ (not be) great. Then PHMC [10]_____ (stop) looking at the survey numbers and [11]_____ (read) their patients' comments instead. They [12]_____ (discover) that their patients [13]_____ (write) a lot about two things: communication and good relationships. So PHMC [14]_____ (change) the meetings. They [15]_____ (talk) about ways to improve relationships and communication. People [16]_____ (bring) new ideas to the meetings and [17]_____ (share) best practices. Patient satisfaction [18]_____ (rise).

Speaking: Motivating projects

10 Think of a project you worked on in the past where you felt very motivated. It could be a work project or something you did in your free time. Answer these questions about it and make notes.

1 What was the project about? What were the goals?

2 What gave you motivation and why? Was it a person? (who?) Was it an idea? (what?) Or was it something you wanted to do? (what?)

3 What was the result of the project? Did anything change? Explain what happened.

11 Work in pairs or small groups. Take turns to describe your projects. Whose project was the most motivating?

TALKING POINT
- Is compliance important in your business?
- How does your organization make sure its employees follow rules?

Listening: A career story

1 Choose two or three things which are most important for success in your job.

1 a good education and passing examinations

2 knowledge of your business and the market

3 being passionate about your job and doing what you love

4 having lots of business contacts

5 the ability to keep trying even when things are difficult

6 something else (what?)

2 Work in pairs. Compare your answers and explain your choices.

3))) **1.9** Listen to an interview with Adam Pritchard, the founder of *Pomegreat*, a successful fruit juice distribution company. Which things were important for his success?

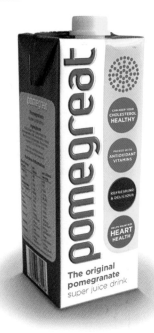

4 Are these statements true (T) or false (F)? Correct the ones that are wrong.

1 Adam went to business school.

2 Adam's first business was a company to sell cars.

3 Adam failed his stock-broking exams.

4 The second business he set up was a telephone counselling service.

5 He invested and lost £40,000 in his second business and had to sell his car.

6 Adam spent a year researching the fruit juice market before he started Pomegreat.

7 His turnover last year was £13m.

5))) Listen again and complete these questions.

1 Adam, _____ you _____ to business school?

2 So _____ did you _____ _____ your first company?

3 How _____ it _____?

4 So what _____ you _____ after that?

5 That's a difficult job. _____ you _____ the exams?

6 So what _____ next?

7 _____ that successful?

8 _____ did you _____ the idea for *Pomegreat*?

9 _____ it _____ you long to set up the company?

6 Work in pairs. Take turns playing the role of Adam Pritchard. Practise asking and answering the questions in exercise 5.

Grammar: Past simple questions

7 Look at the table. Then complete the questions and answers.

Past simple: Yes/No questions		
Verb *be* Change the word order *It was a disaster.*	***Was* it a disaster?** ***Were* you successful?** _____ it easy to sell cars? _____ the exams difficult?	**Yes, it was.** **No, we weren't.** **No, it _____.** **Yes, they _____.**
Other verbs Use *did* + the infinitive form of the verb	***Did* Adam *pass* his exams?** ***Did* he *go* to business school?** _____ Adam _____ £40,000? _____ he _____ from his mistakes?	**Yes, he did.** He **passed** them all. **No, he didn't.** He **went** travelling. **No, _____ _____.** He **lost** £50,000. **Yes, _____ _____.** He **learnt** a lot.

8 Complete the questions with the words in the box.

> Where ~~When~~ Why What What How How much

Question words	
1 _When_ did Adam set up his first company?	When he was twenty-four.
2 _____ was it a failure?	Because he didn't know the market.
3 _____ money did he invest?	£30,000.
4 _____ was his next business idea?	It was a telephone counselling service.
5 _____ did it go?	It was another failure.
6 _____ did he get the idea for Pomegreat?	In Pakistan.
7 _____ happened next?	He turned Pomegreat into a success.

! Don't use *did* in the question: *What happened?*

9 Work in pairs. Ask similar questions about your careers. Begin with the questions below and think of more things to ask. Talk about a member of your family, using *he/she*, if you prefer.

1 What exams did you take at school?

2 When did you leave school?

3 What was your first job?

4 What was your next job?

10 Here is another person who had to keep trying before he became successful. What do you know about him?

11 Work in pairs. Share information about Paul Potts' early life. Student A: Turn to File 40, page 145. Student B: Read the text below and then ask your partner questions to complete the missing information.

B: Where did Paul grow up?

A: He grew up in …

Paul grew up in _____ (where) in South West England. His father was a bus driver and his mother worked in a _____ (where). He had a difficult time at school because _____ (why) and he didn't have much confidence. But he loved singing and joined _____ (what) at school. He graduated from university in _____ (when) but he had difficulty finding a good job. He got a job in a _____ (where), putting things on shelves. He saved every penny he could and bought _____ (what). He sent _____ (what) to talent agents, but he didn't get one reply. Illness was also a problem for Paul. He developed a tumour and had to spend time in hospital. Another time he was off work for _____ (how long) because _____ (why). Paul and his wife had very little money and lots of credit card debts. Then in 2007 he decided to _____ (what/do).

12 Continue to work with your partner. Now share information about the day Paul's life changed. Student A: Read the text below. Then ask your partner questions to complete the missing information. Student B: Turn to File 24, page 143.

A: How did the judges feel?

B: They felt …

It was audition day and the judges of the TV talent show felt _____ (how). There were singers, dancers, fire eaters and comedians but nobody was very good. Then Paul Potts walked onto the stage. He looked _____ (how). He didn't have a tie. His suit cost _____ (how much) and he had a broken tooth. He told the judges _____ (what). 'I'm going to sing opera,' he said. The judges _____ (what/do). They didn't expect his audition to be good.

Then Paul began singing and everything changed. The audience stood up and clapped and cheered because _____ (why). The video of his performance appeared on _____ (where) and millions of people watched it. He won a place in the semi final, and the final, and then he won the competition. He received _____ (how many) votes from viewers. Paul won _____ (how much money) and a recording contract. Later that year he performed _____ (where). Paul's first CD was a number one hit in 13 countries and today he's a successful opera star.

13 Do you know any other people with a similar story to Paul's? What happened to them?

Speaking: Life and career game

14 Play a game with the class.

1 Write three sentences about your past life and career. Two sentences should be true and one sentence should be false. Try to think of unusual things you did in your past.

I trained as an engineer.

I took part in a TV quiz show.

I worked in a toy factory.

2 Take it in turns to read your sentences to the class. The class can ask four questions about each sentence. Then they must decide which sentence is false.

A: I trained as an engineer

B: Where did you go to school?

A: In Rome.

C: When was that?

A: In 2006 and 2007.

D: Did you pass your exams?

TALKING POINT • What's the best teacher: school or experience? Why?

• What were the most important things you learnt at school? Why?

Listening: Good news, bad news

1 What kinds of things do you and your colleagues talk about during work breaks? Think of some different conversation topics. Make a list.

- *stories in the news*
- *the match last night*
- *the cost of living*

2 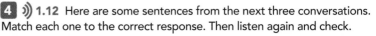 **1.10** Listen to five conversations. Match each conversation to the correct photo below. Then decide if it is about good news or bad news.

3 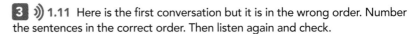 **1.11** Here is the first conversation but it is in the wrong order. Number the sentences in the correct order. Then listen again and check.

That's a pity. ☐

You poor thing. Are you better now? ☐

Yes, I'm fine, thanks. ☐

Tired? ①

That's nice. Did you have a good time? ☐

Not really. I had to leave early. ☐

Yes, I had a bad headache. ☐

Yes, a bit. I went to a party last night. ☐

4 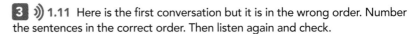 **1.12** Here are some sentences from the next three conversations. Match each one to the correct response. Then listen again and check.

1 Someone drove into her car this morning.

2 Her Honda's badly damaged.

3 I couldn't go.

4 I had to take my daughter to the hospital.

5 The interview went very well.

6 In fact, they offered me the job.

7 Yes, I'm really excited about it.

a Oh, nothing serious I hope.

b Wow! That's terrific! Congratulations!

c Good!

d Yes, I can imagine.

e Are you serious?

f That's a shame.

g Oh no! It's a new car.

5 Look at the responses in exercise 4 again and answer these questions. Which ones sound …

1 surprised?

2 pleased?

3 delighted?

4 shocked?

5 sympathetic (kind and understanding when they hear about a problem)?

A ☐

B ☐

C ☐

D ☐

E ☐

6 🔊 **1.13** Here is the final conversation but some responses are missing. Complete the conversation. Then listen again and check.

A: Did you do anything nice this weekend?

B: We went to Brighton.

A: _____ Brighton's a fantastic city.

B: But we couldn't find anywhere to park.

A: _____ Did you try the multi-storey?

B: Yes. All the car parks were full.

A: _____

B: We spent two hours looking. It was very frustrating.

A: _____

B: Then we found a spot in a back street.

A: _____

B: So we went shopping, and when we came back, we had a parking ticket!

A: _____

B: A fifty pound parking fine!

7 Write these expressions in the table. Then compare your answers with the class. Do you agree?

> That's a pity   That's terrible   Oh dear   Congratulations
> That's terrific   That's nice   That's a nuisance   Fantastic!

8 Think of some more expressions to add to the table. Which expressions do you think are most useful? Why? Are there any you wouldn't want to use? Why?

Reacting to new information			
Wonderful news	**Good news**	**Bad news**	**Awful news**
Wow!	Good.	That's a shame. You poor thing!	Oh no!

⚠ English speakers' voices often go up when they are interested or surprised.

9 Practise the expressions with a partner. Read one of the stories below while your partner reacts with appropriate expressions.

> A: I had an interesting day at work …
> B: That's nice.

Student A:

> I had an interesting day at work … My boss liked a report I wrote … But then she found a mistake … She told me to write it again … Then a customer called and placed a big order … But then he called again and cancelled it … I felt really disappointed … Then the computer system crashed … Tech support came right away … They knew exactly what was wrong … But it took three hours to fix it …

Student B:

> I had an interesting day at work … I got a pay rise … But it wasn't very large … Then I got stuck in the elevator for 20 minutes … The CEO was in the elevator with me … We spent the time talking … on our mobile phones … Then I told him about the idea I had for speeding up production … He asked me what my name was … I was delighted … but then the elevator doors opened and he left …

Speaking: Developing conversations

10 Work in pairs. Practise developing conversations.
Student A: Ask questions to find out what Student B's weekend was like.
Student B: Look at the information below and give answers. Then change roles.
Student B:

1 An old friend came to stay.

2 You lost your car keys.

3 Someone broke into your car and stole your GPS.

4 You saw a good movie.

5 Your sister had a baby.

6 You had toothache.

7 You found a bag containing €100 in the street.

8 Your boss called you at home.

9 You had an argument with your neighbour.

10 You won the lottery.

> A: Did you have a good weekend?
> B: Yes, an old friend came to stay.
> A: That's nice. What did you do? ◄── React + ask another question
> B: We went shopping together.
> A: Great.

Reminder

Grammar reference page 166

The past forms of the verb *be* are *was(n't)* and *were(n't)*. We form questions by changing the word order.
Was he successful?
Where were you yesterday?

Regular verbs end *-ed* in the past tense. We use *did/didn't* to form questions and negatives.
What did you do?
It didn't take long.

Speaking: A good investment?

1 Read a story about Thomas J. Watson, the founder of IBM. Do you think he did the right thing or not?

Thomas J. Watson

Many years ago, a junior executive at IBM made a mistake and lost $600,000 in a risky business deal. The young man was very worried. 'I expect you want to fire me,' he said. 'Are you serious?' Watson replied, 'We just spent hundreds of thousands of dollars training you!' He gave the young man another project.

2 Which do you think people learn from more: their mistakes or successes? Why?

Listening: A mistake

3 1.14 You are going to hear someone talking about a mistake they made at work. Listen and make notes below.

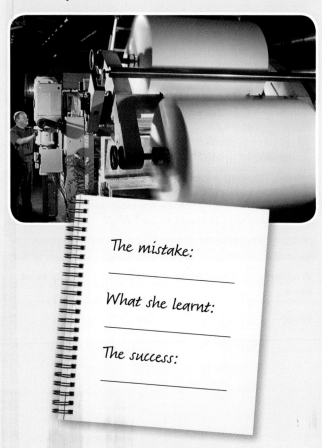

The mistake:
_____

What she learnt:
_____

The success:
_____

4 Compare your notes with a partner. Do you agree?

5 Listen again and answer these questions.
1 What project was Monika in charge of?
2 Why did she think the new technologies were great?
3 How much did the new technologies cost?
4 What did her project plan say?
5 How long did it take to install the first technology?
6 What happened the next day?
7 How did she solve the problem?
8 Did she complete the project on time?
9 Did she achieve the targets?

6 What can we learn from Monika's story? Are there any useful lessons here for your job?

Word focus: Verb–noun collocations

7 A collocation is a combination of words that are often used together. Form some verb-noun collocations. Complete the sentences with the correct words or phrases in the box.

| $5,000   production   our targets   tests   some problems   the deadline |

We speeded up We slowed down	_____ .	We ran We did	_____ .
We had We ran into We solved	_____ .	We spent It cost	_____ .
We met We achieved We exceeded	_____ .	We met We missed	_____ .

8 Which sentences in exercise 7 describe failures? Which describe successes?

9 Write three true sentences about things that have happened in your life using the collocations in exercise 7.

Speaking: Lessons from experience

10 Look at the groups of questions in the table. Then answer questions a–e below.
Which ones are about …
a time?   **b** money?   **c** the things people did?   **d** problems?   **e** final results?

| 1
What went wrong?
What was the problem? | 3
How did it go?
Was it successful?
Did you achieve your goals?
Did your customers like it? | 4
How much did it cost?
How much did you spend? |
| 2
What did you do?
What did you learn? | | 5
Did it take long?
How long did it take? |

11 Work in pairs. Use the questions in exercise 10 to discuss some lessons you have learnt from life.

1 Think of a situation in the past where you experienced or saw a failure. For example, someone made a mistake, technology didn't work, someone missed a deadline, customers weren't satisfied.

2 Describe what happened and answer your colleague's questions.

3 Discuss what you learnt from the failures.

12 Join with another pair. Student A: Tell the new pair the story your partner told you. Student B: Listen to your partner tell your story. Did he or she get it right and remember everything? Change roles so you hear everyone's stories. At the end, correct anything that is wrong and add anything they forgot.

13 Whose story was the most interesting and why? Who do you think learnt most from their experience and why?

Writing: Explaining what happened

14 Your boss asked you to create a spreadsheet and send it to her yesterday. Unfortunately, something happened so you missed the deadline. Write an email to your boss.

- Apologize for the delay. (Begin: *I'm sorry I didn't …*)
- Explain why. (Begin: *Unfortunately …* and say what happened – invent an excuse)
- Say when you will send it. (Begin: *I'll …*)

4

A Comparative adjectives
B Comparative and superlative adjectives
C **Communication strategies** Thanking
D **Interaction** Deciding on priorities

What's best?

Comparative adjectives

Reading: Happiness

1 How happy are you? Discuss these questions with a partner.

1 Are you generally happy and satisfied with life? Are you happier than most people?

2 What makes you happy: a sunny day, a pay rise? Think of five things.

2 What things affect how happy people feel? Tick (✓) the things that make a difference.

1 education level ⬭

2 gender (male/female) ⬭

3 age ⬭

4 having an interesting job or hobby ⬭

5 having close friendships or a satisfying marriage ⬭

6 having children (or not) ⬭

7 genes* ⬭

8 having lots of money ⬭

9 having more money than other people ⬭

10 something else (what?) ⬭

genes: parts of a cell that controls what living things are like. Parents pass their genes on to their children

3 Read the research results of some scientists and psychologists below and find out if you are right.

4 How many answers did you get right? Which answers were most surprising?

What makes us happy?

PERHAPS IT'S SURPRISING, but research shows that most people are happy most of the time. Ninety per cent of Americans say they are 'very happy' or 'fairly happy' and nearly all of them think that they are happier than average.

Education level has no effect on happiness. Women are a little happier than men, and old and young people are a little happier than middle-aged people. But the differences are very small (less than two per cent). It's much more important to have work and leisure activities that interest you. Having a happy marriage or close friendships is very significant, too, but having children isn't.

People usually have the same level of happiness throughout their lives. Big events like winning the lottery or the death of a husband or wife have an effect. But after six months or a year, people usually return to the same level of happiness and feel no better or worse than before. Happiness is genetic. So if your mother and father were happier than average, you're probably more satisfied with your life, too.

Money makes a difference, but only if you're very poor. If you feel safe and have food and a roof over your head, money isn't important. But interestingly, a person's position in the pay scale is significant. People are happier if they think their salary is higher than their colleagues'. But they're less happy if they think their colleagues are earning larger salaries than they are. Happiness is comparative.

Grammar: Comparative adjectives

5 Read the research results again. Then underline the comparative adjectives in the text in exercise 3.

6 Look at the examples in the table. What word do we use after comparative adjectives? Complete the rule.

Comparative adjectives

Examples:

*Women are a little **happier than** men.*

*Genes are **more significant than** age.*

*Having money is **less important than** having close friends.*

Rule:

After comparative adjectives we use the word _____ .

Short adjectives			Long adjectives	
high	+ er	higher	important	more/less important
large	+ r	larger		
big	+ ger	bigger	satisfied	more/less satisfied
happy	– y + ier	happier		

Special cases

good	better
bad	worse

>> For more information on comparative adjectives, see page 173.

7 Complete these questions. Use the comparative form of the adjectives in brackets. Then ask and answer the questions with a partner. The answers are in the text in exercise 3.

1 Are people _____ (happy) if their education level is _____ (high) than average?

2 When you're 15 years _____ (old) than you are now, will you enjoy life less?

3 How long does it take for people to feel _____ (good) after the death of their husband or wife?

4 Which is _____ (important) for happiness: having good friends or having children?

5 Are wealthy people _____ (satisfied) with their lives than poor people?

6 Are people unhappy if they think their salary is _____ (low) than their colleagues'?

Speaking: The economics of happiness

8 Look at these four questions and make a note of your answers.

Which is better?

1 Is it better for organizations to …
  a publish their pay scales so everyone can see them?
  b keep their pay scales secret?

2 Is it better for society when …
  a wealthy people pay higher taxes?
  b wealthy people pay the same taxes as everyone else?

Which would you like?

3 Would you like to have …
  a a job with a higher salary but longer working hours?
  b a lower-paid job where you can spend more time with your family and friends?

4 Would you like to earn …
  a $100,000 when your colleagues earn $200,000?
  b $50,000 when your colleagues earn $25,000?

9 Work in pairs or small groups and compare your answers. Do you agree? Explain your reasons.

  A: *How do you feel about the first question? Is it better for organizations to publish their pay scales?*

  B: *Yes, I think so. What do you think?*

  C: *I'm not sure. I don't want everyone to know how much I earn.*

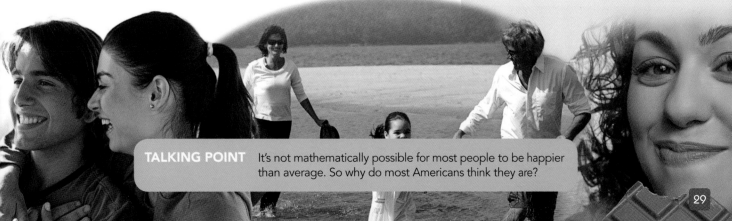

TALKING POINT It's not mathematically possible for most people to be happier than average. So why do most Americans think they are?

Listening: Gift giving

1 People all over the world give gifts but customs for giving them are sometimes a little different. Discuss these questions.

1 When do people generally give presents in your culture? For example, at certain times of the year, at graduations*, weddings or funerals*, when someone receives a promotion or retires, when they want to say sorry for something they did.

2 What gifts are appropriate for particular occasions? For example, when someone moves house, when someone has a baby, when you visit someone's home.

3 Are there any presents that aren't appropriate? For example, knives and scissors aren't appropriate in some cultures because they could signal cutting off the relationship.

graduation: when someone completes a university degree
funeral: a ceremony for someone who has just died

2 Look at the five gifts below and answer these questions. Which ones …

1 would you like to receive? Why?

2 wouldn't you like to receive. Why not?

3 would you give to someone else? Who and why?

3 🔊 **1.15** Listen to people talking about the gifts in exercise 2 and match each speaker to the correct photo. Did they give or receive it?

Speaker	Photo	Give	Receive
Speaker 1			
Speaker 2			
Speaker 3			
Speaker 4			
Speaker 5			

4 🔊 **1.16** Listen to the first two speakers again and answer these questions.

1 Why can't the first speaker give expensive gifts to customers?

2 What did his agent tell him to do with the sweatshirts, and why?

3 Who did he give the sweatshirts to, and how did they react?

4 Who made the glass vase, and why?

5 Why was it a problem on the journey to Korea?

6 Why was the vase a good gift?

5 🔊 **1.17** Listen to the next two speakers again and complete these sentences.

1 But _____ _____ gift I had came from my friends in the post room.

2 It was _____ _____ _____ gift but it's the one I enjoy the most.

3 I didn't care because _____ _____ _____ people in my field were there.

4 It's _____ _____ necklace I own.

6 🔊 **1.18** Listen to the final speaker again and answer these questions.

1 What was the speaker's most unusual gift this Christmas?

2 Who paid for the goat, and who received it?

3 What did his wife think?

4 What did he think?

Grammar: Comparative and superlative adjectives

7 Look at the table and complete the rules. Then complete the superlative forms of the adjectives.

Comparative and superlative adjectives

Superlative:

*The **most unusual** gift we received for Christmas was a picture of a goat.*

Comparative:

*It was **nicer** than last year's present.*

Rules:

1 We use _____ adjectives when we are comparing two things.

2 We use _____ adjectives when we are comparing three or more things.

3 We usually use the word _____ in front of superlative adjectives.

Adjective	Comparative	Superlative
big	bigger	_biggest_
important	more important	_____
pretty	prettier	_____
unusual	more unusual	_____
expensive	less expensive	_____

Special cases:

good	better	_____
bad	worse	_____

>> For more information on comparative and superlative adjectives, see page 173.

8 Complete these sentences. Use the comparative or superlative form of the adjective in brackets. Then discuss the sentences with a partner. Which ones do you agree with and why?

1 The _____ (good) gifts are often surprises.

2 The thought behind a gift is _____ (important) than its price.

3 The _____ (useful) present you can give when times are hard is money.

4 Promotional items with company names and logos make the _____ (bad) gifts.

5 It's _____ (good) to give money to charity than gifts at Christmas.

6 Tickets to events make great gifts. They're _____ (exciting) than things like socks.

7 Don't give me chocolate again! I want to be _____ (thin) not _____ (fat).

8 The _____ (nice) gifts often come in the _____ (small) packages.

Speaking: Choosing presents

9 Work in pairs or small groups. Your company is working on a joint venture with a company in China. You are visiting their offices next month and you want to take gifts for your colleagues there. If possible, you want to take things from your local region or country. Brainstorm some possible gifts.

1 Make a list of …

   a three things your colleagues can wear.

   b three examples of local handicrafts.

   c three items your colleagues can use in their office.

   d three things for your colleagues' homes.

   e three things to eat or drink.

   f three things to play with.

2 Look at your list of possible gifts and compare them. Consider …

   a Price:
   Which gifts are the cheapest and which are the most expensive?

   b Transportation:
   How easy will they be to carry? Which gifts are the largest, heaviest, easiest to break, etc.?

   c How pleasing they are:
   Which gifts are most useful and why? Which ones would you like most and why?

3 You have one suitcase and your budget isn't large. Decide what to take. You need …

   a one very special gift for the CEO.

   b six medium-priced gifts for the executive team.

   c twenty-four small gifts for everybody else.

10 Tell the class what gifts you decided on. Whose gift ideas were the most original? Whose gift ideas were the best?

E

PEARSON
Longman

TALKING POINT
- What's the best gift you've ever received? Why?
- What's the most unusual gift you've ever received?

Listening: You're a lifesaver!

1 Read and discuss this problem.

You are starting a new job next week. Today is your last day in your current place of work. Your colleagues give you a goodbye card and a present. The present is a sweater. It looks expensive but it is a strange style and colour. You don't like it at all and you will never wear it. Do you …

1 say that you love the sweater?

2 say the sweater is interesting?

3 say you don't like it and ask if they have the receipt?

4 do something else (what)?

A

'Is it OK? I didn't know what colour to get.'

2 Look at the photos on the right and read the comments. How would you respond to these people?

> A: *Is it OK? I didn't know what colour to get.*
>
> B: *Oh, I love the colour. It's beautiful! Thank you so much.*

3))) **1.19** Listen to five conversations. Do the people respond in ways you suggested?

4))) Listen again and complete these sentences.

B

'That was a great presentation. Well done!'

	Thanking	Responding
1	Yellow is 1_____! It's 2_____ _____ I 3_____. I love it.	Oh, I'm so 4_____. Does it 5_____?
2	I was very 6_____ and I think I spoke too fast, but it's very 7_____ of you to 8_____ _____.	No, no, 9_____ _____ _____. It was really very good.
3	Are you 10_____ that's all right? I'll 11_____ _____ _____ as soon as I can. Thank you so much!	Don't 12_____ _____. We're happy we can help.
4	Oh, wow! You're a 13_____.	No problem. I'm going your way, 14_____.
5	Oh, it's 15_____, but you 16_____ _____ _____ go to all this 17_____.	You're 18_____. Now take a deep breath …

C

'It's a check – to help with the school bills.'

5 English speakers often use these strategies to say 'thank you'. Match each one to the correct conversations in exercise 4.

a expressing delight and saying you like something

b promising to repay

c saying the other person is nice

d saying it wasn't necessary

e exaggerating and saying someone is more helpful than they really are

D

'It's raining out. Let me give you a lift.'

6 Work in pairs. Practise thanking and responding in these situations.

1 A friend goes to Brussels and brings you back some Belgian chocolates.

2 Your boss congratulates you on a report you wrote.

3 Your partner cooks your favourite meal.

4 Your mobile phone battery is flat and you need to make an urgent call. A friend lends you theirs.

5 You forgot to bring your wallet to work. A colleague buys your lunch.

E

'Come and blow out the candles. We've made you a birthday cake.'

Reading and speaking: Bosses' Day

7 Read about 'Bosses' Day' in the United States. Do you celebrate 'Bosses' Day' in your country? Would you like to?

October 16th is 'Bosses' Day' in the United States, and some employees send their boss a greeting card. Some even hold small parties for their boss or give them small gifts. Greeting card companies sell a variety of cards for employees to express their appreciation.

8 Look at the Bosses' Day cards. Which card is most appropriate for your boss? Choose one. Do you want to change the words? If so, how? What will you write inside?

9 Work in groups. Discuss these questions.

1 You're the boss and your employees give you these cards. What do you say and think?

2 Is Bosses' Day just a way for greeting card companies to make money, or does this idea have value?

10 Think of someone you want to thank and design a thank-you card. Plan what it will say on the front and what it will say inside.

Writing: A thank-you email

11 You visited your London office last week. One of your colleagues invited you to their home and you had a meal with their family. You are now writing to say thank you. Think of different words and phrases to complete the sentences.

Dear Chris,
Thank you so much for
¹ *inviting* me to your home
last ²_____. It was very
³_____ of you. The meal was
⁴_____ and I really enjoyed
meeting ⁵_____.
When you come to ⁶_____,
you must allow me to ⁷_____
your hospitality. I would like to
cook ⁸_____ for you.
Please say thank you to
⁹_____ for me. It was very
kind of her to ¹⁰_____.
Once again, thank you so much.
¹¹_____

A

Boss

For the best Boss
in the World

Thank you for
being so wonderful
to work with.
Have a great day!

B

Best Boss

You encourage us all
and reward success.
You believe in professionalism
and hard work, but you
understand that your
employees have lives
outside work, too.

We love working for you!

Thank you for being
so supportive!

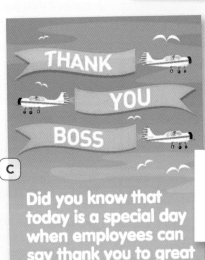

C

THANK YOU BOSS

Did you know that
today is a special day
when employees can
say thank you to great
bosses like you?

You did? Well then,
did you also know that
big bonuses and pay rises
make happy workers?

We use comparative adjectives when we are comparing two things.
*Katrina is **older** than me and **more experienced**.*

We use superlative adjectives when we are comparing three or more things.
*Mohammed is **the youngest** person on our team. He's also **the most energetic**.*

Reading: Entrepreneurs

1 These entrepreneurs have all started successful businesses. What do you know about these people? What field of business are they in?

2 Match these descriptions to the correct entrepreneurs in exercise 1.

1 Born in France of Iranian parents, this entrepreneur moved to the US when he was six years old. He built an online market place to connect buyers and sellers from all over the world.

2 This entrepreneur was born in Milan and his grandmother was an Italian princess. She founded a cosmetics company that is now part of Revlon. He now lives in the US and he has also founded a cosmetics company. But his company sells body and skin care products for pets, not people.

3 Thailand is famous for its beautiful hotels. This entrepreneur built the country's leading hotel chain from nothing. She didn't have much education, but she learnt on the job.

3 What other famous entrepreneurs do you know? What personal qualities do people need to become successful entrepreneurs?

4 Read the article. Does the writer mention any qualities you thought of? Suggest adjectives to fill in the gaps.

5 Use these adjectives to complete the article.

> stupid energetic determined innovative
> motivated optimistic

6 Discuss these questions.

1 Are people born entrepreneurs? Or can people learn to be entrepreneurs from training and experience?

2 Most people have some entrepreneurial qualities. Which ones do you have?

3 Which qualities do you want your children to have, and why? Are there any that you don't want your children to have? Why not?

Pierre Omidyar

Lorenzo Borghese

Chanut Piyaoui

What makes a successful entrepreneur?

Are they born or are they made? Do you need a particular personality to start a successful new company or is it something you can learn? Nobody knows, but here are some things many entrepreneurs have in common:

> Entrepreneurs are 1_____ . They love new ideas and enjoy doing things in different and better ways.

> Entrepreneurs generally have good judgement. They're not super-intelligent but they aren't 2_____ either.

> The future is uncertain, but this doesn't worry entrepreneurs. They're 3_____ and they believe that the right actions today will lead to a better tomorrow.

> Entrepreneurs are 4_____ and full of life. They generally work very hard and for long hours.

> Entrepreneurs are very 5_____ . When someone tells them 'You can't do that,' they don't listen and they go ahead and do it anyway.

> Entrepreneurs are highly 6_____ , but not by money or power. They want to create things and achieve things and they just happen to make money at the same time.

Word focus: Describing people

7 What personal qualities does someone need to be successful in your job? Look at the qualities in the box. Which ones are necessary or helpful and why?

> reliable* fair intelligent tidy patient good listener experienced honest strong technical skills helpful efficient loyal* polite well-educated generous* tolerant* good sense of humour

reliable: if someone is reliable, you can trust them to do what you want them to do

loyal: always supporting your friends, colleagues, etc.

generous: giving a lot of money, presents or help to other people

tolerant: letting other people do or say what they want, even if you don't like it

8 Put the qualities in exercise 7 into different groups. Many groupings are possible. For example, you could put together words connected with …

- personality
- work skills
- people skills
- moral values
- something else (what?)

9 Answer these questions.

1 Which words in exercise 7 have opposites beginning with *un-*, *in-*, *im-* or *dis-*?

> unreliable, inexperienced …

2 Think of other words with similar meanings.

> unintelligent - stupid …

Speaking: Top qualities

10 Read the qualities of an ideal boss. Add two more qualities to the list. Then rank them in order of importance. Write 1 for the most important and 12 for the least important.

The ideal boss		
	My ranking	Group ranking
expert in their field		
good communicator		
honest		
energetic and hard-working		
patient		
well-educated		
good sense of humour		
intelligent		
efficient		
generous		

11 Work in pairs or small groups. Compare your rankings and agree on a group ranking. When you disagree, justify your ranking. Try to persuade the other students to change their minds.

12 Work in pairs or small groups. Brainstorm qualities that the two people below need. Which are the three most important qualities for each of them?

fair

patient

loyal

intelligent

helpful

kind

The ideal husband

The ideal teacher

tidy

optimistic

attractive

wealthy

Review 1-4

1 Complete this text. Put the verbs in brackets in the correct tense: either present simple, present continuous or past simple.

Amanda Smith is the owner of a business which ¹_____ (make) greetings cards. Her first job was as personal assistant to a sales team but she ²_____ (not like) it very much. Four years ago, she ³_____ (take) the decision to leave and she ⁴_____ (start) up her own company. At first, she ⁵_____ (not have) any other staff but now the company ⁶_____ (employ) two other people. At present, she ⁷_____ (experience) some difficulties because of the current financial situation but she ⁸_____ (believe) the company can survive. 'All of us ⁹_____ (work) very hard in this period to find new customers,' she says. 'We ¹⁰_____ (love) the work and we won't let the business fail.'

2 Complete this text with the verbs in the box in the past simple.

teach win not be pay not earn
specialize decide not include set need borrow
sell do grow up leave not want

Rahul Pillai was born and ¹_____ in Kochi, in India. His family ²_____ rich at all. His mother ³_____ on an adult education programme but she ⁴_____ much money. She ⁵_____ a second income, so in the mornings she ⁶_____ idlis, a kind of Indian cake, on the streets to make some extra money.

Rahul ⁷_____ well at school and later he ⁸_____ a scholarship to attend a business college. The scholarship ⁹_____ living costs so Rahul ¹⁰_____ a lot of money from the bank in this period. When he ¹¹_____ business school, he ¹²_____ that he ¹³_____ to work in a company or a bank. Instead, he ¹⁴_____ up a catering company which ¹⁵_____ in producing traditional Indian products, including idlis using his mother's recipe. The company was a success and Rahul soon ¹⁶_____ off all his debts. Now he aims to help other young people from poor backgrounds to become entrepreneurs.

3 Use the correct word from the box to complete each question.

Do Is Am Did Does Were Are Was

1 _____ you in the office last Monday?

2 _____ your new boss know your name?

3 _____ the new product selling well?

4 _____ the computer system down yesterday?

5 _____ you go to the conference last week?

6 _____ you working on any special projects at the moment?

7 _____ I late for the meeting?

8 _____ you belong to any professional organizations?

4 Complete these sentences. Put the adjective in brackets into the correct comparative or superlative form.

1 My wife earns a _____ (high) salary than me.

2 Of all our products, this one is definitely the _____ (successful).

3 It's _____ (easy) to find work here than in many parts of the country.

4 Last summer was the _____ (wet) for twenty years.

5 It's _____ (important) to have a job you enjoy than to earn lots of money.

6 I'll remember this as one of the _____ (good) days of my life.

7 This new system is a disaster. It's much _____ (bad) than the old one.

5 Put each word in the box into the correct group according to its stress pattern.

colleague success maintenance acquaintance
strategy average delay support warranty
compliance equipment licence deadline
achievement benefit address (BrE)

Oo	Ooo
student	exercise

oO	oOo
hotel	profession

6 Complete these sentences. Choose the correct prepositions.

1 I'll look *out / into / up* the problem and get back to you.

2 I can't work *off / out / up* what's wrong with your computer.

3 Please could you pick me *out / up / off* from the airport?

4 I'll try to find *out / up /on* the answer to your question.

5 We ran *into / up / out* a lot of problems with the new technology.

6 Hang *up / in / on* a moment, and I'll come with you.

7 Complete this crossword puzzle.

(Crossword grid with numbered cells: 1, 2, 3, 4, 5, 6, 7, 8, 9)

Across

2 Someone who looks after you on a plane is a flight _____.

6 On a plane, if you don't want to sit next to the window, you could ask to sit next to the _____.

7 A piece of paper which shows how much you paid for something.

8 All the bags you carry with you when you are travelling.

9 You will need to pack this before you go on a business trip.

Down

1 Before you can get on a plane, you need to show your _____ pass.

3 Something you can use to carry your bags at the airport.

4 A building where people get onto planes.

5 The activity of visiting interesting places as a tourist.

8 A ride in a car.

8 Complete these sentences. Choose the correct word.

1 I don't have my mobile with me. Can I *lend / borrow* yours?

2 I'm *expecting / waiting* to hear from the suppliers this morning.

3 It's very important to *meet / run into* this deadline.

4 He was *determined / generous* to start his own company and no one could stop him.

5 Last month's figures were really good and we *solved / exceeded* our targets in some areas.

6 The surname is Gilbert-Smith. That's Gilbert, then Smith with a *colon / hyphen* between them.

9 Match each adjective to the correct negative prefix.

honest tolerant polite fair experienced patient reliable loyal

un	*in*	*im*	*dis*

10 Match each phrase 1–8 with the most suitable response a–h.

1 Is this a good time to discuss things?

2 Do you mind if I borrow your pen?

3 Could you sign here, please?

4 I'm sorry to trouble you.

5 I missed the concert last night.

6 I passed my exam.

7 Nice place, isn't it?

8 I don't know how to do this.

a Yes, it's lovely.

b Yes, of course.

c Not really. Can I call you back?

d That's a shame.

e That's terrific. Congratulations!

f No, not at all.

g I'll show you.

h That's quite all right.

11 Write each collocation with the verb *have* in the correct place on the word diagram.

trouble with something lunch a biscuit a headache difficulty a party a cold a cup of coffee a good time toothache

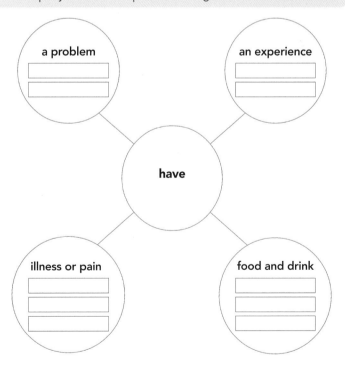

5

A *going to*
B *will*
C **Communication strategies** Offering help
D **Interaction** Making plans

Organized chaos

Reading: Untidiness

1 Are you generally tidy? Do you think these statements are true? Discuss them with a partner.

1 Women are usually tidier than men.

2 Older people are tidier than younger people.

3 Well-educated people are generally tidy.

2 Read the blog posting and find out what the writer thinks.

3 Answer these questions.

1 What do professional organizers do?

2 Why doesn't Jimmy tidy his office?

3 What does Jimmy's wife say about messy desks?

4 Are Jimmy and his wife going to hire a professional organizer?

4 Complete these sentences using words from the text.

1 When you _____ someone, you pay them to work for you.

2 If you feel _____ , you are uncomfortable about what other people think of you.

3 _____ people have received good teaching and learnt a lot.

4 _____ people are very intelligent.

5 If a place is a _____ , it means it's untidy and possibly dirty.

JIMMY'S LIFESTYLE BLOG
– the place to find new ideas on life and living

Mess is best

My wife wants to hire a professional organizer. These are people who go into homes and offices and tell people how to tidy up. What a strange job!

My office is untidy but I'm not embarrassed about it. I work better this way. I'm very productive. I have files and papers that I use regularly and I'm not going to waste time putting them on shelves and then taking them down again.

I read that men are more untidy than women and we become less tidy as we get older. Well-educated people are more untidy, too. In fact, some of the most intelligent and creative people in the world are untidy. Take a look at this desk. Was the owner smart or not?

Unfortunately, my wife doesn't agree with me. She thinks it's more efficient to keep things tidy and she says a messy desk means a messy mind (then what does an empty desk mean?)

Albert Einstein's desk

So we're going to pay for a stranger to come into our house and tell us how to clean up. I know where everything is now. How am I going to find anything when we tidy up?

Grammar: *going to*

5 Find three examples of *going to* in the blog. When do we use it? How do we form questions and negatives? Check your answers in the table below.

going to		
We often use *going to* to talk about future intentions and plans.		
+ She's		*tidy up.*
– I'm not	*going to*	*waste time putting them on shelves.*
? How are we		*find anything?*

> ⚠ **Pronunciation**
> People often say *going to* very quickly so it sounds like *gonna*.

>> **For more information on *going to*, see page 168.**

6 Say what is or is not going to happen in these situations. Use the words in brackets and make positive or negative sentences.

1 You don't need these papers any more. (throw away)
   We're going to throw them away.

2 We don't need these books any more. (keep)
   We aren't going to keep them.

3 Harry's computer hard drive is full. (delete some files)

4 Peter's workspace is a mess but he has no time to do anything about it. (tidy)

5 We have a lot of glass bottles that we don't need any more. (recycle)

6 One of the company cleaners will be 66 next week, but he doesn't want to stop work. (retire)

7 Louise decided to employ a professional organizer to tidy up her home. (do it herself)

8 Mary wants some coffee but her cup is dirty. (wash)

9 Jodie doesn't like her job but she can't find another one at the moment. (leave)

10 Mary wrote her password on a Post-it note and stuck it on her computer. Her supervisor is angry about it. (take it down)

Speaking: Tidy up!

7 Your company's offices are very untidy. Management thinks it creates a bad impression on visitors and is having a negative effect on productivity. Work in pairs. Plan how to make everyone tidy up.

1 Are you going to hire professional organizers to come and tell everyone how to keep things tidy? Why?/Why not?

2 Are you going to …
   a reward employees who are tidy?
   b punish employees who aren't tidy?
   c Both a and b?
   How are you going to reward/punish them?

3 What rules are you going to establish for keeping individual workspaces tidy?

4 How are you going to enforce the rules? Are you going to …
   a have official inspections at the end of each day?
   b create a secret team of 'tidy police' who check at unknown times on different days?
   c do something else (what)?

5 One of your untidiest employees is also one of your most productive employees. He works in a back room where nobody important sees the mess. Are you going to …
   a ignore the problem (why)?
   b insist he keeps things tidy, too (why)?

8 Compare your decisions with another pair. Explain what you are going to do and why. Did you decide to do the same things?

9 Tell the class what you are going to do. Who has the most creative ideas?

TALKING POINT
• Would you like to hire a professional organizer? Why?/Why not?

• Does your organization have a clean-desk policy, so employees must put away all paperwork before they leave their desk? Do you think it's important? Why?/Why not?

Reading: Multitasking

1 See if your brain can multitask (do more than one thing at the same time). Try these experiments.

1 Rub your stomach with your right hand. Keep rubbing and then start to pat your head with your left hand. What happens? Now change the movements so that you pat your stomach and rub your head. What happens?

2 Lift up your right foot and turn it round and round clockwise. Keep turning your foot and then lift your right hand and draw a circle anticlockwise in the air. What happens?

2 Which of these actions can you do at the same time? Which can you not do together? Why not?

1 write a letter and listen to music

2 talk on the phone and write an email

3 listen to the radio and watch a film

4 drive a car and talk on your mobile phone

5 chop an onion and watch TV

3 What happens to efficiency when people multitask? Read the article and find out.

4 Find the words and phrases in the article with these meanings.

1 at the same time

2 finishing dates for something which give you very little time

3 change

4 to become worse

5 difficult

6 gave most of their attention to something

5 Answer these questions.

1 Why do people need to multitask?

2 Why is multitasking inefficient?

3 Where is the part of the brain we use to multitask?

4 Who are better at multitasking: older or younger people?

5 How did great engineers and inventors complete difficult tasks?

One thing at a time

ARE YOU GOOD AT multitasking? Many people need to be these days because it's part of their job. They have to work on two or three projects simultaneously and work to tight deadlines, too. So they rush through the day, taking calls, writing emails and eating their sandwiches at the same time and as a result they make mistakes. The brain needs time to switch from one task to another so multitasking means things take longer than they should. Researchers estimate it costs companies an average of 2.1 hours of work each day.

The area of the brain that we use for multitasking is just behind the forehead*. It allows us to leave something unfinished and then return to the same place later to continue. Unfortunately this part of the brain is the first to deteriorate as we grow older. Young people who can multitask now won't be so good at it in 20 or 30 years' time.

So will employers continue to ask us to work on more and more projects at the same time? They shouldn't because they'll find it leads to more mistakes and lower productivity. Our brains don't work well that way. Employers should remember that the great engineers and inventors of the past didn't multitask. When they had a challenging task, they concentrated all their thoughts and energy on it until the job was completed. Focus, not multitasking, brings success.

forehead: the part of your face above your eyes

Grammar: *will*

6 Look at the examples in the table and complete the rules.

will

We use *will* to talk about the future and make predictions.
Will employers continue to ask us to work on different projects?
They'll find it leads to lower productivity.
*They **won't** be so good at multitasking in 20 years' time.*

Rules:
1 We make questions with *will* by …
   a using *do / does.*
   b changing the word order.
2 The contracted form of *will* is _____ .
3 The contracted form of *will* + *not* is _____ .

! Pronunciation
Contracted forms of *will* are very common in spoken English and they're often difficult to hear. Say these contractions:
I'll, You'll, It'll, He'll, She'll, We'll, They'll, There'll

>> For more information on *will*, see page 169.

7 Make predictions about the future. Give your own opinion. Complete these sentences with *will* or *won't*.

1 People _____ multitask more in the future. (need to)
People <u>will need to</u> multitask more in the future.
2 Companies _____ more older workers in the future. (employ)
3 Most people _____ work before they're 70. (stop)
4 I _____ change jobs many times in my career. (need to)
5 The ability to learn new things fast _____ more important in the future. (become)
6 Children _____ more years in school. (spend)
7 The skills workers need now _____ very different in the future. (be)

8 Compare your predictions with a partner. Do you agree?

Listening: Changing times

9 🔊 **1.20** Listen to three different people talking about skills that workers will need in the future. Make notes of the skills they talk about.

Speaker	Skills
1	
2	
3	

10 Did they think the skills would be more or less important in the future?

11 🔊 Listen again and note down the reasons the speakers give. Do you agree?

Speaking: Future skills

12 Look at these skills. Do you think they will be more important in the future (M) or less important (L)? Then compare your opinions with a partner and explain your reasons.

- writing in clear handwriting
- remembering facts like names and dates
- remembering passwords
- speaking another language which is not English
- speaking to a camera
- doing mathematical calculations in your head
- reading long documents very quickly
- reading maps
- time management skills
- creative thinking skills

TALKING POINT Do you think women are better at multitasking than men? Why?/Why not?

Listening: Offering things

1 Who is the most generous and helpful person you know. Why? In what ways have they helped you and other people?

2))) **1.21** Listen to a conversation and match it to the correct photo. Does the woman sound helpful and generous? Why?/Why not?

C *Are these chocolate biscuits?*

D *Are you making tea?*

A *Is anybody else here hot?*

E *Have you finished with that newspaper?*

F *My memory stick's full. Do you have space on yours?*

3))) Listen again and answer these questions.

1 What was the first question the man asked?

2 What was his second question? What was his third?

3 Why did the woman misunderstand him at first?

4 People often make requests in an indirect way. They say things like 'Do you have any chocolate?' instead of 'Can you give me some chocolate?' Why do you think that is?

5))) **1.22** Listen to four more conversations where people offer things. Match each conversation to the correct photo in exercise 2.

6))) Listen again and complete these offers. Then decide which ones are offering things and which are offering to do things.

1 Do _____ _____ _____ _____ make some for you, too?

2 Would _____ _____ _____ ? Please help yourself.

3 Yes. _____ _____ _____ a copy?

4 _____ you like me to _____ _____ _____ ?

Indirect requests

7 Which group (A or B) are direct and which are indirect? Complete the table. Then match the requests in A to similar requests in B.

Requests	
A _____	**B** _____
1 *Are you going to pass a postbox on your way home?*	a *Would you make me a sandwich?*
2 *It's cold in here. Is that door shut?*	b *Can you post a letter for me?*
3 *What time are you leaving?*	c *Could you shut the door?*
4 *I'm hungry.*	d *Do you mind if I borrow them?*
5 *I have a headache.*	e *May I borrow your mobile?*
6 *Is anyone using these scissors?*	f *Could you give me a lift?*
7 *My battery's run out.*	g *Can you get me an aspirin?*

8 Reply to the indirect requests in exercise 7. Make offers beginning with:

   Do you want me to …?

   Would you like me to …?

9 Do people make indirect requests in your language? Think of some examples.

Speaking: Responding to requests

10 Look at the picture above. How can these people say what they want more directly?

Is anybody else here hot? = Can I turn the fan on?

11 Match these replies to the comments in exercise 10.

1 It's easy. Would you like me to show you?

2 Yes. Do you want to check the football results?

3 I'm afraid I left mine at home today.

4 Oh, sorry. Do you want me to move them?

5 Yes, but they're not ours so you can't have one.

6 Oh, sorry. I borrowed it. I'll put it back.

7 Yes, I'll hang it up in a minute.

8 Yes, would you like a cup?

9 Yes, do you want me to put the fan on?

10 No, but please bring it back when you've finished with it.

11 Yes, why? Do you want me to give you a lift home?

12 I'm really busy just now. Will it take long?

12 Read the notes on saying 'yes' and 'no'. Do you do anything similar in your language?

Saying 'yes' and 'no'

Notice how we agree to requests.

A: Can I turn the fan on?

B: Yes, certainly. / Yes, of course.

We often agree to indirect requests with an offer.

A: Is anybody else here hot?

B: Yes, do you want me to put the fan on?

We often apologize if we have to refuse direct requests.

A: Can I have a biscuit?

B: I'm sorry but I made them for my children's school.

With indirect requests, it's easier to refuse.

A: Those biscuits look nice.

B: Yes, I made them for my children's school.

13 Work with a partner. Use the picture to make up more conversations. Think of more ways to say 'yes' and 'no' to the requests.

Writing: Making offers

14 Several months ago, your friend lent you a book to help you with a research project. You finished using the book weeks ago but forgot to return it. Today you received an email from your friend. Read the email and use the notes to write a reply.

Hi,
How is your research going?
Is the book helpful and are you
still using it?
Cheers,
Jody

In your reply ...

● apologize for keeping the book so long.

● offer to return it in two different ways (for example, in person; by post; by giving it to another friend to pass on to her).

● thank her and say how useful the book was.

Reminder

Grammar reference
pages 168 and 169

going to vs will
We can use *going to* and *will* to talk about the future and in many cases it doesn't matter which.
She's going to be thirty next month.
She'll be thirty next month.

We often use *going to* when we already have a plan.
Today's the day! I'm going to do it now. (I've already decided.)
At the time we're making a decision, we generally use *will*.
It looks complicated. I'll have a cup of tea first. (I'm deciding now.)

Reading: Just do it!

1 Match the two halves of these sayings. What do they mean? Which one do you like the most and why?

1 Never put off until tomorrow
2 An hour in the morning
3 You'll always have enough time
4 There's no time
5 Time is a great teacher

a if you use it well.
b but unfortunately it kills all its students.
c like the present.
d what you can do today.
e is worth two at night.

2 Discuss these questions.

1 Think of someone you know who is very efficient and good at managing their time. Who are they and how do they do it?

2 Think of someone who isn't so good at managing time. Who are they and what stops them from being efficient?

3 Read the thoughts of someone with a job to do. What job is it? Do they put things off for good reasons?

4 Find words and expressions in the text that mean the same as these.

1 a person who keeps records of how much money a business or person has received and spent

2 an official piece of paper with spaces to write information in

3 delay something

4 make something have a thin edge or narrow point at the end

5 not simple or easy to understand

Idle thoughts

9:00
I hate doing my taxes. My accountant sent me the form to fill in months ago and I can't put it off any longer. So today's the day! I'm going to do it now. I'll sharpen my pencil. In fact, I'll sharpen all my pencils …

9:10
I had to clear some space on my desk to work and I found the cookbook I lost. It has a great pasta recipe. I'll just take a look …

9:35
Where's my accountant's email? There are 3982 messages in my in box. I'll run some searches …

9:40
Sandy rang me. I left my umbrella in her car. Is it going to rain this weekend? I'll go to *weather.com* and see …

10:30
While I'm online, I'll check the sports news …

11:40
This tax form looks complicated. I'll have a cup of tea first …

12:00
There's a good programme on television about time management. I'll watch it for five minutes …

1:00
I'm hungry. I can do my taxes after lunch.

2:00
I started work, but then an email message arrived from Facebook. Bill wants to be my friend! I'll log in quickly, say yes, and see what everyone else is doing …

3:50
The doorbell rang and it was Kyoko. She's going to be thirty next month so we had a coffee and chatted about her party.

4:50
Oh, my! Where did the time go? I'll have to do the taxes tomorrow instead.

Word focus: *put off*

5 When we *put something off* we don't do it at the time we should. Instead we decide to do it later. Read the notes on *put off* and write down three different things you put off doing.

---

put off

1 *put off* is often followed by an *-ing* form:
He **put off going** to the dentist.
NOT ~~He put off go to the dentist.~~

2 We always separate the verb when we use *put off* with *it* or *them*:
She **put off** doing her homework. → She **put it off**.
I **put off** doing my taxes. → I **put them off**.

---

6 Look at some ways people put off doing things. Find examples of each one in the text in exercise 3.

1 They spend too long reading things – books, news stories, websites, etc.

2 They allow interruptions. Sometimes it's a good idea to take the phone off the hook or disconnect the doorbell.

3 They don't deal with documents that arrive. They need to file them, throw them away or store them.

4 They avoid jobs because they don't like them or they think they're too difficult.

7 Work in pairs. Talk about the things you put off doing and how you put them off.

Speaking: Making things happen

8 Here are some dreams. Which ones would you like to come true for you? Tick the ones you like. Then pick the five you like best.

Experience zero gravity ☐
Learn to sky dive ☐
Stand up on a surfboard ☐
Climb a mountain ☐
Do a bungee jump ☐
Chase a storm ☐
Learn a language ☐
Learn to play a musical instrument ☐
Write a book ☐
Pay off my debts ☐
Read five books this month ☐
Find a new job ☐
Learn to dance the tango ☐
Loose 20 kilos ☐
Fall in love ☐
Travel the world ☐
Run a marathon ☐
Retire early ☐
Get a master's degree ☐
Work from home ☐
Start my own business ☐
Plant a garden ☐
Get better at small talk ☐
Go on a cruise ☐
Meet the Queen ☐
Sleep under the stars ☐
Have more contact with old friends ☐
Play guitar in a band ☐
Make a movie ☐
Get closer to my children ☐
Visit 12 new places in my city/ town ☐
Take a balloon ride ☐
Tidy my desk ☐
Something else (what?) ☐

9 Compare the dreams you chose with a partner. Would you like to change any of the dreams a little? How? (You can change some of the words.)

10 To make dreams come true you cannot put things off. Work in pairs. Plan how you can make your top five dreams happen.

> **A:** *So you want to visit twelve new places in our town. What are you going to do?*
> **B:** *Well, first I'll do an internet search to find some interesting places.*
> **A:** *Good. Will you ask your friends to suggest places, too?*

11 Report back to the class. Tell them what your partner is going to do.

> **A:** *Stephan's going to visit twelve new places in town. He's going to do some internet research to find some interesting places and …*

Interaction

45

Features and benefits

Numbers

Reading: The Loc8tor

1 Think of a time when you lost something you needed. Work in pairs. Ask and answer these questions.

1 What did you lose?

2 Why was it a problem?

3 Did you find it again? Where?

4 What's the worst thing you can lose?

2 Read an advertisement for a device which helps you find things. How does it work?

3 Match the words and phrases in italics in the text to these definitions.

1 special because it's the only one of its kind _____

2 a tool or piece of equipment _____

3 small and designed to take up little space _____

4 a small device you attach to something so you know where it is _____

5 you can buy it at a price of _____

6 follow the movements of something _____

7 make it start working _____

8 things that you have or own _____

9 attach _____

Don't lose it, loc8te it!

You have half an hour to get to the station. You put on your coat, pick up your briefcase and you're ready to leave the house. But where are your house keys? They're not on the table by the door and they're not in your pockets. You don't have much time. You look inside your briefcase but they're not there. You're going to miss your train.

Buy the Loc8tor and say goodbye to stress like this. The Loc8tor is an easy-to-operate RFID (radio frequency identification) *device* that can quickly find your missing *possessions*. *Stick* a *tag* onto an important item and the Loc8tor can *track* it. You just *switch it on* and key in the object you want to find. The tag beeps loudly and the Loc8tor points towards it. It operates at a frequency of 2.45 GHz so it works through walls and floors and it can find things up to 183 m away. It even works with things that move, so you can stick tags on your children and pets.

The Loc8tor is *unique*. No other device has technology like this and it's *compact*. It's only 11 cm long and 5.3 cm wide, so it fits in your briefcase or handbag. Including batteries, it weighs just 70 g. It *retails at* $169.99 and comes with an easy-to-read user guide and four tags.

With the Loc8tor, you never need to worry about losing things again.

4 Complete these specifications for the *Loc8tor*.

1 Length: _____
2 Width: _____
3 Weight: _____
4 Operating range (distance in metres): _____
5 Operating frequency: _____
6 Number of tags included: _____
7 Price: _____

Word focus: Numbers

5 Look at the numbers in exercise 4. How do you say them? Then check the table.

Numbers	
Decimal numbers	In English, write a point not a comma. After the point, pronounce numbers separately. 2.45 → *two point four five*
Fractions	$\frac{1}{2}$ → *a/one half* $\frac{1}{4}$ → *a/one quarter* $\frac{2}{3}$ → *two thirds* $\frac{7}{8}$ → *seven eighths*
Large numbers	In British English we say *and* after the hundreds but we don't usually in American English. 183 → *a/one hundred and eighty-three* Between every three numbers, we write a comma (not a point). 1,000 → *a/one thousand* 1,000,000 → *a/one million*
Telephone numbers	We pronounce numbers individually in groups of three or four. In British English, we often say 'double' or 'triple' with repeated numbers but we don't in American English. 1870 111 7777 → *one, eight seven oh, triple one, double seven, double seven*
Prices	We write the money symbol before the number but say it after. £99.99 → *ninety-nine pounds, ninety-nine pence* Sometimes we don't pronounce the money symbol. £99.99 → *ninety-nine, ninety-nine*

>> For more information on numbers, see page 174–175.

Listening: Collecting numbers

6 🔊 **1.23** Listen to someone describing another kind of Loc8tor. Complete the answers to these questions.

1 What size is it? ___8.6___ cm x _____ cm
2 How much does it weigh? Just _____ g
3 What size are the tags? _____ cm x _____ cm
4 What's the operating range? _____ m
5 How much does it cost? $ _____
6 How many tags does it come with? _____
7 How can I order it? Visit our website or call _____.

Speaking: What's the number?

7 There are some numbers that we never forget. Write down seven numbers that you find memorable.

1 They can be …
• numbers that are personal to you, e.g. your shoe size.
• interesting numbers that you know, e.g. the speed of light.

2 Try to include a …
• decimal.
• fraction.
• price.
• telephone number.
• measurement.
• large number.

8 Work in pairs. Dictate your numbers to your partner. Check they write them down correctly. Then see if they can guess what they are.

A: *My first number is ten and a half.*
B: *Is that the age of your daughter?*
A: *No, it's the number of hours I worked yesterday.*

TALKING POINT • Would you like a Loc8tor? Why?/Why not?
• Is it a good idea to attach the tags to your children? Why?/Why not?

Reading: Product specifications

1 Look at the photo. Is this a real car or a trick photo? Read the article and find out.

2 Find words and expressions in the text to complete these sentences.

1 A _______ is a kind of ship that can travel underwater.

2 Drive a normal car into water and it _______ to the bottom. Drive a sQuba into water and it _______ on the surface.

3 Scuba divers wear _______ over their faces. They carry a _______ of _______ on their back so they can _______.

4 A _____ is something that somebody does or produces only once.

5 A vehicle which has _______ _______ produces no pollution.

3 Here is some technical data on the *sQuba*. What do you think these things refer to?

A: 3.785 m. Perhaps that's its length.

Specifications	
1 _______________	3.785 m
2 _______________	1.94 m
3 _______________	1.117 m
4 _______________	920 kg
5 _______________	10 m
6 _______________	120 km/h
7 _______________	3 km/h
8 _______________	5 electric engines
9 _______________	Not for sale
10 _______________	white
11 _______________	2

4 Here is the missing information from the specifications. Complete the table with the items in the box. What other information would you like to know about the sQuba?

Colour   Weight
Maximum speed on land
Height   Width   Length
Seating capacity   Dive depth
Maximum speed underwater
Price   Power

Making a splash

Many years ago in *The Spy Who Loved Me*, James Bond drove his car into the sea and it turned into a submarine. It was trick photography, but when Frank Rinderknecht, a Swiss inventor, saw the movie, he decided he wanted to build a car like that. It took him thirty years, but the result is the sQuba: the world's first underwater car.

When the sQuba enters the water, it floats on the surface. Then, when the driver decides to let in the water, it sinks to a depth of up to ten metres and travels like a submarine. There's no roof, so the driver and passenger need to put on masks to breathe. The sQuba comes with a tank of compressed air, like the tanks that scuba divers use.

The sQuba is a one-off concept vehicle. So there is only one sQuba and you can't buy it. It's powered by five electric engines and it has zero emissions so there's no pollution. It's a 21st century vehicle.

Listening: Asking for information

5 1.24 Listen to seven different people asking about the sQuba and complete these sentences.

1 I'd like to know its _______. How _______ is it?

2 How _______ can it go when it's travelling on the _______ of the water?

3 I know it goes underwater, but how _______ does it go?

4 How _______ are the engines?

5 How much does it _______ and what does the price _______? Does it _______ with a five-year _______?

6 I'm surprised it doesn't _______ to the bottom of the sea. How _______ does it _______?

7 How _______ can it travel underwater? And how _______ does the air _______?

6 Can you find the answers in the specifications in exercise 3? (It is not always possible.)

Grammar: Question forms

7 Complete the table.

1 Find words in exercise 4 to complete the first column.

2 Complete the second column with these words: *wide, weigh, high, long, heavy, deep.*

3 Are the words you wrote verbs, nouns or adjectives?

Question forms: Dimensions

	What's the l_____?	How _____ is it?
	What's the w_____?	How _____ is it?
	What's the h_____?	How _____ is it?
	What's the d_____	How _____ is it?
	What's the w_____?	How _____ is it? How much does it _____?

How long …?
We use *how long* to ask about dimensions and time.
How long is it?   3 metres.
How long does the air last?   2 or 3 hours.

Speaking: What is it?

8 Here are the specifications for another water transport device. Work in pairs. Student A: Look at the information below. Ask and answer questions and complete the table. Student B: Turn to File 13, page 141.

   B: How fast can it go?
   A: 27 kilometres per hour.

Max speed	27 km/h
Weight	
Materials	Aluminium and fibreglass
Colour	
Seating capacity	1
Height	
Width	2.44 m
Length	
Power	No petrol required – just human jumping power
Price	

9 What do you think the device is? Compare your ideas. Then check your answer: Turn to File 33, page 145. Would you like to buy one? Why?/Why not?

10 Work in pairs. Student A: Look through your briefcase or handbag and find an object. Say why you think the product is useful and why your partner should buy it. Student B: Ask questions about the specifications. Then change roles.

   A: This is a … It's useful because …
   B: How big/wide/long/heavy is it?
   A: …
   B: What is it made of?
   A: …
   B: What colours does it come in?
   A: …
   B: How long will it last?
   A: …

> **!** We pronounce km/h as *kilometres per hour* or *kilometres an hour.*

TALKING POINT   Would you like to drive or ride in the sQuba? Why?/Why not?

Reading: Sales techniques

1 Salespeople use different techniques to make customers buy their products. Work in pairs. Think of some sales techniques. Which ones are most effective?

A: Salespeople often list the price as €9.99, not €10.00 to make the product seem cheaper.

B: They also say things like 'lots of intelligent people are buying the product'.

2 Read about some sales techniques in the article. Did you think of any of these?

3 Find words in the article that mean the same as these phrases.

1 can be trusted

2 other companies offering similar products or services

3 a business agreement that helps both sides

4 amounts of money you have to pay for goods or services

5 think that something is true, although you have no proof

6 can be easily bought or found

7 say nice things about someone, sometimes when you don't really mean it

8 nice things you say about someone that show you admire them

4 Why do you think the sales techniques work?

5 Here are some reasons why psychologists think the techniques work. Match them to the correct techniques in the article.

a Your customer imagines what it will be like to have the product. This makes it easier for them to decide to buy.

b Your customer sees the low price and makes the decision to buy. People don't like to change their mind, so they'll often agree to a higher price later.

c When you give someone a gift, they'll want to respond and give you something, too, or do something you want.

d For some reason, three is a powerful number.

e When products are scarce so there aren't enough of them, they seem more valuable. Time can be scarce, too. People don't want deals to disappear, so time pressure makes them buy.

f Customers like to buy things from people they like. They want to know that people like them, too.

The psychology of selling – six techniques that work

1 List your product's features in threes, for example: 'Our cleaning service is cheaper, faster and more reliable than our competitors'.'

2 Offer a fantastic price like: 'A new floor for only €1,000' so your customer agrees to the deal. Then tell them about the extra charges: 'Delivery is €300 and installation is €500.'

3 Assume your customer's going to buy your product. Don't wait for them to say: 'I'll take it.' Ask questions like: 'When do you want us to deliver it?' or 'What will your neighbours say about it?'

4 Give things away. This is very effective when you don't just give one thing but you give several things away. 'I'm going to give you free batteries and a carrying case.'

5 Say there aren't many products available, or they're only available for a limited time. For example: 'There aren't many left' or 'The sale finishes tomorrow.'

6 Flatter your customers and pay them compliments. Say nice things like: 'That hat really looks good on you.'

Listening: It's now or never

6 🔊 **1.25** Listen to some salespeople at work. Which of the sales techniques in the article is each one using?

a _____   b _____   c _____   d _____   e _____   f _____

7 🔊 Here are some of the things the salespeople said. Match the beginnings to the endings. Then listen again and check your answers.

1 It's really nice talking to someone …	**a** Seventeen hundred covers everything.
2 I checked with our warehouse …	**b** I'm only going to charge thirty pounds!
3 It's going to look lovely above your fireplace. …	**c** and they have one more in stock.
4 Yes, it includes airport taxes, hotel transfers and insurance. …	**d** who's an expert on these things.
5 It comes with a spare battery …	**e** And it'll brighten up your room, too.
6 I'm feeling very generous today, so …	**f** a charger and a 12-month warranty.

8 What are the sentences in exercise 7 about? (More than one answer is sometimes possible.)

a the product   **b** the price   **c** availability   **d** other things the customer wants to hear

Speaking: Persuasive selling

9 Look at these phrases. Which ones could a salesperson use to sell a jacket (J), a car (C) or both (B)?

1 We'll give you a free service, a two-year warranty and a GPS system.

2 Wow! It really looks good on you.

3 What will your friends say when they see it?

4 This is the last one we have left. There are no more in stock.

5 It's very flattering. It makes you look slimmer.

6 I can tell you know a bargain when you see one.

10 Work in pairs. Take turns to be a salesperson and a customer. Student A: Look at the information below. Student B: Turn to File 17, page 142.

1 You need a new car. You'd like something reliable and high tech, and you also want a good deal. You go to the car showroom where Student B works as a salesperson. Take five minutes to think of questions to ask Student B.

2 You work in a department store and sell jackets. Student B is a customer. Try to persuade Student B to buy a jacket. Make sure you're very nice and try to flatter Student B. Take five minutes to plan what you're going to say. Then begin with: *Good morning. Can I interest you in a jacket?*

11 Work in pairs. Choose one of the sales techniques and write another sales conversation to illustrate how the technique works. Read your conversation to the class.

Communication strategies

Product presentations often include facts and specifications.
It's just 12 cm long.

They're also persuasive.
It's a very quick, simple and clever solution.
It will look really good in your living room or bedroom.

Reading: No more wobbling!

1 What do you think this product is for? Compare your ideas with some other students.

2 Read the article and find out if you are right.

A ridiculous idea?

Dragons' Den is a TV programme where people make presentations to a panel of five rich business people, the 'dragons'. They try to persuade them to invest in their business in return for a share of their company. Only a small number are successful and get the investment they want. But sometimes the investors make the wrong decision.

When Andrew Gordon went on the show and presented his new product, Stabletable, all five investors laughed at it. Stabletable is a simple device that you put under a table leg to stop the table wobbling*. It's made up of eight pieces of plastic and it's adjustable, so it works under any table. One investor called it 'the most ridiculous idea' on the show so far.

But Andrew still believed in his idea. He continued to produce and market the product, and sales of Stabletable continued to grow. Now even the British Royal family use it in Kensington Palace and Andrew is on the way to becoming a millionaire.

wobbling: moving unsteadily from side to side

3 These statements are false. Look at the article again and correct them.

1 Most people who appear on *Dragons' Den* get funding.

2 Only one investor liked Andrew Gordon's product.

3 Andrew stopped producing Stabletable after the programme.

4 Sales of Stabletable decreased after the programme.

5 Andrew is now a millionaire.

Listening: A product presentation

4 Here are some things you can do when you present a product. What is the best order to do them in? Compare your ideas with a partner.

a Describe the product.

b Invite questions.

c Introduce yourself.

d Summarize in one sentence why people should buy it.

e Describe the problem the product solves.

5))) **1.26** Listen to someone presenting Stabletable. What order do they do the things in exercise 4?

6))) Listen again and complete these sentences.

1 Today _____ _____ _____ _____ _____ a very simple but very clever product: Stabletable.

2 Picture _____ _____. You're meeting some friends in a bar or restaurant.

3 Here's _____ _____ _____: Stabletable. You can put this _____ _____ under the legs of any wobbly item.

4 It's an _____ _____ for anyone who likes going to bars and restaurants.

5 Stabletable _____ _____ _____ _____ _____ colours.

6 Remember, with Stabletable, _____ _____ _____ _____ sit at a wobbly table again.

7 Now, _____ _____ _____ any questions?

7 The presentation also includes information about the product features (facts and specifications) and also its benefits (the ways it can help). Look at this example. Then match the other features and benefits.

It comes in a range of colours	so	everyone can choose their favourite.
↑		↑
feature		benefit

Features	Benefits
1 It's only 60 cm long and 20 cm thick.	a It's easy to order.
2 It's adjustable.	b You can afford to buy one for all your friends.
3 Different print designs are available.	c You can carry it on a key ring.
4 A pack of ten retails at under £20.	d You can personalize it with your company's logo.
5 You can buy it from our hotline or website.	e You can make it the right height to stop the wobbling.

Word focus: -able and -ful

8 Something you can adjust is *adjustable* and something with lots of uses is *useful*. Add *-able* or *-ful* to these words to make more adjectives you can use in presentations. You may need to change the spelling.

1 fashion	_____	6 value	_____
2 power	_____	7 profit	_____
3 beauty	_____	8 delight	_____
4 comfort	_____	9 success	_____
5 help	_____	10 rely	_____

9 Think of more words ending with *-able* and *-ful*.

> **!** *-y* often changes to *i*: *Beauty → beautiful*.
> Sometimes we drop the final *-e*: *desire → desirable*

Speaking: A winning presentation

10 Work in pairs. Read some information about another product and prepare a presentation to persuade people to buy it.

Think about …

• the stages of the presentation.

• sales techniques you can use to be persuasive.

• how to divide the different parts of the presentation. Both presenters should do part of it.

Pair A: Read about the Flower quiver: File 16, page 142

Pair B: Read about the Q-top: File 11, page 141

Pair C: Read about the Beanock: File 28, page 144

11 Form groups with two other pairs and give your presentations.

12 Discuss these questions.

1 Who gave the best sales presentation and why?

2 Which product is the most useful and why?

3 Each of the three products appeared on *Dragons' Den*. A dragon promised to invest in one of them. Which do you think it was? (To find out turn to File 22, page 142.)

Writing: A PowerPoint presentation

13 Choose a product from exercise 10 or another product you like, for example a gadget you enjoy using or would like to use. Write some PowerPoint slides to accompany a sales presentation for the product.

Write slides about …

• the problem it solves.

• its features and benefits.

• its specifications.

Interaction

7

A Modals of obligation
B Modal question forms
C **Communication strategies** Instructions
D **Interaction** Learning from play

Playing by the rules

Modals of obligation

Reading: Workplace rules

1 Do you or your colleagues work under pressure? What do people do to relax and relieve stress at work?

2 Read about three companies with unusual ways to relieve workplace stress. Which idea do you like most and why?

3 Find words or expressions in the article which mean the same as these phrases.

1 the level of positive feeling that people have about their work

2 producing or achieving a lot

3 restrict, keep something below a certain amount

4 unhappy because you know you have done something wrong

5 a short sleep

4 Answer these questions.

1 Who benefits when employee morale is high and why?

2 What are Burton Snowboards' employees allowed to do? What do they have to do?

3 What limit does the Dutch insurance company put on playing computer games?

4 Why does the managing director of Vielife think taking a nap is a good idea?

5 Could the ideas work in your workplace? Would they make you more productive? Why?/Why not?

Relax the rules and boost productivity

When employee morale is high, everyone benefits. Happy employees are more enthusiastic about their work. That means they're more productive, so employers are happy, too. But it's difficult to be enthusiastic when you're working long hours under pressure. Here are three companies that have found unusual ways to put smiles on their employees' faces. They've relaxed the rules and increased productivity at the same time.

Animals are welcome at Burton Snowboards' headquarters in Vermont and employees are allowed to bring their pets to work. They don't have to worry about getting home on time to feed or take care of them and that helps when they need to work late. It costs the company nothing and improves morale. The only rule is 'You must clean up after your pet'.

In most companies, workers can't play computer games because employers think they're a waste of time. But an insurance company in the Netherlands finds that games like patience* help their workers to relax. They have to limit how long they play but if it's  one hour or less a day, productivity increases. Perhaps more organizations should try it.

'You mustn't sleep on the job' is the rule in most companies, but you don't need to worry about it at Vielife, a London-based consulting firm. They have a dark room with a comfortable chair and soft music where employees can go for a short sleep when they're tired. The company's managing director says employees return to work with more energy, so they shouldn't feel guilty about taking a nap in the middle of the day.

patience: a card game you can play on your computer
AmE: *solitaire*

Grammar: Modal verbs

5 Complete the table with the verbs in the box.

> must   mustn't   ~~can~~   can't   have to   don't have to
> need to   don't need to   should   shouldn't

Modals of obligation	
Possible or allowed	can
Forbidden or not allowed	
Necessary or obligatory	
Not necessary	
A good idea or the right thing to do	
Not a good idea or the wrong thing to do	

>> For more information on modal verbs, see page 170.

6 Here are some more ideas for improving morale in the workplace. Choose the best verbs to complete the sentences.

1 An email-free day
This is a day when nobody is allowed to send emails. When they *mustn't / need to* communicate with someone, they *must / don't have to* ring them or go and speak to them face to face.

2 A casual dress day
Forget the dress code on Fridays. If employees don't want to wear a suit and tie, they *mustn't / don't have to*. They *can / should* even wear jeans if they want.

3 'Great job' emails
You *should / shouldn't* send these messages when you want to thank a colleague that helped you. The computer system automatically forwards them to your colleague's manager, so they *can / don't need to* hear about their good work.

4 A beautiful baby competition
Everyone *needs to / mustn't* bring a photograph of themselves as a baby to work. Then you put them on the wall and everyone *has to / doesn't have to* guess whose photos they are.

5 Physical exercises
The employees get together before the work day begins and do physical exercises for half an hour. Everyone *shouldn't / has to* join in.

6 A potluck lunch
You *don't have to / mustn't* eat in the company canteen on potluck days. It's not necessary because everyone brings a dish of food that you *don't need to / can* all share.

7 Stand-up meetings
Long meetings are boring. To keep them short, tell everyone that they *can't / need to* sit down. If they're still too long, tell everyone they *must / don't have to* stand on one leg.

Speaking: Improving morale

7 Work in pairs or small groups. Discuss each of the ideas in exercise 6.

1 Do you do these things or similar things in your organization?

2 Would you like to introduce these ideas in your workplace? Why?/Why not?

8 Think of some more things organizations can do to reduce stress and improve employee morale. Share your ideas with the class. Explain why you think they are a good idea.

TALKING POINT   What rules would you like to change in your workplace? What rules don't you want to change?

Reading: Working from home

1 Work in pairs. Think of five things companies often do when they want to cut costs. Then tell the class your ideas.

2 Read about what happened at Acuity, an insurance company in Wisconsin, USA. Do you think their productivity fell or improved as a result? Why?

> In the late 1990s Acuity wanted to cut costs. To save money, it closed and sold 12 of its 13 branch offices and told its employees that they had to work from home instead. Flexitime and telecommuting became part of the corporate culture. Employees who needed to travel received a company car, a lap top, a cell phone and pager and $100 to buy audio books. The company paid for internet access and computer software but not for office space.

3 In fact productivity improved and Acuity has won many awards for being one of the best companies to work for in the US. Read about another company where employees do not work fixed hours. How is it similar to or different from the organization you work for?

> Best Buy, the leading electronics retailer in the US, has a new way to manage its staff. It focuses on results and not on how long employees spend at work. Employees mustn't miss their targets but they can work when they want and where they want. The system seems to be working. Staff turnover is down and productivity is up by 35 per cent on average.

Listening: Changing times

4)) **1.27** Listen to Best Buy employees talking about the system. Are these statements true (T) or false (F)? Correct the ones which are wrong.

1 Everyone has targets that they need to meet.

2 Employees can only work from home if their manager agrees to it.

3 They have to attend important meetings.

4 They mustn't talk about the hours they work.

5 Some managers think that people should work in the office.

6 It's easy for everyone to switch off from work.

> **!** Americans don't use the contracted form *mustn't*. Instead they often say *'not allowed'*.
> We're **not allowed** to talk about the hours anybody works.

5)) Listen to the interview again and complete these questions.

1 So, _____ work from home any time you want?

2 _____ ask for permission from your manager first?

3 _____ go into the office for meetings?

4 So, _____ allow their employees to work from home?

6 Work in pairs. Discuss these questions.

1 How many hours do you work a week? Officially and actually?

2 Does your company log your time? For example, do you have to fill in time sheets?

3 How do your managers judge your productivity?

4 Could the Best Buy system work in your workplace? Why?/Why not?

Grammar: Modal question forms

7 Look at the table and complete the rules.

Modal question forms

Can you work from home?	Yes, we *can*.
Do you **need to** ask for permission?	No, we **don't**.
Does she **have to** go in for meetings?	No, she **doesn't**.
Should all companies do this?	Yes, they **should**.

Rules:

1 With semi-modals like _____ and _____ we use *do* or *does* to form questions and short answers.

2 With full modals like _____ and _____ we change the word order to form questions and short answers.

>> For more information on modal question forms, see page 170.

8 Work with a partner. Ask and answer questions about rules in your place of work or study. Use the verbs in brackets.

A: *Can you work from home some days?*

B: *Yes, I can, but I have to get permission first.*

1 work from home some days (can)

2 show a security pass to enter the building (have to)

3 smoke in the buildings (can)

4 wear any special clothing (need to)

5 be in the office at a particular time each morning (have to)

6 send joke emails to your colleagues (can)

7 belong to a trade union* (have to)

8 attend many meetings (need to)

trade union: a workers' organization

Speaking: Meeting guidelines

9 Work in pairs or groups. Find out about some of the meetings your colleagues need to attend.

1 Who are they with?

2 What are they about?

3 Are any meetings in English? What languages do people speak?

10 Discuss how people should behave in meetings. Should these things be allowed or forbidden? Or does it depend on something? If so, what?

1 arriving late

2 shaking hands with everyone before the meeting begins

3 switching off your mobile phone

4 calling people by their first names

5 smoking

6 disagreeing openly with the boss

7 eating snacks

8 talking about the subjects on the agenda and nothing else

11 Create some meeting guidelines.

1 Agree on some ways people should behave in meetings. Write them down.

People need to arrive on time.

2 Read your guidelines to the class. Decide which five are the most important.

Writing: Describing changes

12 You have a new boss and they have made some changes to the way you do things at work. Write an email to a friend telling them about it.

1 Choose to write about two good changes or two bad changes, for example, changes to working hours, dress code, security procedures, meeting procedures, etc.

2 Select from the alternatives below and fill in the gaps.

Hi, _____
Thanks for your email. It was nice to hear from you.

Work *is / isn't* going well at the moment. things are different with out new boss. He's made some *terrific / terrible* changes. Last year we *could / couldn't* _____ but now we *can / have to / don't have to* _____ . Another change is that now we *can / should / don't need to* _____ .

Everyone *likes / is complaining* about the new rules. I think they're a great *improvement / big mistake*. What do you think?

All the best / Love,

_____

TALKING POINT What are the advantages of employees working from home? What are the disadvantages?

Listening: Giving instructions

1 Work in pairs. How do you like to receive instructions? Answer these questions.

1 You buy a piece of furniture that you need to assemble. What will you do when you open the box and why?

a Read the instructions.

b Look at the pieces and try to work out how they fit together.

c Something else (what?)

2 A co-worker needs to teach you how to do something on the computer. What would you like them to do and why?

a Take the mouse and show you.

b Give you the mouse and tell you what to do.

c Something else (what?)

3 Your boss needs to explain a complicated process to you. How do you want them to begin and why?

a Start with the first step, and then go on to the second step.

b Ask you what you already know about the process and start from there.

c Something else (what?)

2)) **1.28** Listen to someone explaining a work task. Complete the missing instruction. Do you think they explained it well?

> ### How to schedule a meeting
> 1 Open Meeting Manager.
> 2 Select the date, room and time.
> 3 _____.
> 4 Click 'enter'.

3)) Listen again and complete these sentences.

1 Oh, it's easy. First, _____ _____ _____ open up your Meeting Manager program.

2 _____ select the date. _____ _____, choose a room …

3 Now select a time. _____ _____. Now click 'enter'. _____. Oh, that's strange.

4 Hang on. _____ slow down.

5 _____ _____ _____ click too fast.

6 I see the problem. _____ _____ _____ type the cost centre number in the box on the left.

7 Then _____ _____ _____ ask your manager to give you one.

4 Compare the written instructions in exercise 2 with the spoken instructions in exercise 3.

Which ones are …

1 shorter?

2 more detailed?

3 more friendly?

5 Here are some things people often do when they give spoken instructions. Find examples of these things in exercise 3.

1 They explain in what order to do things.

2 They say 'You'. So instead of 'Do this', they say 'You need to do this' or 'You want to do this'.

3 They also say 'We …' and 'Let's …' when they're working together with someone.

4 They say 'Try not to …' to warn about things you shouldn't do.

5 They give praise.

6 Complete the table with words and phrases from the box.

Let's try   After that   That's great   You want to …   Try not to …   Now

Giving instructions	
Explaining the order of steps:	First, …, Then …, ¹_____ …, Next …, ²_____ …
Explaining what to do:	³_____ select the date. Then you need to select the time.
Working together:	⁴_____ again. We have to type the number in the box.
Giving gentle warnings:	⁵_____ forget the number.
Giving praise:	That's right. / ⁶_____ . / Good!

Word focus: Computer terms

7 Match the verbs to the icons.

1	save	7	paste
2	print	8	zoom in
3	delete	9	zoom out
4	highlight		
5	cut		
6	copy		

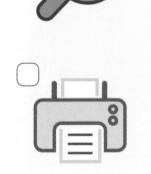

8 Think of ways to change these written instructions into things people might say. Use phrases from the box in exercise 6. Then read them to your partner. Try to sound encouraging and helpful.

1 Select 'page layout'. Go to 'size'. Click on 'A4'. Save the changes. Print the document.

2 Delete the file. Create a new one.

3 Copy the picture. Paste it into a new document.

4 Don't choose a password that's easy to guess.

5 Zoom in. Highlight the text. Zoom out.

Speaking: Teach me how

9 Work in pairs. Look at these written instructions for using chopsticks. Think of ways to say them and sound friendly. Then practise giving the instructions to each other. You can use pencils to practise in place of chopsticks.

How to eat with chopsticks

Step 1
Take a chopstick and hold it between your thumb and middle finger. The chopstick shouldn't touch your forefinger.

Step 2
Take another chopstick and place it between your thumb and forefinger. The two chopsticks must be parallel.
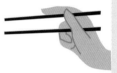

Step 3
Keep the first chopstick stationary and practise moving the second chopstick towards the stationary one. Don't move the first chopstick.

Step 4
Position the chopsticks around a piece of food, and move the sticks together.

Step 5
Hold the food firmly and lift it towards your mouth. Don't drop it.

10 Think of some things you know how to do well.

For example, how to ...

- cook spaghetti.
- change a car tyre.
- take a photograph with your phone.
- win at chess.
- make a paper aeroplane.
- hit a golf ball.
- sell things using the internet.

11 Look for a partner you can exchange your skills with. Find someone who can teach you something you want to learn and who wants to learn one of your skills. Take turns teaching one another your skills.

12 When you have finished, ask your partner for feedback.

Do they think ...

1 your instructions were clear?

2 you sounded friendly and helpful?

Communication strategies

Reminder

Grammar reference page 170

We use *must, have to* and *need to* to say when things are obligatory or necessary. We use *mustn't* and *can't* to say when things are forbidden or not allowed.

We use *don't have to* and *don't need to* to say when things are not necessary. We use *should* when something is the right thing to do and *shouldn't* when it is the wrong thing.

Reading and speaking: Mind games

1 Read a dilemma and discuss the questions.

> You're choosing between three candidates for a job. They are all well-educated and they all have the right experience and personality. You look at their applications and notice that one candidate's hobby is basketball, another's is video games and the third one enjoys playing chess.

1 Will their hobbies affect your choice? Why?/Why not?

2 Does it make a difference if you're selecting …

a an executive for a job that requires strategic thinking?

b a doctor who needs to perform keyhole surgery (an operation where the surgeon uses cameras and makes very small cuts)?

c the president of your country?

d something else (what)?

3 Which hobby would you like your husband/wife to have? Why?

2 Read this article. Does it make you want to change your mind about your answers in exercise 1?

3 Are these statements about the article correct? Write *yes, no* or *doesn't say.*

1 Michelle Obama played basketball with Barack to find out what he was like.

2 Michelle's brother approved of Barack.

3 Video games develop important skills for keyhole surgeons.

4 Research shows that most surgeons enjoy video games.

5 You have to evaluate threats and respond fast to play bridge.

6 Students at Hampton University's business school only play chess with each another.

7 Students can learn many business and life skills from chess.

4 Work in pairs or small groups and discuss these questions.

1 Which games are popular in your country? Make a list. Include card games, board games and sports.

2 Which games can develop business skills and how?

3 Which games do you enjoy playing and why? Which don't you enjoy, and why not?

4 Think of some games you played as a child. What useful skills did they teach you about business and life?

5 Plato, the Greek philosopher, said, 'You can discover more about a person in an hour of play than in a year of conversation.' Do you agree? Why?/Why not?

6 What have you learnt about people from playing games with them?

Learning from play

You can learn a lot about people from playing games with them. Before Michelle Obama married Barack, she sent him to play basketball with her brother. Barack didn't know, but it was a test. She wanted to know what he was like as a person. After the game, her brother told her Barack was a good team player. He shared the ball, but not too much and he liked him. The rest is history.

You can also learn a lot of practical skills from playing games. Researchers have found that people who are good at video games often make the best surgeons. In one study, keyhole surgeons who played video games were 27 per cent faster and made 37 per cent fewer errors in the operating room than those who didn't.

Different games develop different skills. For example, to play backgammon you need to think quickly and calculate risks. To play the card game bridge you need social interaction and communication skills. Chess requires strategic thinking. In fact for many students at Hampton University's business school, chess isn't just a game they play for fun. It's a game they must play to get their MBA. As part of their first year course, students need to play 20 strangers over the internet. The school believes that chess teaches important skills like strategic planning, problem solving and time management. The students have to learn to lose, laugh, and fight again, so it also teaches skills for life. ■

Speaking: The 'name it' challenge

5 Work in pairs or small groups. Get ready to play a game. First, read the rules. Is everything clear?

6 One important rule is missing. Decide what it should be. Come to a joint decision.

> What should you do when someone gives a wrong answer?
> **a** Give them no points?
> **b** Make them lose points? How many?

Rules

1 The person with the largest feet starts. The person with the smallest feet keeps score.
2 Toss a coin to move around the board. Heads: move one square. Tails: move two squares.
3 Try to complete the challenge on each square. If you're successful, you score the point(s). If not, you get no points.
4 When you take too long to complete a challenge, you lose a point.
5 If you land on a square someone landed on before, you can choose to move onto the next square, or try the challenge, too.
6 The person with the most points at the end is the winner.

7 Now play the game. If necessary, make up more rules as you play.

FINISH Congratulations! Now add up your score.	**35** Name something you shouldn't try to repair yourself. 2 points	**34** Can you say the English alphabet backwards in less than 30 seconds? Do it! 5 points	**33** Name three things you want to buy but can't afford. 2 points	**32** Think of three things you shouldn't say to a customer. 3 points	**31** Name three people who have to wear uniforms. 1 point
25 Name three things you have to do when you get home tonight and two things you can do. 3 points	**26** Name three things you can't do in a library. 2 points	**27** What kinds of documents do you have to shred (cut into very small pieces)? 2 points	**28** Name three things you can do to save money. 3 points	**29** Name something you can't wear at work. 1 point	**30** Name four different ways you can get to work without going by car. 2 points
24 Name three things you should pack when you go on a trip abroad. 1 point	**23** Find out what time everyone has to be at work tomorrow. 2 points	**22** Name three things you need to do to improve your English. 3 points	**21** Name something you have to do this weekend and something you don't have to do. 3 points	**20** Name three things you can do at work to help the environment. 2 points	**19** Name three security procedures you have to follow at work. 2 points
13 Think of three things you shouldn't say to your boss. 3 points	**14** Name a document you mustn't throw away. 3 points	**15** Name three things people do when they can't sleep at night. 2 points	**16** Name two things you should check regularly. 3 points	**17** Ask another student to lend you €5. You can only score points if they do. 5 points	**18** Name two things you can't do when you're driving. 2 points
12 Name something you have to keep locked and something you have to keep locked up. 3 points	**11** Name something you don't have to pay for. 2 points	**10** What mustn't you do when you see this sign? ℗ 1 point	**9** Name three different kinds of tax you have to pay. 2 points	**8** Name two things you have to do and two things you can do before you get on a flight at the airport. 3 points	**7** Can you say the months of the year backwards in 20 seconds? Do it! 4 points
1 **START HERE** ☞	**2** Explain what you must do when a fire alarm goes off. 1 point	**3** Explain what you have to do if you're sick on a workday. 1 point	**4** Name three things you can do in your coffee breaks. 1 point	**5** Name three days when you don't have to work. 1 point	**6** Explain what you should do before you send an email. 1 point

8 What did you learn from the game?

1 Did you learn any English that's useful for your job? What?

2 Did you learn anything about the other players? Who was …

  a the most competitive player?

  b the most imaginative player?

  c the best team player?

Interaction

8

A Present perfect
B yet and *already*
C **Communication strategies** Sharing ideas
D **Interaction** Dealing with change

What's the big idea?

Present perfect

Reading: Feature overload

1 Think of some hi-tech products that you have bought. Was it easy to learn how to use them? Why?/Why not?

2 Read the article. What did the writer buy and what problem did they have?

Hi-tech headaches

I've just bought a new digital video recorder. It can store 350 hours of programmes and record two programmes simultaneously. But the remote control has 70 buttons and I can't work out which ones to press to record anything.

I know I'm not alone. A study by Philips Electronics showed that more than half the products that people returned had nothing wrong with them. The problem was *consumers* couldn't work out how to use them. Now the company has begun a 'sense and simplicity' campaign to make its products less *complicated*.

Technology *upgrades* are cheap so *manufacturers* have loaded products with too many features. It's time to send a message to the designers: KISS (Keep it *simple*, stupid).

3 Complete these sentences with the words in italics in the article.

1 Designers are the people who design products, _____ make them and _____ are the people who use them.

2 I like it when there are _____ for my computer. Everything works better and I can do more things.

3 It's difficult to follow instructions when they are _____. Manufacturers need to keep their instructions _____.

Grammar: Present perfect

4 Read the examples and complete the rule.

Present perfect

We use the present perfect when past actions are important in the present.

*Designers **have loaded** products with features.*
(The features are available now.)

*The company **has begun** a campaign.*
(The campaign is running now.)

We often use the present perfect to give news. If something has happened a very short time ago, we can add *just*.

*I've **just bought** a new digital video recorder.*

Rule:

We form the present perfect with _____ or _____ + past participle.

Use a list of irregular verbs to find out which ones have different past participles.

>> For more information on the present perfect see page 165.

Listening: New products

5 🔊 **1.29** Look at these hi-tech products and listen to four different conversations. Match each conversation to the correct photo. What is good or bad about each product?

6 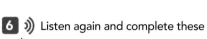 Listen again and complete these sentences.

1 Oh, yes. _____ _____ now. _____ you _____ inside?

2 I _____ _____ it but I need to.

3 But _____ _____ problems making calls.

4 This one's great. _____ _____ it for about a month.

5 _____ _____ _____ reliable?

7 Find examples of questions and negative forms in exercise 6. Then complete these rules.

Present perfect questions and negatives

Rules:

1 We use *hasn't* and _____ in negative sentences.

2 We change the word order to form _____.

8 Complete these sentences. Use the verbs from the box in the present perfect.

> install   program   break down   show
> buy   (not) work out   (not) use

1 Tom's car _____. Its computer says there's something wrong with the steering lock and it won't start.

2 _____ Peter _____ you how to use the television? I'm afraid it's a bit complicated.

3 They _____ a new voicemail system at work. We have to press ten buttons before we can hear our messages.

4 My car has a computerized electronic locking system. I _____ it yet because I'm worried that I'll lock myself in.

5 My husband bought a new electric toothbrush with computer sensors a month ago. He still _____ how to use it.

6 _____ you _____ a new stereo? I think you had a different one last time I was here.

7 I _____ the coffee maker. Tomorrow morning it's going to wake us up, play us music and make us cappuccino.

Speaking: Updates and upgrades

9 Look at this web page and say what changes Cool Presents has made to their products. Use these verbs

> reduce   improve   upgrade   add   introduce   simplify

10 Work in pairs. Take it in turns to be a Cool Presents salesperson and a customer calling to place an order. The Salesperson's information is below. Customer 1's information is in File 14, page 141. Customer 2's information is in File 19, page 142.

Salesperson
Your partner will call you to place an order. Tell them about the improvements you've made to your products and try to persuade them to buy as many things as possible.

Use the information on the web page and make up any other information you like. Take a few minutes to prepare what to say before they call. Answer the phone with: *'Cool Presents. How can I help you today?'*

TALKING POINT   Who is to blame for products that are difficult to use:

    a designers who make them too complicated?

    b manufacturers who add cheap features?

    c consumers who want products with more features (until they get them home and try to use them)?

Reading: Creativity

1 Are these statements true or partly true? How? Or are they myths (stories that are false, although many people believe they are true)?

1 People are more creative when you offer them money for their work.

2 People are more creative when they work under time pressure.

3 Most people aren't very creative. Creative people are special.

2 Read the article below and find out if you are right.

3 Find words and expressions in italics in the article with these meanings.

1 something you receive for doing something good

2 worried

3 arrangements of shapes and colours

4 think of (an idea or answer)

4 According to the article, can these things improve creativity? Write *yes, no* or *doesn't say.*

1 caring about your work   _____

2 sharing ideas with others   _____

3 getting a reward like money   _____

4 having the right opportunity   _____

5 feeling worried   _____

6 being alone for long periods   _____

7 having more time   _____

5 What things could make you more creative in your work? And what about in your life outside work?

Creativity myths

SUCCESSFUL COMPANIES are creative companies where everyone has useful ideas. Employers need to encourage creativity in the workplace but there are lots of myths about it. Here are some myths that research has shown are wrong.

1 Money encourages creativity.

As part of his research into animal behaviour, the zoologist* Desmond Morris worked with chimpanzees who enjoyed playing with paint and making coloured *patterns*. When he offered them a *reward* for their work, they lost interest. People (and chimps!) are most creative when they care about their task and not about the money.

2 People are more creative under time pressure.

Researchers have discovered that people *come up with* their best ideas when they have time to focus. Sometimes it's not easy to pick up a pen and begin a job, and in that situation a deadline can help. But it only works when we've already had time to think. The *anxious* feeling that we have when our boss asks 'Have you finished yet?' doesn't help at all.

3 Most people can't be creative.

Researchers have found that anyone of normal intelligence can be creative in the right environment. Perhaps their bosses haven't given them the opportunity yet but everyone can have great ideas. Offer people the chance to try new things and watch them change the world.

zoologist: a scientist who studies animals and their behaviour

Grammar: *yet* and *already*

6 Look at the examples and complete the rules with *yet* and *already*.

> **yet and already**
>
> We often use *yet* and *already* with the present perfect tense.
> *We've **already had** time to think.*
> *We've **had** time to think **already**.*
> ***Have** you **finished yet**?*
> *Perhaps you **haven't given** them the opportunity **yet**.*
>
> **Rules:**
> **1** We use _____ when something has happened before now – earlier than someone expected.
> **2** We use _____ in question and negative forms. It means that something hasn't happened up to now.
> **3** We can put _____ before the main verb or at the end of the sentence.
> **4** We can only put _____ at the end of the sentence.

7 Write some sentences with *yet* and *already*. Use the verbs in the box.

> see eat write give think ring

1 You gave your colleague a book to pass on to your friend. You don't know if he has. What do you ask?

> *Have you given that book to Peter yet?*

2 You asked your assistant to phone your advertising agency. You don't know if she has. What do you ask?

3 You finished writing a report for your boss yesterday. Today he asks, 'How are you getting on with that report?' What do you say?

4 Your boss wants to know what your colleague thinks about the new product design. You haven't shown it to him. What do you say?

5 Your colleague asks if you want to go to the restaurant for lunch. You had your sandwiches half an hour ago. What do you say?

6 Your boss told you to think of a name for a new product. You're trying but it's difficult and it could take another week. Your boss asks, 'What are we going to call this product?' What do you say?

8 Work with a partner. Choose two or three of the situations in exercise 7 and roleplay the conversations.

Speaking: Explaining decisions

9 Work in pairs. Decide what to do in these situations. Choose *a* or *b* or think of an idea of your own.

1 You want someone to write a radio ad for your product. Will you …
  a contact an advertising agency?
  b have a competition to see which employee can write the best one?

2 You need to cut costs. Will you …
  a send an email to all employees asking for cost saving ideas?
  b put some suggestion boxes around the office?

3 Your marketing team haven't been very creative recently. Will you …
  a offer a bonus for the best creative idea?
  b fire the marketing manager?

4 You need to think of a name for your new product. Will you …
  a organize a meeting to brainstorm ideas?
  b look at the names of other products and choose something similar?

5 You want to organize a staff training day on creativity. Will you …
  a contact a staff training organization?
  b ask HR to think of some ideas?

10 It is now a week later. Join with another pair and discuss what you have done.

> **A:** *What have you done about the radio ad? Have you contacted an agency yet?*
> **B:** *No, we think that'll be too expensive, but we've organized a competition to see who can write the best one.*

TALKING POINT Are there any parts of a company or organization that shouldn't be too creative?

Reading: Good design

1 Think of something you use that is well designed, for example, something you use in your kitchen, in your workplace, or in your bedroom. Why do you like the design?

2 Read about some good design ideas in a hospital. What problem did they solve?

3 Answer these questions.

1 How did the designers find out about the patients' experience?

2 Why were the videos boring?

3 What did the nurses suggest and propose and why?

4 What did the consultants recommend and why?

> **!** *suggest, propose, recommend*
> **1** Use an *-ing* form (*doing*) after these verbs.
> *They suggested/proposed/recommended attaching mirrors.*
> NOT ~~They suggested to attach mirrors~~.
> **2** These verbs are all formal. We use them to report what people said when we are writing. We generally use different expressions when we are speaking.

Why don't we attach mirrors?

Let's attach mirrors.

How about attaching mirrors?

They recommended attaching mirrors.

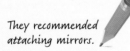

4 Work in pairs. Look at the article again. What do you think the nurses and design consultants actually said?

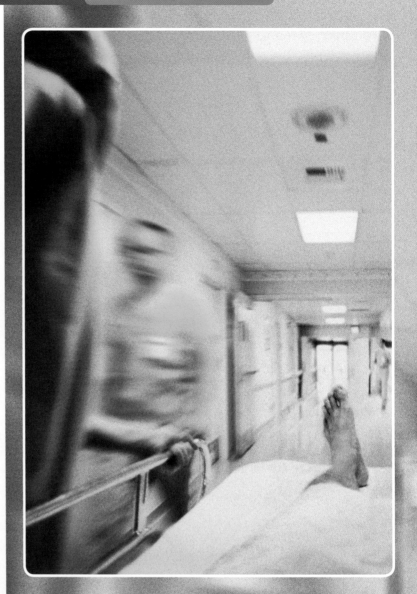

Seeing things through the users' eyes

A large healthcare organization in Minnesota employed some design consultants to help improve its patients' experiences. The designers looked at its hospitals through the eyes of its patients and made videos of the things they saw. The results were a surprise. Patients spend most of their time in bed, so they look at the ceiling or walls for hours and hours. The videos were very boring.

One nurse suggested sticking pictures on the ceilings. Another proposed putting whiteboards on walls in patients' rooms. Visitors could write on them with coloured pens and when they left, the patients could see their messages and pictures. The consultants recommended attaching mirrors to the ends of the gurneys* the hospital used to move patients from one place to another. The patients could look in the mirror, see their nurse and have a conversation.

All these ideas worked and the patients liked them. Good design is about understanding human beings and seeing things from the user's point of view.

a gurney (AmE): a table with wheels, used for moving sick people in a hospital

Listening: Sharing ideas

5 🔊 **1.30** Listen to the managers of a retail store discussing a problem. Which photo shows what they are talking about? What is the problem?

6 🔊 Listen again and complete these sentences.

	Making suggestions	Responding
1	_____ _____ _____ ask them to leave?	I _____ _____ that's a good idea. They look a bit _____.
2	_____ _____ calling the police?	_____, _____ they're not doing anything wrong.
3	_____ _____ speak to our neighbours about it?	There aren't _____ places for young people to go in this town.
4	_____ _____ _____ install a device that makes a high-frequency noise?	How _____ it _____?
5	_____ look into it.	OK, _____ find out more about it.
6	Or _____ _____ install speakers in the doorway and play classical music.	That's a _____ idea. Most young people _____ _____ Mozart.

7 Look at the expressions in exercise 6 and answer these questions.

1 What phrase for making suggestions is followed by an *-ing* form?

2 Which response …

   a is most positive?

   b asks a question?

   c offers to do something

   d says 'no' to the suggestion?

   e says 'yes', then 'no'?

   f changes the subject?

3 English speakers sometimes change the subject to be polite. So when someone suggests something they don't like, they talk about something else. That way they don't have to disagree. Do people do anything similar in your language?

Speaking: Suggesting improvements

8 Match these problems to the other photos in exercise 5.

1 Employees complain that the lifts in your building take a long time to travel from floor to floor. You can't afford to install more lifts and your engineers can't speed them up. How can you improve the users' experience of waiting for, and riding in, the lifts?

2 Employees are not allowed to smoke in your building so they go outside. They leave cigarette ends on the ground, which looks messy. How can you solve this problem?

3 You use electric fork-lift trucks to lift and carry goods in your warehouse. People sometimes don't hear them coming and truck drivers don't always notice people either. There have been some near accidents. How can you improve safety?

4 Patients at your surgery sometimes have to wait a long time to see a doctor. The waiting room is uncomfortable and they get bored and complain. How can you improve your waiting room?

9 Work in pairs or small groups. Choose some, or all, of the problems in exercise 8 and suggest different ways to solve them. When you have finished, tell the class what you have decided to do.

Reminder

Grammar reference page 165

We use the present perfect when past actions are important in the present.

We've changed the design of this product. (It's different now.)

We often use the present perfect to give news.

We've decided to hire an advertising agency. We haven't chosen which one yet.

Word focus: Collocations with *idea*

1 Use the words and phrases in the box to make expressions with similar meanings.

> think about   brilliant   come up with   original
> ridiculous   dismiss

Collocations with *idea*			
verbs		**adjectives**	
think of 1_____	an idea	a great a 4_____	idea
consider 2_____	an idea	a new an 5_____	idea
reject 3_____	an idea	a crazy a 6_____	idea

2 Complete these sentences with verbs and adjectives from exercise 1. Write the correct form of the verbs.

1 What a/an _____ idea. Now why didn't I _____ that?

2 I know this sounds like a/an _____ idea but I don't think we should _____ it completely.

3 That's a/an _____ idea. I don't think anyone has _____ that one before.

4 I'll _____ your idea but I'm not sure it will work.

Reading: Marketing methods

3 Look at the picture. What is the product and what is it for? Then read the article and find out if you are right.

4 Choose the best answers.

1 When you put Alka-Seltzer into water it …

  a floats.

  b dissolves – mixes with the water and becomes part of it.

2 The advertising agency suggested the makers told customers …

  a to buy more Alka-Seltzer.

  b to use more Alka-Seltzer.

3 Sales increased because they persuaded …

  a new customers to buy the product.

  b their existing customers to use more.

Plop plop, fizz fizz

Alka-Seltzer is a medicine that people take when they have a headache or an upset stomach*. Many years ago, its makers wanted to increase sales so they hired an advertising agency in New York. The agency came up with the slogan *Plop, plop, fizz, fizz, oh what a relief* it is! *Plop* was the sound of the tablet falling into a glass of water and *fizz* was the sound of the bubbles it produced when it dissolved. But the most important thing about the slogan was it said the words twice.

Before the new campaign, the makers sold Alka-Seltzer with the instruction 'take one'. The advertising agency recommended changing it to 'take two', and the new slogan suggested people should take two as well. It was a simple but very clever marketing trick. The slogan appeared in all of their advertisements and later in TV commercials. Sales of the tablets didn't quite double but they came very close.

an upset stomach   an illness that affects the stomach and makes you feel sick

relief   the feeling you have when something painful or worrying stops

5 Unscramble the letters in italics to make words to do with marketing. The words are all in the article.

1 A *ongals* is a short phrase which a company uses to advertise something.

2 A business which organizes your advertising for you is called an advertising *ecanyg*.

3 If you plan special advertising activity for a particular period, this is called an advertising *gimancap*.

4 An advertisement on TV is called a TV *lemocimrac*.

6 A slogan usually says something about a product's unique selling point – the thing that makes it different from the competition. Match these slogans for cleaning products with their unique selling points.

1	Clean floors cost less	**a**	It's environmentally friendly.
2	Just one wipe	**b**	The price is lower than the competition's.
3	The greener clean	**c**	It contains an air freshener.
4	Fresh as a sea breeze	**d**	You don't need different versions for different jobs.
5	One house, one bottle, one cleaner	**e**	You don't have to work very hard.

Speaking: Changes to the brief

7 Find some other students to work with and form a team. Decide on a name for your team.

8))) **1.31** Management wants you to come up with a marketing campaign. Listen to your manager and complete the missing information in the brief.

■ The brief

The product:

1 _____

Target market:

2 _____

Points to be decided:

- A name for the product
- The price
- The packaging
- A slogan
- A unique selling point

9 You have five minutes to come up with some ideas. When you have finished, tell the class what you have decided.

10))) **1.32** There is a change to the brief. Listen to your manager. What is the change?

11 You have five minutes to change your plan. When you have finished, tell the class what you have changed.

12))) **1.33** Listen to your manager one last time. What is the news?

13 You have five minutes to change your plan. When you have finished, tell the class what you have changed.

14 Discuss the task you have just done.

1 How did you feel about the way the brief kept changing?

2 How did you manage the changes? Did you …
   a change your original plans?
   b throw out your original plans and start again?
   c do a mixture of a and b?
Why?

3 Do projects you work on ever change in similar ways? How?

4 What advice and suggestions do you have for people who work in situations where things change fast?

Writing: An update

15 Your boss wants to know your marketing plans for the new aftershave. Write an email telling her what you have decided to do.

Dear …
Re our meeting on the marketing campaign:
After some discussion, we've decided …

Review 5–8

1 Complete these sentences. Choose the correct modal verb.

1 There is no dress code so employees *can / must* wear casual clothes if they want.

2 They lock the building at five o'clock, so everyone *can / must* be out before then.

3 All visitors *can / need to* sign the book, or the security staff won't let them in.

4 Customers like personal contact so all customer service staff *can / should* wear a name badge.

5 We work flexible hours so you *mustn't / don't have to* be on the premises at fixed times.

6 You *shouldn't / don't have to* put drinks near your computer keyboard.

7 The food in the canteen is free today so you *mustn't / don't need to* bring any money.

8 You *can't / don't have to* smoke in here. It's a non-smoking building.

2 There is one extra word in each of these sentences. Correct each sentence by crossing it out.

1 The delivery trucks are 4.5 metres in high.

2 How long time does the guarantee last?

3 You should to turn off your mobile phone during meetings.

4 You can switch it on the machine by pressing this button.

5 Do we must have to sign the book at reception?

6 Have they are come to see the new building?

7 The deadline has passed but they haven't already finished the work yet.

8 Let's to find out more about the cost before we decide.

3 Complete this text. Put one word (or a contraction like *I'm*) in each gap.

I can remember a time when nobody used email. Now it's the most common way to communicate with friends and colleagues. But ¹_____ also become a big problem. Take today, for example. It's only ten o'clock and I've already ²_____ 11 emails. And no, I haven't answered them ³_____. I'm ⁴_____ to wait until the end of the day and do all my emails together.

Some people in my company have suggested ⁵_____ the number of emails people can send each day. But the problem with emails is not just that we send too many. They arrive immediately, so people think they ⁶_____ to answer them immediately, too. But in fact, you ⁷_____ have to read them the moment they arrive. When an email comes, you ⁸_____ interrupt what you're doing. Instead, tell yourself, '⁹_____ deal with that at the end of the day.' That's a more productive way of working – and ¹⁰_____ feel less stressed, too.

4 Match each sentence with the correct product from the box.

> picture   sunglasses   memory stick   printer   electric car
> briefcase   holiday   jacket

1 The price includes airport taxes and insurance.

2 It'll brighten up your room.

3 It really suits you.

4 It has zero emissions.

5 The lenses are unbreakable.

6 It holds up to four gigabytes.

7 You can shrink or enlarge copies.

8 It has an adjustable shoulder strap.

5 Complete these sentences. Choose the correct word.

1 The economic situation is bad and I'm afraid it's going to *improve / deteriorate* further.

2 He always tries to *put off / put on* doing the unpleasant jobs.

3 If you want to apply, you need to *fill in / fill on* this form.

4 This model is available in a wide *range / spread* of colours.

5 If you want to copy the paragraph, you need to *brighten / highlight* it first.

6 I don't think anyone has *come up with / come out of* that idea before.

7 You'll need to *upgrade / upset* your hard drive before you run this software.

8 James had a really *shiny / brilliant* idea for our new slogan.

6 Match each phrase 1–8 with the most suitable response a–h.

1 Have you got a moment?

2 Are those chocolates?

3 I'm feeling a bit cold.

4 What does the price include?

5 You want to hold the camera like this.

6 How about giving away some samples?

7 We could contact some agencies.

8 Why don't we find out more?

a It comes with a user guide and a spare battery.

b OK, I'll look into it.

c I'm afraid I'm really busy right now.

d I see.

e That's a good idea. People like anything free.

f Do you want me to close the window?

g Yes, but they're very expensive.

h Yes, would you like one?

7 Read the written instructions. Then complete the dialogue. Write one word in each gap.

Insert a comment

1 Click on the end of the text.

2 Go to the review tab and click 'new comment'.

3 Type the comment text in the balloon.

A: Adrian, I need your help.

B: Sure, what's ¹_____?

A: I don't know how to insert comments in this text.

B: It's ²_____. First, you ³_____ to click on the end of the text.

A: OK.

B: ⁴_____ you click on the review tab.

A: Right.

B: That's ⁵_____. Now we just ⁶_____ to click on 'new comment'.

A: Like this?

B: That's it. Now you can write your comment and after ⁷_____ you can save it.

A: Oh, thanks, Adrian.

B: You're ⁸_____.

8 Match each word in the box with a word with the same vowel sound in the table.

deep depth height weight piece float wide threat myth show paste width

late	size	sell
cheap	sink	post

9 Find sixteen adjectives in the word square which could be used to describe a product. Read across, down and diagonally. One is done for you.

C	X	C	P	O	W	E	R	F	U	L
X	O	O	L	U	N	I	Q	U	E	A
S	X	M	X	E	X	X	E	S	X	D
I	F	P	F	X	V	L	X	E	X	J
M	G	A	X	O	B	E	L	F	X	U
P	O	C	S	A	R	B	R	U	L	S
L	O	T	U	T	A	T	K	L	O	T
E	D	L	X	I	X	C	A	X	V	A
X	A	X	L	X	I	X	X	B	E	B
V	B	E	A	U	T	I	F	U	L	L
X	R	X	Q	C	H	E	A	P	Y	E

10 Match each adjective in box A with a possible opposite in box B.

A

tidy heavy valuable common guilty casual simple rude

B

complicated light innocent cheap polite scarce messy formal

11 Write each collocation with the verb *take* in the correct place on the word diagram.

a photo an aspirin long ages a nap a call a holiday a look a tablet a moment

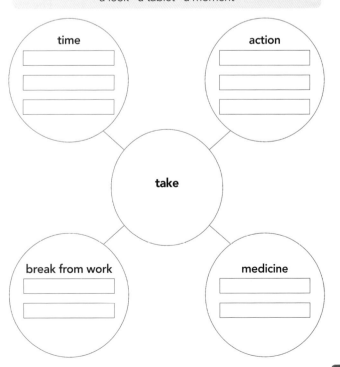

time

action

take

break from work

medicine

9

A Modals of possibility
B Future arrangements
C **Communication strategies** Saying 'no'
D **Interaction** Planning a social event

Put it in your diary

Modals of possibility

Reading: What's 'late'?

1 You have these appointments in your diary. What time will you really arrive? Be honest. Are you generally punctual?

1 a 10 a.m. job interview

2 a 9 a.m. meeting with your team

3 a 7 p.m. party invitation

2 Do you know any countries where people have different attitudes to time keeping? Read the article and find some.

3 Find words and phrases in the article that mean the following.

1 two

2 at the right time, without being late

3 a very sad event that shocks people

4 arrive

5 not polite (find two words)

4 Answer these questions.

1 Why isn't it polite to complain if someone arrives ten minutes late in some countries?

2 How far behind schedule was the Japanese train? In your opinion, was it late?

3 How late might guests arrive at a party in Peru? Do people generally arrive on time for events in your country?

4 What does 'late' mean to people in your country? And what does it mean to you personally?

What do you mean by 'late'?

Y OU'VE ARRANGED TO meet a friend at a certain time. They call you and say, 'I may be a couple of minutes late'. Will they be just two minutes late? Or might they mean ten or 15 minutes? Could they mean an hour?

Your answer may depend on where you live because what's 'late' in one culture may be perfectly OK in another. In countries with strict timekeeping, a 9 a.m. business meeting will start promptly at nine and it's rude to arrive late. But in other countries there may be a ten-minute 'courtesy time', so when people show up at 9:10 a.m., you shouldn't suggest that they are late.

In Amagasaki, Japan, a train driver was worried that his train was 90 seconds late and he speeded up. It was a tragedy. The train derailed* and 94 people died. But 90 seconds might not matter in other parts of the world. Some people could think that a train that's 90 seconds late is still 'on time'.

Take Peru, for example. The expression *hora peruana* (Peruvian time) means about one hour behind the time on the clock and *mañana* (tomorrow) means an indefinite time in the future. Guests often turn up several hours late for a party and it's not impolite. The party happens when it happens.

derailed: came off its tracks

Grammar: Modal verbs

5 Look at the examples in the table and complete the first set of rules with *may*, *could*, *might* and *will*.

> **Modals of possibility: *may*, *could*, *might* and *will***
>
> I **may** be a couple of minutes late.
> **Could** they mean an hour?
> 90 seconds **might not** matter in other parts of the world.
> In countries with strict time keeping, a 9 a.m. business meeting **will** start promptly at nine.
>
> **Rules:**
>
> **1** When we're sure something is going to happen, we use _____ .
> When we're unsure and we're talking about possibilities, we use _____ , _____ and _____ .

6 *May*, *could*, *might* and *will* are all modal verbs. Choose *a* or *b* to complete the second set of rules.

> **2** Modal verbs are followed by …
>   **a** an infinitive with *to* (*to do*).
>   **b** an infinitive without *to* (*do*).
>
> To form questions with modal verbs we …
>   **a** use *do*.
>   **b** change the word order.
>
> To form negatives we use …
>   **a** not.
>   **b** don't.
>
> >> For more information on modal verbs, see page 169.

7 Make sentences using the modal verbs from the table.

1 Think of something that you feel sure you will do tomorrow.
I will attend a nine o'clock meeting.

2 Think of three things that might/could/may happen when you do them.
Some people may be late.

3 Think of two things that *might not* or *may not* happen.
The meeting might not start on time.

Speaking: Solving problems

8 Work in pairs or groups. Have you ever had a similar problem to this?

One of your colleagues regularly turns up an hour late for work and your manager is ignoring the problem. You need to process the work she completes but she doesn't pass it to you promptly because she arrives late. You have asked her to arrive on time but she ignores you.

9 Here are some things you could do. Discuss which ideas might and might not help. Then tell the class which actions you think could be most effective and why.

> • Ignore the problem.
> • Copy her and show up late, too.
> • Ask your manager to change her working hours.
> • Buy her an alarm clock as a present.
> • Find out why she's late.

A: We could complain to the manager.
B: That might work. She won't listen to us but she'll have to listen to the manager.
C: Yes, but she could be angry with us for complaining about her.

10 Describe a problem you have at work. What different things could you do about it? Which ones might and might not work?

TALKING POINT Think of someone you know who is a poor timekeeper. Why do you think they're often late?

Reading: Virtual assistants

1 Discuss these questions with a partner.

Have you ever …

1 forgotten a family member's or close friend's birthday? Whose?

2 left an important document that you needed at home? What happened?

3 arrived at the wrong time for an appointment? What happened?

2 Read this article and find out how you can become more organized.

3 Answer these questions.

1 Where's Judith going next week?

2 What's happening next Thursday?

3 How much does Judith pay Gyan?

4 How has Gyan changed Judith's life?

5 What's Gyan doing tomorrow?

Grammar: Future arrangements

4 When do we use the present continuous? Is it when we're talking about now, future arrangements or both? Look at the table and find out.

> **Future arrangements**
>
> We use the present continuous to talk about …
> **1** things that are happening now.
> *It's 7:30 a.m. and Judith's **speaking** to her assistant.*
> **2** future arrangements.
> *Tomorrow, I'**m reading** a bedtime story over the phone.*
>
> **>> For more information on the present continuous, see page 165.**

5 Find more examples of the present continuous in the article. Find negative and question forms, too. Do they refer to present time or future time?

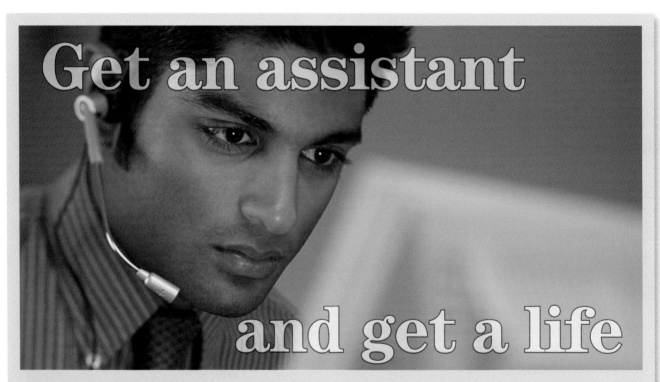

Get an assistant
and get a life

It's 7:30 a.m. and Judith Harwood, an account manager in Los Angeles, is speaking on the phone to her assistant.

'Where am I staying in Dallas next week?'

'The Marriot. I've reserved a room. Your client isn't meeting you at the airport so I've booked a rental car. And it's your aunt's birthday on Thursday, but don't worry. I've ordered flowers.'

Fantastic! Gyan has organized everything, but the strange thing is Gyan and Judith have never met. Gyan lives over 140,000 kilometres away in Mumbai, India, and they communicate over the internet. He's Judith's virtual assistant.

'Before I found Gyan, my life was a mess,' says Judith. She works 60 hours a week and pays about eight dollars an hour for Gyan to take care of travel arrangements, hairdresser's appointments and restaurant reservations. 'It's worth it,' says Judith. 'My life isn't falling apart* anymore.'

So is business booming for virtual assistant companies? Gyan says it is. Many busy executives now use their twenty-four-seven services to pay their bills, manage their correspondence and even write their job applications. 'There are all kinds of things we do,' explains Gyan. 'Tomorrow, I'm reading a bedtime story over the phone to my client's kids.'

Judith agrees. 'I'm travelling on business 15 days next month and I couldn't do that without Gyan. He's my lifesaver!'

falling apart: becoming impossible to manage

6 Work in pairs. Look at Judith's diary. Then ask and answer questions about her schedule.

> **A:** What's she doing on Thursday morning?
> **B:** At eight o'clock she's taking part in a web conference with the Spanish team, and at ten she's working on …

■ Thursday 20th March	
8:00	Web conference with the Spanish team
9:00	
10:00	Work on the marketing plan with Pilar
11:00	
12:00	
1:00	Update website
2:00	Prepare for tomorrow's presentation
3:00	
4:00	
5:00	
6:00	
7:00	Parents' evening at Timmy's school
8:00	
9:00	

■ Friday 21st March	
8:00	
9:00	
10:00	
11:00	Presentation to HKOM team
12:00	
1:00	Training course on the new CRM software
2:00	
3:00	
4:00	
5:00	Give telephone interview (Business Week Magazine)
6:00	
7:00	
8:00	
9:00	

Listening: Scheduling times

7))) **1.34** Listen to Gyan scheduling two appointments for Judith. Write them in her diary. What's the problem?

8))) **1.35** Below is the next call Gyan made but it is in the wrong order. Put it in the correct order. Then listen and check.

_____ Ah. Do you want to schedule another time, then?

__10__ Bye.

__1__ Paul Jones.

_____ Hey, it's no problem. I'm glad to help.

_____ I'll email you to confirm, and thank you for being so flexible.

_____ Good. Thanks. I'm sorry to mess you around like this.

_____ Yeah, Friday's open. So that's Friday at four at Judith's office, then.

_____ Paul, it's Gyan again. I'm afraid something's come up and Judith can't meet you on the 20th.

_____ Yes, please. Are you free at the same time on Friday the 21st?

_____ You're welcome. Take care.

9 Work in pairs. Turn to the audio script on page 153 and read Gyan's three telephone conversations.

Make a note of useful phrases to …

1 arrange a time or place.

2 check or confirm arrangements.

> **!** The expressions British and American speakers use when they're making arrangements can be a little different. For example:
> *Does six o'clock suit you?* (British English)
> *Does six o'clock work for you?* (American English)

Speaking: Making arrangements

10 Work in pairs. Prepare to act out some telephone calls.
Student A: Turn to File 20, page 142.
Student B: Look at the information below.
Then change roles and make the calls again.

> **Student B:**
> You're Gyan, Judith's virtual assistant. Schedule some more appointments for Judith. Your partner will play the roles of the different people you need to call. Write the appointments you make in the diary in exercise 6. Spend a minute preparing what to say before making each call. Judith's instructions are in the email below.

> Gyan.
> Please schedule some appointments for me on Thursday and Friday:
>
> 1 I have a terrible toothache. Please call my dentist and make an appointment ASAP.
> 2 It's my wedding anniversary on Friday. Can you book a table for two at Salento's Restaurant for Friday evening? Try to make it early in the evening.
> 3 My son Timmy needs some help with his school science project. I think it will take about an hour. Can you call him and schedule an hour when we're both free – and if I can't help him, can you?

TALKING POINT Would you like to employ a virtual assistant? Why?/Why not? If so, what jobs would you like to give them?

Reading and listening: International misunderstandings

1 Work in pairs. Read these situations. What do you think went wrong, and why?

1 I invited Mr Chen to join us for lunch. He hesitated before he replied and he was very vague. He didn't say it was impossible but he said it was inconvenient. I didn't understand so I asked what the problem was. Why did he seem uncomfortable?

2 I called and asked, 'Can I speak to Herr Schmidt, please?' His assistant said, 'No, he's out today but you can leave a message on his voicemail.' I'm a good customer, so why didn't she apologize and try to help me herself?

3 My Iranian neighbour often invites me in for a chat and offers me something to eat. If I say 'no thanks', ten minutes later she brings me something anyway. And when I eat it, she puts more on my plate. I don't want to be unsociable but do I have to eat everything she gives me? I'm putting on weight.

4 I got a little lost in Mumbai so I stopped a man in the street and asked, 'Can you tell me how to get to Rula College?' He didn't know the way, but he didn't tell me that. Instead he gave me wrong directions and 20 minutes later I was really lost. Why didn't he say, 'No, I can't help'?

5 I met John at a friend's house. We talked about Birmingham because it's John's home town and I often go there on business. He asked me to visit him next time I go. We didn't know one another well but I didn't want to be rude, so I asked for his address. Why did he seem surprised?

6 Maria's party was on the same day as my sister's wedding so I had to turn her invitation down. Maria was disappointed and she said, 'But you must come, all my close friends will be there.' She told me to slip away from the wedding early but how can I do that? Why did she insist?

2 Find words and phrases in the situations that mean the same as the following. The first letter of each word is given.

1 stopped for a moment before saying something   h_____
2 unclear, usually because someone does not give detailed information   v_____
3 not useful because it doesn't suit your plans or save you time   i_____
4 refuse an invitation   t_____ it d_____
5 unhappy because something you hoped for didn't happen   d_____
6 disappear from an event in secret, so that nobody notices   s_____ a_____
7 demand that someone should do something   i_____

3))) 1.36 Listen to some other views of these misunderstandings. Match each one to the correct situation in exercise 1. Why did the misunderstandings happen?

4 Discuss how people give and turn down invitations in your country. Do they …

1 give indefinite answers like 'I'll try' when they mean 'no'?
2 give detailed excuses or vague ones?
3 insist and say things like 'You must come' when they know it's impossible?
4 always know if people have said 'yes' or 'no' to an invitation?

Listening: Refusing invitations

5 When did you last refuse an invitation? What was the event and why did you turn it down?

6))) 1.37 Listen to Tim inviting someone to a barbecue. Why do they turn him down?

7))) 1.38 Listen to Tim inviting some other people. Do they accept? Why?/Why not?

8))) 1.39 Listen to the conversations again and complete the phrases in the table.

Invitations		
Preparing to invite	1 Are you _____ anything this weekend?	
	2 What _____ _____ _____ on Saturday?	
Inviting	1 _____ you _____ to come?	
	2 _____ you _____ to come?	
Positive responses	1 Oh, it's _____ _____ of you to invite us.	
	2 _____ be great! _____ love to.	
Saying 'no'	1 I'm _____ she's not well enough for a party.	
	2 _____ be lovely, _____ we're already booked.	
Responding to 'no'	1 Oh, that's a _____.	
	2 Not to _____.	
Suggesting alternatives	1 _____ love to come _____ time.	
	2 _____ _____ the weekend after next _____?	

9 Compare the phrases in exercise 8.

1 How well does Tim know the people he's inviting in the two conversations?

2 Which phrases (1 or 2) do we use with people who are socially distant or socially close?

Speaking: Invitations

10 Read some advertisements. Tick (✓) the events you would like to attend and cross (✗) the ones you would not. Think of reasons not to do the events you crossed out.

I'm scared of heights, so I don't think I'd like bungee jumping.

I'm going to my friend's wedding so I can't go to the Karaoke night.

11 Work in pairs. Take turns inviting each other to the events in exercise 10. Accept if you like the event, or refuse and give reasons if you do not.

Slide Show

Share your holiday photographs with other members of the Smalltown Geographic Society

Poetry reading

Elouisa Hawkins reads poetry from her latest book:

'Time and memories'

Taxation & Local City Government in the 17th Century

A History Society talk by Professor Crookshank

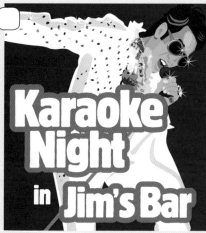

Karaoke Night in Jim's Bar

CLASSICAL MUSIC CONCERT:

THE LONDON CITY ORCHESTRA

PLAYS

Mozart

DISCOVER EXCITEMENT

BUNGEE JUMPING

ONLY $100

YOUR SAFETY GUARANTEED

Relax!

Spend an afternoon at the sauna and get your life back into balance

Latin American dance classes

7pm every Wednesday at the New Black Cat

Dracula meets Frankenstein

THE MOVIE YOU CANNOT AFFORD TO MISS

CATCH YOUR DINNER

DEEP SEA FISHING

BOAT LEAVES AT 5:39 A.M.

Reminder

Grammar reference
pages 168 and 169

English speakers use a variety of forms to talk about the future. For example:
He's arriving at eight. (It's a planned arrangement.)

It will be a wonderful surprise. (I'm certain.)
He could/may/might arrive late. (It's a possibility.)

Reading: A birthday celebration

1 What's the best birthday you have ever had? Tell another student about it. How did you celebrate? Why was it special?

2 Imagine you have $8,000 to spend on a birthday celebration. What might you do? Then read the article and find out what a Californian businessman did.

3 Work in pairs. Answer these questions.
1 Why did Taj celebrate his birthday in this way?
2 What gifts did he give his guests?
3 How much did the party cost?
4 Would you like to give a party like this? Why?/Why not?
5 What charities would you like to help and how?

A millionaire's party

Taj Chal likes to celebrate his birthdays in style. One year he hired limousines to take his friends to San Francisco. Another year he flew to Las Vegas. But when Taj and his brother sold their company, BlueLithium, to Yahoo for $300m, Taj wanted to give something back. He wanted to do something really nice for people who need help.

So Taj worked with Martha's Kitchen, a charity that gives meals to homeless people. Together they entertained 300 homeless guests at a surprise party. His guests enjoyed ravioli and meatballs, salad, garlic bread and, of course, birthday cake. Everyone also received presents: a lunch box and a bag containing a towel, toothbrush and other useful things. And Taj didn't just pay the $8,000 bill. He also helped serve the meal.

Word focus: Expressions with *give*

4 Look at ways in which we use expressions with *give*. Then think of more expressions with *give*.

> **Expressions with *give***
>
> We use the verb *give* when we talk about putting things into people's hands.
>
> *She **gave** me a birthday present.*
>
> But we use *give* in many other expressions, too.
>
> *He **gave** a party for 300 homeless people.*

5 Complete these sentences. Make common expressions with the correct form of *give* and the phrases in the box.

> us some help   him a lift   a speech   you more information
> you some advice   us permission   us any explanation
> me a chance   me a kiss

1 The minister _____ on the environment at last year's conference.

2 Can you _____? We need to carry these boxes upstairs.

3 Let me _____: wear a suit and arrive early for the interview.

4 I know I can do the job. Why won't they _____?

5 His train leaves in half an hour. Could you _____ to the station?

6 She laughed and _____ on the cheek.

7 They _____ to use their parking space while they were on holiday.

8 The guide will _____ about the area when you get to your hotel.

9 We don't know why our flight's delayed. Nobody _____.

Listening: Planning a party

6))) 1.40 Listen to two people planning another surprise birthday party and answer these questions.

1 Who's the party for?

2 How are they going to get him to the party without him suspecting anything?

3 What's the extra surprise?

7))) Listen again and decide if these plans and arrangements are definite (D) or only possibilities (P).

1 Prepare for at least 30 guests.

2 Cook the food on Saturday morning.

3 Decorate the flat.

4 Make a video of the party.

5 Invite Ivan to play squash.

6 Tell Ivan some sports equipment is at Caroline's flat.

7 Pick up Ivan's sister at the airport.

8 Caroline and Terry sound like they have everything organized but things might still go wrong with their plans. What could go wrong?

9 Work in pairs. Practice making telephone calls.
Student A: Turn to File 27, page 143. Student B: Turn to File 37, page 145.

10 Tell the class what happened when you made your calls. Did Ivan agree to go out with Terry? Why?/Why not?

Speaking: Planning a surprise

11 Work in pairs or groups. Think of someone you want to surprise with a party, celebration or special event. For example, a friend, a family member, your boss or a colleague.

12 Plan how to surprise them.
Decide …

1 the date, time and place.

2 things you need to do (food, music, decorations, etc.)

3 who is doing what.

4 how you can take the person to the event without telling them about it.

13 Tell the class about your plans. Explain what is happening. Listen to other students' plans and think about what could go wrong. Then ask them questions.

Writing: Refusing an invitation

14 You are based in London and your friend Robert lives and works in Brussels. You have just received this email from him. Unfortunately, you cannot meet him because you are doing something else at that time. Reply to his email.

- Apologize and explain why you can't meet. Invent a good reason.

- Suggest another time when you could meet.

- Wish him good luck for the interview.

> Hi there!
> I'm coming over to London on 26 March for a job interview. It will be a really quick visit because I have to get the train back that evening but it would be really nice to see you. The interview is at 2:00 so I'll be free between about 4 and 7. How about a drink or a bite to eat?
> Hope we can meet up.
>
> Robert

10

A Countable and uncountable nouns
B *too* and *enough*
C **Communication strategies** Complaints
D **Interaction** Collecting information

Special places

Countable and uncountable nouns

Reading: Big decisions

1 What is the biggest decision people make in life and why?

Is it deciding …

a what career to follow?

b who to marry?

c where to live?

d something else? What?

2 Read the article. Does the writer agree with your answers in exercise 1?

3 According to the writer, are these statements true (T) or false (F)?

1 The place we live in affects our salary.

2 People can work efficiently in any place that has good communications.

3 Living near talented, creative and productive people gives us more opportunities.

4 The job and marriage market aren't important when we're selecting a place to live.

4 Discuss these questions.

1 How much time did you spend deciding where to live? Did you research other places or did it just happen?

2 How do you feel about the place where you live? When you get home from work, do you feel glad you live there?

A major decision

How much time did you spend deciding where to live? Did you collect information on different places and make comparisons? A lot of people don't give it much thought but it's a really important decision. It affects how much money we earn, the friends we make and the opportunities our families have. In many ways it's more important than deciding on a career or who to marry.

Living in the right town or city feels good and gives you lots of energy. Some people think you can work efficiently anywhere these days if you have equipment to access the internet. But this isn't really true. Talented, creative and productive people often live near one another in the same cities or regions. That means some places have lots of opportunities but there aren't so many in others. Also, the sad fact is that jobs end and relationships break up. We all hope it won't happen but if it does, we need to be in a place where it's easy to find a new job or partner. Deciding where to live is a major life decision. ■

Listening: Finding a place

5 🔊 **1.41** When you are choosing where to live, what are your priorities? For example, is it having lots of job opportunities or having good schools nearby? Listen to an estate agent talking about a house to a potential buyer. What is the buyer interested in?

6 🔊 Listen to the conversation again and answer these questions.

1 According to the estate agent, what changes have taken place in this area?

2 What changes will take place in the future?

3 Do you think the client will buy the property? Why?/Why not?

Grammar: Countable and uncountable nouns

7 Look at these nouns from the article. Are they countable (C) or uncountable (U)?

> time information place decision money friend opportunity
> energy equipment crime shop nightlife bus traffic entertainment

8 Complete the rules. Choose the correct answers.

Countable and uncountable nouns

Rules:

1 *Countable / Uncountable* nouns can be singular or plural.

place → places

bus → buses

2 *Countable / Uncountable* nouns cannot be plural.

money → ~~*monies*~~

traffic → ~~*traffics*~~

3 We use *singular / plural* verb forms with uncountable nouns.

*There **is** a lot of nightlife.*

*Crime **doesn't** worry me.*

4 We use *much / many* with countable nouns and *much / many* with uncountable nouns.

*There aren't **many** opportunities.*

*There isn't **much** entertainment.*

5 We generally use *much* and *many* in *positive sentences / questions* and negative sentences.

*How **much** time did you spend deciding where to live?*

6 *A lot of* and *lots of* mean the same thing. We use these expressions with *countable nouns / uncountable nouns / both countable and uncountable nouns.*

***A lot of** people don't give it much thought.*

*The right place gives you **lots of** energy.*

> **!** Some nouns are countable or uncountable, with a change in meaning.
> *How much **time** do we have?*
> *How many **times** have you been to England?*
>
> *Person* is a countable noun in English. The normal plural form is *people*.

>> **For more information on countable and uncountable nouns, see page 172.**

9 Describe the area you live in.

Make sentences about it beginning:

1 There is/are a lot of …

2 There isn't much …

3 There isn't/aren't any …

There are a lot of shops and restaurants.

10 Work in pairs. Roleplay this situation. Then change roles.

Student A:
You're trying to sell your house or apartment. Student B is a possible buyer. Think of all the good things about living in your area of the city and try to persuade Student B to buy it.

Student B:
You're interested in buying Student A's house or apartment. You want to know more about the area. Ask about …

- local schools.
- crime.
- parks and green spaces.
- the nightlife.
- nearby shops.
- traffic.
- public transport.
- sports and leisure facilities.
- job opportunities.

Begin questions with:

> Is/Are there a lot of/lots of …?
> Is there much/any …?
> Are there many/any …?

Speaking: A second home

11 Work in pairs or small groups. You have decided to combine your savings to buy a second home together. You have US$1,000,000 to spend. Decide together on the ideal place.

Discuss these questions …

1 Do you want to buy a place in your country or a different one? Why?

2 Do you want a place in a city or the countryside? Why?

3 What things are most important to you? For example, peace and quiet, good transport links, nightlife.

TALKING POINT   What's the most important decision you've made in your life so far?

Reading: International complaints

1 A choir is a group of people who sing together. Have you ever sung in a choir? Do you know of any famous choirs?

2 Read about some unusual choirs. What do they sing about?

Singing the blues

'Valituskuoro' is a Finnish expression which means 'complaints choir'. In Finland, people use it to describe a situation where a lot of people are complaining simultaneously. But now it has another meaning as well. Two Finns, Tellervo Kalleinen and Oliver Kochta-Kalleinen, had the idea of creating real complaints choirs – groups of local people who come together and sing about their complaints.

They spoke to arts organizations in different cities and the first place to try it was Birmingham in the UK. A group of people met and wrote the lyrics. Then they put them to music and performed for fun. A video of their song was an immediate hit on YouTube and now many other cities have formed complaints choirs, too.

Sometimes the choirs complain about the particular place where they live. So in Finland they sing about poor sauna etiquette and in Singapore they sing about humid weather that spoils your hairstyle. And some of the complaints are about life in general, like high taxes and lost car keys.

So it just goes to show that complaints aren't always negative things. People can form creative friendships and have a lot of fun when they get together and complain.

3 These statements are false. Correct them.

1 The singers in the first complaints choir came from Finland.

2 Not many cities have complaints choirs.

3 Complaints choirs only sing about the city where they live.

4 Find words in the article that mean the following.

1 the words of a song

2 a song that's a big success and very popular

3 the rules of polite behaviour

4 hot and wet in an unpleasant way

5 has a bad effect on something so it's no longer attractive

Listening: Common complaints

5 🔊 **1.42** Listen to part of a radio interview about complaints choirs. How many complaints do they mention?

6 🔊 Work in pairs. Try to remember all the complaints the people mentioned. Then listen again and check.

Word focus: *too* and *enough*

7 Look at the expressions with *too* and *enough*. Then answer the questions.

---

too, too much and *too many*

Too and *too much/many* mean 'more than we want' or 'more than there should be'.

There's **too much** traffic on I95 in the mornings.

There are **too many** red lights.

My vacations are **too** short.

Rules:
Match the beginnings and endings of these sentences to complete the rules.

1 We use *too* …   a before plural nouns.

2 We use *too much* …   b before adjectives.

3 We use *too many* …   c before uncountable nouns.

---

enough

Enough means 'as much as we want' or 'as much as we need'.

There are**n't enough** Sundays in the week.

My voice is**n't** good **enough**.

Rules:
Choose the correct words to complete the rules.

4 We place *enough before / after* a noun.

5 We place *enough before / after* an adjective.

! *Too* does not mean *very*.

8 Here are some complaints from choirs around the world. Complete the sentences with the correct phrase from the box.

> is too   are too   is too much   are too many

1 There _____ bills to pay. (Malax, Finland)

2 Meetings _____ long and boring. (Bodøe, Norway)

3 There _____ glass on the cycle path. (Rotterdam, The Netherlands)

4 Public transport _____ expensive. (Budapest, Hungary)

5 There _____ commercials on TV. (Wroclaw, Poland)

6 Television commercials _____ long. (Singapore)

7 There _____ mosquitoes. (St Petersburg, Russia)

8 Tax forms _____ complicated and there _____ bureaucracy. (Hamburg, Germany)

9 Add the word *enough* to complete these complaints. Rewrite the sentences. Make sure you put *enough* in the correct position in each sentence.

1 McDonald's doesn't give you ketchup. (Jerusalem, Israel)

2 My vacuum cleaner lead isn't long. (Helsinki, Finland)

3 There isn't space on the C drive. (Wroclaw, Poland)

4 I don't get paid. (Helsinki, Finland)

5 There aren't winning tickets in the lottery. (Bodøe, Norway)

6 Our breaks aren't long. (children at Polikkilaaso school, Finland)

Speaking: Making complaints

cul-de-sac: a road that's closed at one end so it goes nowhere

10 🔊 1.43 Listen to part of the Birmingham complaints choir song. Work in pairs or groups. Write the words for a similar song with complaints about your city or life. Use these structures.

> I want …
> My job's …
> And the buses/trains/taxis …
> Why don't they …?
> … was good before.
> And I'm …

11 Now write some more complaints. You can use these structures or others that you know.

> There 's too much …
> There are too many …
> There aren't/isn't enough …
> The … isn't/aren't … enough.

12 Practise reading your complaints together. Then read them to the class. Which pair/group had the best ones?

TALKING POINT   Would you like to join a complaints choir? Why?/Why not?

Reading: A difficult customer

1 Discuss these questions.

1 Which group of people is most important to the organization you work for: employees, customers, shareholders (the people who own shares or parts of the business) or someone else?

2 Many people say, 'The customer is always right.' What do they mean? Do you agree?

2 Read this article about an airline company. Which group is most important there?

3 Answer these questions.

1 Why does the writer think companies should put their employees first?

2 Where is Southwest Airlines based?

3 What record does it hold?

4 What didn't Mrs Crabapple like about the company?

4 What did Herb Kelleher say to the difficult customer?

5 Who do you think said these things: Herb (H), Mrs Crabapple (C) or a Southwest Airlines employee (E)?

1 ☐

> There's another complaint from that woman.

2 ☐

> I didn't like the colour of my seat and the seat belt was uncomfortable.

3 ☐

> It's better to lose a bad customer than good employees.

4 ☐

> Other airlines provide food, so why can't you?

5 ☐

> Could you deal with this one?

6 ☐

> Be good to your employees and they will be good to your customers.

The customer is always right – or are they?

Put your employees first and they will put your customers first. Then the customers will come back again and the shareholders will be happy, too. That's what Herb Kelleher, the former CEO of Southwest Airlines thinks, and it certainly seems to work. The small Texas airline he founded in 1971 carries over 100 million passengers to 63 cities across the U.S. each year. It also has the best customer satisfaction record for any airline in the country.

But even Southwest can't please everyone. The company once had a difficult customer who was always disappointed. After every flight she wrote a letter with a long list of complaints. She didn't like the fact that the airline didn't assign seats or serve meals. She didn't like the boarding procedures and she didn't like the flight attendants' uniforms. One day someone passed one of her letters to Herb. It didn't take him long to deal with it. He wrote back:

'Dear Mrs. Crabapple, We will miss you. Love, Herb.'

So remember what Herb says: 'The customer is sometimes wrong.'

Listening: A complaint

6))) **1.44** Listen to a customer complaining. What are they complaining about and to whom?

7))) Number these things 1–6 in the order they happened. Then listen again and check. What excuse did the bus company offer for the mistake?

a The bus company charged the customer twice. _____

b The customer clicked 'confirm'. _____

c The customer called and someone booked the tickets for them. _____

d The customer complained and the bus company refunded them. _____

e The customer went to the bus company's website to book some tickets. _____

f Nothing happened and the screen froze. _____

8 Complete the expressions in the table. Use the words in the box.

> delete frustrating satisfied refunded apologize problems solve

Dealing with complaints	
Showing sympathy	Oh dear. That's annoying Oh, that's ¹_____ for you.
Saying sorry	We're really very sorry about this. I do ²_____.
Explaining	We're having some ³_____ with our computer system.
Putting things right	I can ⁴_____ that charge. I've ⁵_____ you in full.
Saying it won't happen again	We're installing new software which will ⁶_____ this problem.
Checking the customer is happy	Are you ⁷_____ with this solution?

9 Work in pairs. You work for a hotel and there is a problem with the hotel's in-room movie system. Think of some suitable responses to a guest's complaint.

Guest: *I wanted to watch a movie last night so I clicked on 'play' but nothing happened.*

You: 1_____.

Guest: *And now I see you've charged me for watching the movie.*

You: 2_____.

Guest: *Are other guests going to have this problem?*

You: 3_____.

Guest: *Good.*

You: 4_____.

Guest: *Yes, make sure you remove the charge and it'll be OK. Thanks for your help.*

Arcadium Hotel
Shepherds Bush
MJ1 40J
London, England
Tel: 44 (0) 123 456 7833

ARCADIUM

Room 323
Room Rate   £180

	Description	Charges
24/2	Room charge	£180
24/2	Health club	£20
24/2	Breakfast	£25
24/2	Laundry	£280
24/2	Internet	£5
25/2	Room charge	£180
25/2	Health club	£20
25/2	Breakfast	£25
25/2	In-room movie	£5
25/2	Room service	£35
	SUBTOTAL	£495
	Taxes	£94
	TOTAL	£789

Speaking: Dealing with a complaint

10 Work in pairs. A hotel guest has found some mistakes in their bill. Take turns to act out the conversation between the guest and hotel manager. Manager: Look at the information below. Guest: Turn to File 23, page 143.

Hotel manager:
You work for the Arcadium Hotel and your partner is a guest. This is their hotel bill but they aren't happy with it. Find out what's wrong and apologize where necessary. You can remove any charges you think are unfair. You'd like the customer to leave happy. Take a few minutes to think about what you will say, then begin: *Can I help you?*

Room rate – This is just the room rate. It doesn't include breakfast.

Laundry – You charge £2.80 per shirt.

Internet – You charge £5.00 per hour.

Health club – The hotel has a swimming pool, sauna and gym with lots of exercise equipment.

Reminder

Grammar reference page 172

We use *a lot of* and *lots of* with countable and uncountable nouns.

We use *how many, not many, too many* with countable nouns.

Are there many museums and art galleries here? How many?

Not many tourists know about this place.

We use *how much, not much, too much* with uncountable nouns.

There isn't much nightlife/crime/ unemployment.

It costs too much money. How much?

Listening: What are the sights?

1 Is tourism an important source of income for your city or region? What sights do visitors enjoy? Are there any interesting places that not many tourists know about?

2 Here are three tourist attractions that sometimes surprise visitors. Which ones would you like to visit? Why?

A

Lots of tourists visit the ancient Inca city of Machu Picchu in Peru each year. But the surprising thing is nobody knew the place existed for hundreds of years.

B

There's a lot of woodland and beautiful scenery on the little island of Eilean Shona off the north east coast of Scotland, but no television. It's ideal for quiet holidays when you want to get away from it all.

3 🔊 **1.45** Listen to some people talking about the places in exercise 2. Match each conversation to the correct place. Which place sounds most interesting? Why?

4 Which places are these things connected to, and how?

1 a rowing boat
2 a bookcase
3 a castle and cottages
4 smallpox (a serious disease that causes spots on your skin that leave marks)
5 a password
6 coloured pieces of string with knots

5 🔊 **1.46** Listen to the first conversation again. Write down all the numbers you hear. What do they refer to?

6 🔊 **1.47** Listen to the second conversation again and answer these questions.

1 Why is it hard to find The Safe House?
2 What's in the room at the entrance?
3 How can you get the password?
4 Why do people clap, cheer or boo?
5 What kinds of gadgets are inside the club?

7 🔊 **1.48** Listen to the third conversation again. Are these statements true (T) or false (F)? Correct the ones that are wrong.

1 Machu Picchu is over 500 years old.
2 Not many people died from smallpox.
3 There were a lot of skilled writers in Inca society.
4 They had systems for accounting.

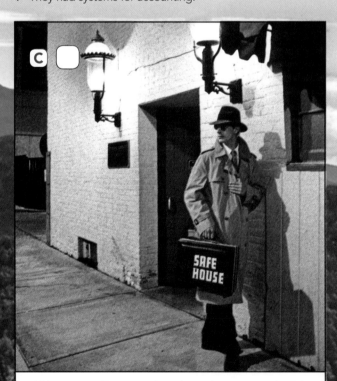

Shhh. Don't tell anyone, but The Safe House nightclub and restaurant in Milwaukee, USA has a spy theme. It's the perfect place to visit when you want to pretend you're James Bond – 007.

Speaking: Visitor information

8 Work in pairs. Act out a conversation and exchange information about interesting sites to visit. Then change roles.

Student A:
You're staying in Student B's home town/city/region for a few days and it's your first visit. You'd like to see the tourist attractions and also some places tourists don't normally go.

1 Ask questions about the things you can see and do. For example:

Is there much/Are there many …
- *historical places and buildings to visit?*
- *culture?*
- *good restaurants?*
- *nightlife?*
- *parks and gardens?*
- *interesting shops?*

2 Find out about the economy of the place as well. For example:

Is there much/Are there many …
- *industry?*
- *unemployment?*
- *public transport (buses, trains, taxis), etc?*
- *crime?*
- *tourists at this time of year?*

Take a few minutes to plan what you'll say, then start asking questions.

Student B:
Student A is visiting your home town/city/region for a few days. It's their first visit and they want to know about …

- interesting sights (including places that tourists don't usually visit).
- historical places and buildings.
- the public transport system.
- your city's main industries.
- how safe the city is.
- things they can do in the evenings.

Take a few minutes to think of useful information you can give them. Then answer their questions. Try to be helpful. Also give them information about places they shouldn't visit, perhaps because they're not safe, too crowded or cost too much.

Writing: A website review

9 There is a website where people send reviews of places they have been on holiday. Write a short description of your favourite holiday destination for the website. Describe the place and some of the things visitors can see and do there. Say why you like it.

Begin: *We've just had a wonderful holiday in …*

Interaction

11

A First conditional
B *if* and *when*
C **Communication strategies** Agreeing and disagreeing
D **Interaction** Introducing changes

Making changes

First conditional

Listening: The fisherman's story

1 You are going to listen to a story about a fisherman, a business consultant and the things in the photos below. What do you think will happen in the story?

2 Who do you think will be smarter, the business consultant or the fisherman? Why?

3))) **2.1** Now sit back, listen and enjoy the story. You can close your eyes if you want.

4 Why did the fisherman say, 'Thanks, but no thanks' and walk away at the end of the story?

Grammar: First conditional

5))) Listen again. Complete the sentences in the table. Then answer the question.

if + present, *will/can*
After *if* we usually use a present tense to refer to the future.
1 If you _____ longer, _____ _____ more fish and then you can sell them.
2 If you _____ more money, _____ _____ _____ another boat.
3 _____ _____ the number of fish you catch if you _____ another boat.
4 If your business _____ _____, you _____ _____ your company's shares on the stock market.
These conditional sentences have two clauses. Does the *if*-clause always come first?

>> For more information on conditional sentences, see page 171.

The stock market

A fish business

A fishing boat

A tropical island

Money

6 Work in pairs or small groups. Create some more stories with *if* + present, *will/can*.

Here are some possible story beginnings:

- If the weather's nice tomorrow …
- If I lose my job …
- If I save more money …

   A: If my boss gives me a pay increase, I'll have more money.

   B: If I have more money, I can buy a new car.

   C: If I buy a new car, I'll drive to …

Word focus: *worth*

7 Read the examples. Then make similar sentences with *worth*.

---

worth

1 We use *worth* + an amount to say how much money people will pay for things.

   *Your business will be **worth** millions of pounds.*

2 We say something is *worth doing* if it will be useful or enjoyable.

   *It's a very good movie. It's definitely **worth seeing**.*

   *It's **worth staying** late tonight if it means we can finish the job.*

3 We say something is *worth it* if it is important and good enough to spend time and effort on.

   *The fisherman could follow the consultant's advice but it **isn't worth it**.*

---

8 Work in pairs. Ask and answer these questions.

1 How much will your car be worth in ten years time?

2 Is it worth paying extra for brand name goods in a supermarket?

3 If we get up an hour earlier each day, we can go to the gym and work out. But is it worth it?

4 How much will your computer be worth in three years time?

5 Is it worth going to the office Christmas party? It will be very boring but the boss expects us to be there.

6 If I rent out the spare room in my house, I can make some extra money. But is it worth it?

Speaking: Weighing alternatives

9 Work in groups of three and discuss some problems.

Problem 1

A local university is offering an evening MBA course. I could do it but it will take six years and it's very expensive. Should I take the course, and is it worth it?

Student A: You are the person with this problem. Ask Student B and Student C for advice. First, take a few minutes to prepare some questions to ask, e.g. *How much extra will I earn if I have an MBA?*

Student B: Turn to File 35, page 145.
Student C: Turn to File 35, page 145.

Problem 2

My husband/wife and I are expecting a baby. Hooray! At the moment, we both work. If we lose an income, it will be hard to live on one salary. Should one of us stop working and take care of our baby, or should we both continue to work and pay for childcare instead?

Student B: You are the person with this problem. Ask Student A and Student C for advice. First, take a few minutes to prepare some questions to ask, e.g. *If one of us stops working, how much money will we save in taxes?*

Student A: Turn to File 38, page 145.
Student C: Turn to File 38, page 145.

Problem 3

The company I work for has financial problems and it's trying to reduce its workforce. If I offer to resign (officially say that you're going to leave your job), I'll receive a small redundancy payment. If I don't resign now I won't receive any money if they make me redundant later (stop employing me because there is no work any more). Should I resign or should I keep working and hope someone else will lose their job instead?

Student C: You are the person with this problem. Ask Student A and Student B for advice. First, take a few minutes to prepare some questions to ask, e.g. *Will I find another job if I resign?*

Student A: Turn to File 1, page 140.
Student B: Turn to File 1, page 140.

TALKING POINT   What's the moral of the fisherman story? Can it teach us any useful rules for life?

Reading: Getting things done

1 Have you ever worked with any unreliable people (people you could not trust or depend on to do things)? In what ways were they unreliable?

2 Read some problems and decide how to handle them. Then compare your answers with a partner.

1 Your water heater has broken down and you want some plumbers to give you a price estimate to repair it. You called two different plumbers and they promised to come yesterday. You waited in all day but they didn't show up.

2 You are a publisher. One of your writers is very talented and writes excellent books but he often misses his deadlines. What can you do?

3 Your department's secretary is very pleasant. When you ask her to help, she always says 'yes'. But sometimes she doesn't do things she agreed to do. That's a problem because you're never sure if she's booked a meeting room or flight, or ordered the supplies you need.

3 Read an article. Do you agree with the writer? Why?/ Why not?

How to handle unreliable people

Douglas Adams was the writer of the science fiction comedy *The Hitchhiker's Guide to the Galaxy*. He was a successful writer and everyone liked him, but he often missed deadlines. His publishers once had to lock him in a hotel room for three weeks to make him finish a book.

Unreliable people are often very nice people. They want to please everyone so they don't say 'no'. That means they *take on* more work than they can handle and then they miss deadlines and *drive us crazy*.

Douglas Adams

The best way to deal with them is to say you *value* their work. Set mini-deadlines and get them to agree. Then *point out* the problems you'll have if they don't do what they say. Call them regularly to check their progress and make sure they don't *take on* too much work. And *just in case*, be ready to do the job yourself if they don't.

4 Use the words and expressions in italics in the article to complete these sentences.

1 If you _____ something, then you tell someone something that they didn't already know.

2 If you agree to do too much work, then you _____ too much.

3 If you think that something is very important or useful, then you _____ it.

4 If you think it might rain, you should take an umbrella _____ .

5 If you make us feel very annoyed you _____ .

5 Could any ideas in the article help you deal with the problems in exercise 2? How?

Listening: Working under pressure

6 🔊 **2.2** Listen to some people getting ready for a conference. What do they need to do?

7 🔊 Listen again and answer these questions.

1 When did the men arrive?

2 When will Jasper arrive?

3 Have they spoken to Gary?

4 Is Anna coming?

5 What job is the woman going to help with?

6 And what's Jasper going to do?

7 Would you like to work with the two men? Why?/Why not?

Grammar: Conditional sentences

8 Read the notes on conditional sentences.

Conditional sentences

In most sentences with *if*, we use normal verb forms. So, for example, we use present forms to talk about the present and future forms to talk about the future.

*If you **help** Pete with the cables, I **can** set up the cameras.*

*If you**'re going** to set up in time, you **need** help.*

*If he **hasn't left** yet, he **won't be** here for at least half an hour.*

We use *when* in situations where we're sure something will happen and *if* in situations where we're not.

*Jasper can do the microphones **when** he arrives.* (I'm sure he will arrive.)

*Tell Gary to hurry up **if** he calls.* (I don't know if he will call.)

! We do not normally use *will* in the same clause as *if* or *when*. Instead we use a present tense.

*Tell Gary to hurry up **if** he calls.* NOT ~~Tell Gary to hurry up if he will call~~.

>> **For more information on conditional sentences, see page 171.**

9 Match the beginnings and endings of these sentences.

1 If we're going to meet this deadline,
2 If you've had a difficult day at the office,
3 If I drink coffee at bed time,
4 If she can't pay her credit card bills,
5 If you want to learn how to relax,
6 If their flight leaves at noon,
7 If you eat too much salt,
8 If you smile at other people,
9 If I have to sit through one more boring meeting,
10 If everyone else is panicking and you're not,

a she needs some financial advice.
b we need everyone to work overtime.
c they generally smile back.
d perhaps you don't know what the problem is.
e I think I'll go crazy.
f they should leave the house before 10 a.m.
g come to my yoga class with me.
h I can't sleep at night.
i it raises your blood pressure.
j the last thing you want is a flat tyre on your way home.

That's the last thing I wanted.

10 Look at the sentences in exercise 9 again. Find examples of different tenses and modal verbs in the *if-* clauses. In which sentences can you replace *if* with *when*?

Speaking: Finding solutions

11 Here are some situations that put people under pressure. Are you or your organization facing any similar problems? How?

A **The 24-hour day**
Our organization has employees and customers all over the world, operating in different time zones. The 9–5 day has disappeared. Employees need to be available to answer urgent questions 24/7.

B **New skills**
The skills our organization needed five years ago are not the same as the skills they need today. Employees have to constantly update their skills to be ready for the future.

C **Poor communication**
Many of our employees are specialists and nobody else can do their job. Sometimes people don't work well in teams because they don't understand what their colleagues need them to do.

D **Inefficiency**
Some employees take longer to do things and make more errors than others. This puts pressure on their more efficient colleagues who have to do more work.

12 Read some responses to the problems in exercise 11. Match each response to the correct problem.

1 We should create a new organization chart and our employees should reapply for their jobs. We should give our employees no special favours. New external job applicants should have an equal chance of getting the jobs.

2 Employees should rotate jobs with another team member every month. Nobody should stay in a job for longer than 30 days.

3 Management should record all employees' telephone calls and every keystroke they make on their computers. Then it should analyse the data, identify inefficient employees and fire them.

4 The company should give its employees mobile phones which they must leave on at all times.

13 Work in pairs or small groups. Discuss each response in exercise 12.

1 Will they solve the problem? What will happen if organizations do these things and what will happen if they don't?

2 Can you suggest better solutions?
   A: *If people don't have the right skills, they'll have to go.*
   B: *Yes, but some of them have worked here for years.*
   C: *Morale will fall if everyone has to reapply for their jobs.*

TALKING POINT

In your job, what's the most stressful …
- time of the day?
- day of the week?
- time of the year?
Why?

Writing: Raising objections

14 Choose one of the responses in exercise 12. Write an email to your boss saying why you do not think it is a good solution. Explain what will happen if the organization decides to do this.

Begin: *I am concerned about the proposal to … If we do this, …*

Reading: Shoplifting

1 Imagine you are a store detective. Which people in the picture do you need to watch carefully? Why?

2 Read about how to spot a shoplifter and find out if you are right.

How to spot a shoplifter

Shoplifters come in all ages and sizes and you have to watch carefully to catch them. Look for unusual behaviour. They might walk strangely, seem nervous or spend more time looking for CCTV cameras than looking at goods. They might go into a fitting room carrying clothes on hangers and come out later with nothing but a bag.

Shoplifters sometimes work in pairs. One can engage a sales assistant in conversation while the other steals the goods. Of course, they need places to hide the things they steal. They sometimes have a large bag that they place at their feet and drop things in. Some wear large coats with big secret pockets inside. They can also slip small items into an umbrella or a newspaper. Baby buggies* are another good hiding place, especially if the baby is sitting on a blanket*.

Shoplifting costs UK stores £1.6 billion every year. And unfortunately, shoplifters aren't the only thieves. Dishonest shop staff cost stores another £1.4 billion. In some ways, theft by employees is worse. The stores are paying their wages, after all.

buggy: a light folding chair on wheels that you push small children in
blanket: a thick warm cover for a bed

3 Complete these sentences with words from the text.
1 People who s_____ something are t_____ and the crime they commit is t_____.
2 S_____ is the crime of stealing things from shops and the people who do it are s_____.

4 Circle all the examples of possible shoplifting behaviour in the picture. Can you see any possible employee theft? Which one do you think is hardest to spot? Why?

Listening: Security issues

5 Think of some different things a department store can do to prevent theft. Make a list.

6))) **2.3** Listen to some store managers discussing the problem. What ideas do they discuss? Do they suggest any ideas you thought of?

7))) Listen again and answer these questions.
1 What don't they like about electronic tags? (Name three things)
2 Why is a digital security camera system better?
3 Why don't they want to install one?
4 What kinds of searches does the woman suggest?
5 Why don't her colleagues agree?

Agreeing and disagreeing

8 Look at B's responses in the examples below. Decide if they are agreeing or disagreeing with A.

Agreeing and disagreeing

1 **A:** *I really don't like the idea. The tags look ugly.*
   B: *And they're not cheap.*

2 **A:** *We can't afford it.*
   B: *Yes, it's too expensive.*

3 **A:** *We could just put tags on expensive items.*
   B: *Yes, but they don't always work.*

4 **A:** *They won't agree to that.*
   B: *No, they won't like it.*

5 **A:** *A digital system's better. You can store more data.*
   B: *And the pictures are clearer.*

Yes commonly signals agreement in English.
A: *We can't afford it.*
B: *Yes, it's too expensive. (Yes = I think you're right.)*

But with negative statements like this, we can commonly signal agreement with *no* as well.
A: *We can't afford it.*
B: *No, it's too expensive. (No = No, we can't afford it.)*

9 Discuss these questions.

1 The most common way English speakers disagree is by saying 'Yes, but …' and raising an objection. Find an example in the table above. Do people say anything similar to 'Yes, but …' in your language?

2 When English speakers agree, they sometimes repeat or add to ideas. Look at the examples where B is agreeing with A. Is B repeating A's idea or adding to it?

10 Match these opinions to the correct agreements.

1	It costs too much.	a	No, it's too much effort.
2	That's impossible.	b	No, it'll take too long.
3	We won't have time.	c	Yes, it's really expensive.
4	It isn't worth it.	d	Yes, we can't do that.
5	They won't like it.	e	Yes, that'll work.
6	That'll solve the problem.	f	No, they'll complain.

11 Work in pairs. Practise disagreeing and agreeing with your partner. Read the problem and take turns to argue for the proposals 1–4 below. Your partner should raise some objections with 'Yes, but …' After one or two objections, agree with one another.

Problem:
You work together in an office where things have disappeared recently. Someone has stolen money from employees' bags and desk drawers and a computer disappeared the other day. You don't know if an employee is responsible or visitors.

1 We should ask the management to install video cameras in the office.

2 We could put electronic tags on all our belongings and equipment.

3 Why don't we search visitors' bags and belongings before they leave the building?

4 How about leaving some trick money on a desk? If you pick it up, it goes BANG! and covers you with red dye (colouring you can't wash away).

Speaking: Preventing theft

12 Look at some ways to prevent theft in a department store. Can you add more ideas?

Employee theft
Higher pay
Background checks on job applicants
Searches of employees' belongings
CCTV cameras in the staff rest area
Reward staff who report employee theft

Regular stock* checks
More CCTV cameras
Take thieves to court
Better staff training

Shoplifting
Plain-clothes store detectives
Uniformed security guards at the door
Warning notices
Electronic tags
Hiring more sales assistants

stock: a supply of things that a shop has available to sell

13 Work in pairs. You are the managers of a department store that needs to reduce theft. Discuss ways to prevent theft by employees or discuss ways to prevent theft by shoplifters.

1 Discuss the advantages and disadvantages of the ideas in exercise 12.

2 Decide on the three best actions to take.

14 Join with another pair. Explain what you plan to do. Do they think you have made the best decisions or do they have any objections?

Communication strategies

Reminder

Grammar reference page 171

We can use *if* to talk about future possibilities.

If you take more exercise, you'll improve your health.

We don't usually use *will* in the same clause as *if*.

If you exercise more, you'll be healthier.
NOT *If you will exercise more …*

Reading: Counting footsteps

1 Discuss these questions with a partner.

1 What kinds of things do you do in a normal day that keep you fit?

2 How could you take more exercise and be fitter?

2 Read the first part of the article. What is the experiment about?

3 Here are some of the occupations ACE studied. Who do you think took the largest number of steps? Who took the smallest number?

1 teachers

2 lawyers

3 postmen/women

4 secretaries

5 police officers

6 nurses

Stepping **out**

◄ Pedometer: a device that measures how far you walk.

Walking is a great way to exercise and it doesn't cost anything. But can you get enough exercise from walking? According to the American Council on Exercise (ACE), it depends on your job.

ACE set up an experiment to find out which jobs involve the most walking. Researchers asked volunteers from a number of different occupations to wear pedometers at work for three days. Then they added up the steps people took and calculated the average.

4 Here are the average numbers of steps the people took. Match the numbers with the occupations in exercise 3.

8,648 4,726 5,336 18,904 5,062 4,327

5 Check your answers with the actual results in File 36, page 145. Do you find anything surprising?

6 Read the rest of the article. What suggestions does the writer make for increasing the number of steps you take at work?

ACE recommends we take at least 10,000 steps a day. This means you're all right if you deliver the post, but what if you work in an office? You won't reach half the recommended total.

But there are lots of things you can do to get more exercise at work. Some just require small changes but together they can make a big difference to your health. For example, if you just take the stairs instead of the lift, or go over to people's offices instead of sending them emails, it can help. A short walk at lunchtime could also make a big difference, and you'll probably return to work feeling more refreshed as well. ■

Listening: A fitness plan

7 🔊 **2.4** Listen to someone talking about a fitness plan. Who is he and what is he going to do?

8 🔊 Answer these questions. Then listen again and check.

1 How does Adam keep fit?

2 Why is he worried about the health of his staff?

3 What is 'operation fitness'?

4 Does he think his staff will like his plans and does he care? Why?/Why not?

5 Would you like to have Adam as your boss? Why?/Why not?

Speaking: Holding a meeting

9 Work in pairs or small groups. You all work for Adam. Read the changes he is planning to make. Go through them one by one and discuss the questions.

1 Do you like them or dislike them?

2 What will happen if he goes ahead with the changes?

3 Are they sensible changes? Why?/Why not?

OPERATION FITNESS

1 Install exercise machines in the staff restrooms.

2 Turn off the electricity supply to the lifts so everyone uses the stairs.

3 Relocate all the meeting rooms to the fifth floor.

4 Stop cars from entering the car park. Provide bicycle racks instead.

5 Turn the extra car park space into a tennis or basketball court.

6 Offer cash or gift vouchers to employees who join a gym.

7 Instruct the staff canteen to stop serving junk food. All meals to be vegetarian.

8 Coffee machines to only serve decaffeinated coffee.

9 No internal phone calls. If employees need to speak to someone, they should go to their desk.

10 All employees to wear pedometers. Employees who don't take 10,000 steps a day to be punished.

11 Start every company meeting with a ten-minute exercise routine.

12 Turn down the heating so everyone has to move about to keep warm.

---

10 Adam has agreed to meet with his employees to discuss the plans before he implements them. Work in pairs or small groups and take a few minutes to prepare for the meeting. Decide who will take which roles.

Adam and his advisors:
Ideally, you would like to make all these changes. But you realize that some of the plans might not work or may lower efficiency. So you're willing to listen to arguments and make necessary changes.

But you are determined that your employees need to change their unhealthy lifestyles and become fitter. Prepare to argue your case for the changes you feel strongly about.

Employees:
You are concerned that some of the changes are not feasible or may damage efficiency. Prepare to argue against the changes you don't like. Where possible, suggest alternatives or alterations to the current plans

11 Hold the meeting. Adam and his advisors: listen to all the arguments and then decide which changes to make.

Interaction

12

A The passive
B Active and passive
C **Communication strategies** Turn taking
D **Interaction** Promoting an event

That's entertainment!

The passive

Reading: Bollywood

1 Think of movies that fit into each of these categories.

1 Action and adventure movie

2 Romantic movie

3 Mystery

4 Musical

5 Fantasy movie

6 Comedy

Mamma Mia is a musical.

2 What kinds of films do you like most? Why? Which ones don't you like? Why?

3 Read an article about Bollywood movies. What kinds of movies are they?

4 According to the article, are these sentences true (T) or false (F)?

1 Bollywood is a place in Mumbai.

2 A larger proportion of a Hollywood movie budget is spent on marketing than a Bollywood one.

3 It takes more time to make a Bollywood movie than a Hollywood movie.

4 More films are made in Hollywood than Mumbai.

5 Bollywood movies are made in English.

6 Bollywood movies are rarely shown outside India.

WHAT'S BOLLYWOOD?

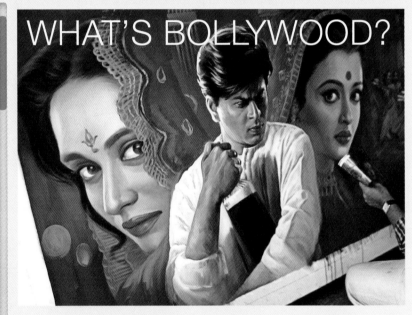

Everyone knows Hollywood. It's the place in California where many of the world's movies are made. 'Bollywood' isn't a place. The term 'Bollywood' is used to describe the very successful film industry that is based in and around Mumbai in India. Bollywood movies are famous for having everything – action and adventure, romance, excitement, music, dancing, comedy, and of course, a happy ending.

In the USA, about 40 per cent of a movie's budget is spent on marketing and many movie stars earn million dollar salaries. In India, movie tickets are much cheaper and production budgets are smaller. Marketing costs account for around 15 per cent of a film's budget. There are fewer high-tech production facilities and films take longer to make. But more than a thousand movies were made in India last year.

That's more than double the number that were made in the USA.

To work in Bollywood, you need English. It's the business language of India, and it's also the language of the Indian film industry. However, over a thousand different languages are spoken in India so Bollywood films are made in local languages. Sometimes they have subtitles in different languages, so people can read the words on the screen. Often they're dubbed – a new recording is made in another language.

Bollywood movies are loved by fans all over the world and they are an important source of foreign income for India. They're very popular in Russia and the Middle East and they also do well in Australia, the UK and the USA. Bollywood was a US$2.1bn industry last year and much of that money was earned abroad. ■

Grammar: The passive

5 Compare these sentences. Which one is passive and which one is active?

1 We use the term 'Bollywood' to describe the Mumbai film industry.

2 The term 'Bollywood' is used to describe the Mumbai film industry.

6 Look at the examples in the table and complete the rules. Then find more examples of passives in the article.

> **The passive**
>
> We use the passive when we are more interested in the action than in the person who does it.
>
> *About 40 per cent of a movie's budget **is spent** on marketing.*
>
> *More than a thousand movies **were made** in India last year.*
>
> *Bollywood movies **are loved** by fans all over the world.*
>
> *Much of that money **was earned** abroad.*

> **Rules:**
>
> **1** We form the passive with the verb _____ and the past participle.
>
> **2** To say who or what does something in a passive sentence, we use the preposition _____.
>
> **>> For more information on the passive, see page 171.**

7 Complete this description of an Indian movie with the passive verbs in the box.

> is based on   is set   was directed
> were actually filmed   is played   was released

The Namesake tells the story of a family that moves from India to America and the changes that happen in their lives over 25 years. The movie ¹_____ by Mira Nair, who also directed *Monsoon Wedding*. It has many wonderful characters to connect with and scenes to make you laugh and cry. The main character ²_____ by Kal Penn, an American actor whose parents were Indian immigrants.

The film ³_____ a book by Jhumpa Lahiri, and she actually plays a small part in the movie. The story ⁴_____ in Calcutta and New York, but some of the New York scenes ⁵_____ in Calcutta to save money. The movie ⁶_____ in 2006 and earned US$13,566,248 in ticket sales.

Speaking: Guess that movie

8 Prepare to tell some other students about a movie you have seen. First write some sentences about it. Use these phrases.

The main character is played by …

It was directed/produced by …

It was shot in/based on/set in/filmed in …

It tells the story of …

It makes you laugh/cry … because …

9 Work in groups. Take turns to describe your movies. See if anyone can guess which movie you are describing.

10 Discuss these questions.

1 Many famous movies are based on books. Think of examples.

2 Is it better to read a book and then see a movie, or is it better the other way round? Why?

3 Do you think people are encouraged to read by movies? Why?/Why not?

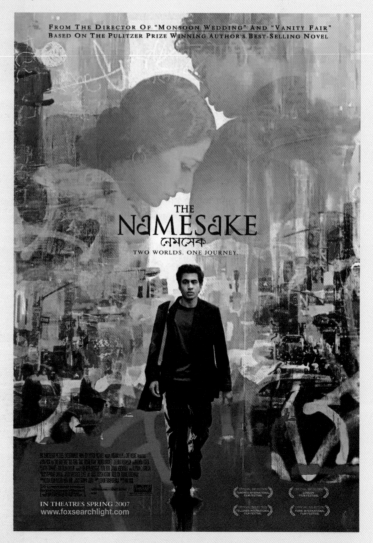

FROM THE DIRECTOR OF "MONSOON WEDDING" AND "VANITY FAIR"
BASED ON THE PULITZER PRIZE WINNING AUTHOR'S BEST-SELLING NOVEL

THE
NAMESAKE
নেমসেক
TWO WORLDS. ONE JOURNEY.

IN THEATRES SPRING 2007
www.foxsearchlight.com

TALKING POINT
• Do you ever watch Bollywood movies? What do you (or would you) like and dislike about them?
• When you're watching foreign movies, do you prefer them to have subtitles or be dubbed? Why?

Listening: Exciting eating

1 What is most important when you eat out at a restaurant? And what is least important? Is it the food, the service, the décor (interior decoration), the price or something else? What?

2 Look at these photos of some unusual restaurants. What do you think goes on in each one?

3 Match these descriptions to the correct photos. Would you like to eat in these restaurants? Why?/Why not?

A

In the fifteenth century in Japan, Ninjas were trained in martial arts like karate and hired to spy on and kill people. But today, they serve food and entertain guests at Ninja restaurants in Japan and the U.S.

B

The first Medieval Times restaurant was opened in Mallorca, Spain in 1973 but now you can find them in the USA and Canada, too. Diners are entertained by a historical show with knights* and horses.

knight: a man from the past who was trained to fight while riding a horse

C

You can find Rainforest Cafés all over the world. They are decorated with plants, waterfalls and robotic animals. They often have a retail store, where rainforest-themed merchandise* is sold.

merchandise: goods that are for sale

D

The world's first fully automated restaurant is located in an industrial park just outside Nuremberg, Germany. Meals are ordered with a touch-screen computer and a system of steel pipes is used to deliver the food.

4 🔊 **2.5** Listen to four conversations. Which restaurant in exercise 3 is each conversation about?

1 _____

2 _____

3 _____

4 _____

5 🔊 Match these sentences to the correct restaurant and answer the questions. Then listen again and check.

1 The restaurant doesn't provide knives and forks? Why not?

2 Customers don't need to leave a tip. Why not?

3 Customers hear some sounds twice an hour. What sounds do they hear?

4 The waiters and waitresses try to scare the guests. How?

Grammar: Active and passive

6 Compare the sentences in group A with group B. Then answer the questions.

Active and passive	
A	**B**
Diners **are entertained** by a historical show.	The waiters and waitresses **entertain** everyone.
Meals **are ordered** with a touch-screen computer.	We **order** the food with this computer.
Steel pipes **are used** to deliver the food.	**Use** your fingers to eat your food.
Themed merchandise **is sold** in the stores.	They **sell** organic beef here.

1 Which sentences (A or B) are more formal?
2 Which sentences (A or B) are passive?
3 Are passives more common in written or spoken English?
4 Do we use the passive when we are more interested in …
   a what someone or something does?
   b what happens to something or someone?

>> For more information on the passive, see page 171.

7 Complete a description of another restaurant. Use an active or passive form of the verbs in brackets.

Dinner in the Sky is a restaurant where 22 guests can enjoy a meal 50 metres in the air. The seats ¹_____ (attach) to the dining table and they all ²_____ (have) a seat belt. When guests arrive, their seat belts ³_____ (fasten) and then the table ⁴_____ (lift) into the air by a large crane*. The food ⁵_____ (cook) before the event and it ⁶_____ (take) up with the guests. The chef and waiters ⁷_____ (serve) the meal from a platform in the middle of the table.

It ⁸_____ (sound) frightening, but most guests ⁹_____ (relax) after a while and start to enjoy the experience. Their seats can turn 180 degrees so they ¹⁰_____ (get) a great view.

The restaurant ¹¹_____ (have) a roof so the guests ¹²_____ (protect) from rain, but it sometimes ¹³_____ (get) windy. The other problem is that there are no toilet facilities in the air so guests ¹⁴_____ (advise) to use the bathroom first.

The restaurant is the invention of David Ghysels. He ¹⁵_____ (base) in Belgium, but he ¹⁶_____ (take) the restaurant all over the world.

crane: a tall machine used by builders for lifting heavy things

Word focus: Restaurants

8 Underline the word that is different in these lists. Why is it different?

1 knife, fork, napkin, spoon
2 onions, eggs, cauliflower, broccoli
3 dessert, meal, starter, main course,
4 meat, lamb, beef, pork
5 bill, receipt, menu, tip
6 waiter, cooker, chef, waitress

Speaking: A themed restaurant

9 Work in pairs or groups. You are going to open a themed restaurant together. Decide on these things.

1 Location and target market
● Where will you open your restaurant?
● Who will your customers be?

2 Entertainment
What will the theme be? For example, the Wild West, the circus, the seaside, snow and ice, the Space Age, or something else (what?).

10 Now plan your restaurant. Decide on these things.
● the décor
● the food and menu
● what waiters and waitresses will wear and do
● themed merchandise you can sell
● other entertainment (what?)

11 Congratulations! Your restaurants are now open for business. Take turns to tell the class about them. Answer these questions.

1 Where is the restaurant located and who are its customers?

2 What is the theme of the restaurant?

3 How is the restaurant decorated?

4 What kind of food is served?

5 What costumes are worn by the waiters and waitresses?

6 What merchandise is sold?

7 Is there any other entertainment?

TALKING POINT Describe an experience you had eating out at a restaurant. Would you recommend the restaurant to other people? Why?/Why not?

Speaking: Secret rules

1 Work in groups of four. You are going to have a conversation about sports. Follow these instructions.

• You can talk about anything you like, for example, sports you play, sports you like watching, or sportspeople you admire.

• Each person must follow a rule.

• **Don't tell anyone** what your rule is.

Student A: Turn to File 2, page 140.

Student B: Turn to File 25, page 143.

Student C: Turn to File 7, page 140.

Student D: Turn to File 34, page 145.

2 Try to guess what rules the other people in your group were following.

3 Discuss these questions.

1 How did your conversation go?

2 Which person had the most pleasant conversation style? Why?

3 Which person was the most difficult to talk to? Why?

Reading: Conversation styles

4 Complete the article about conversation styles. Write the name of a sport in each gap. Then check your answers: Turn to File 26, page 143.

5 Discuss these questions.

1 What kind of conversation style do you think most people have in your culture?

2 Is it generally rude to interrupt in your culture? In what situations is it acceptable?

Playing the conversation game

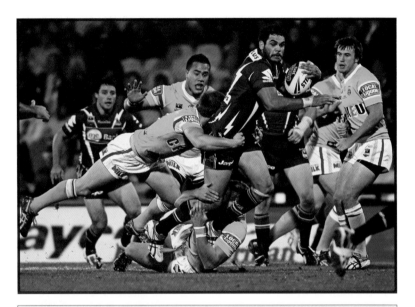

Rugby is a very energetic game with lots of physical contact. There is a strong feeling of belonging to a team.

Bowling is a slow and relaxing game. Players wait for other players to take their turn.

Basketball is a fast game. Players pass the ball from one person to another quickly and take turns to shoot and score points.

It's not just our personalities that determine our conversational style. Researchers have found that culture is important as well. Susan Steinbach, an instructor at the University of California, has an interesting way of explaining the cultural differences. She compares them to different sports.

In some cultures, being considerate in conversations is a top priority. Interrupting is often rude and people may wait for one person to finish before they speak. Who starts a conversation is often important. In Japan or Korea, for example, seniority may matter, so a younger person might wait for an older one to speak first. Susan compares this with the sport of 1 _____.

In other cultures, it's more important to show that you're engaged in a conversation. People might do that with lots of gestures, strong eye contact and also by interrupting. If you're listening to a conversation in Russia, Greece, Africa or Central and South America, for example, you may find more than one person is speaking at a time. Susan compares this with 2 _____.

And some cultures have a mixture of these styles. In the US, UK, Australia and Canada, for example, speakers pass the topic to one another quickly and everyone is expected to take turns. People interrupt each other a lot but only at certain times. They generally wait until someone comes to the end of a thought and then jump in. Speakers overlap* each other briefly* as they change topics. Susan says it's like 3 _____.

overlap: when speakers overlap each other, they speak at the same time
briefly: for a short time

Listening: Developing conversations

6))) **2.6** Listen to a conversation about a football match. Why does the conversation not develop?

7))) **2.7** Listen to another conversation. How does the man help it develop?

8))) Listen to the conversation again and complete the missing words.

A: Great match last night.

B: Yes, 1 _____.

A: I thought Pato played well.

B: Yes he was 2 _____. Definitely their best player.

A: But do you think Milan deserved that second goal?

B: No, I think it was a mistake.
3 _____ _____ _____ _____?

A: Yeah. It was a bad decision by the referee.

B: 4 _____ _____ _____ _____ the Barcelona match tonight.

A: Do you think they'll win?

9 Which of the man's responses comment on what the woman has said? Which introduce a new idea to the conversation?

Speaking: Passing the ball

10 Think of two more hobbies or pastimes to add to this list.

> stamp collecting   golf   reading for pleasure
> video games   gardening   watching television   walking
> cycling   fishing   painting   working on cars

11 Work in small groups and play a conversation game. Your goal is to hold conversations about the hobbies in exercise 10 for as long as possible without interruptions or hesitations.

1 Choose someone in your group to be a timekeeper. They should time how long your conversations last.

2 Take a piece of paper and screw it up to make a ball. From now on, if you want to speak, you must hold the ball.

3 When someone wants to say something, they can hold out their hand so the speaker can pass them the ball.

4 The speaker can also throw the ball to another group member. The person receiving the ball must then ask a question or make a comment to develop the conversation.

5 Long pauses or silence are not allowed. If the person with the ball hesitates for too long, the clock stops and the group has to start again with a new hobby as the topic.

Possible conversation openers:

> I enjoy … because …
>
> I think … is boring because …
>
> An interesting thing about … is …

Reminder

Grammar reference page 171

We use active forms to describe what people and things do.
The town holds a festival every year. It attracts a lot of visitors.

We use passive forms to describe what happens to them.
A competition is held. Prizes are given.

Listening and reading: Festivals

1 Work in pairs. Look at the photos of different festivals. What do you think is happening in each one?

2 In which photo can you see the following?

1 a tuna fish
2 a fight
3 a steep hill (a hill that goes down or up very quickly)
4 a rope
5 a racecourse
6 a piece of cheese
7 squashed (pressed on so they are flatter) tomatoes

A

B

C

D

3))) **2.8** Listen to the interviews about two of the festivals in exercise 1 and answer these questions.

1 Which festivals are they talking about?

2 Where do they take place?

3 What do people have to do?

4))) **2.9** Listen to the first interview again. Are these statements true (T) or false (F)? Correct the ones that are wrong.

1 Leslie was a winner in last year's cheese-rolling festival.

2 The festival is held twice a year.

3 The person who gets to the bottom of the hill first wins.

4 The winner has to catch the cheese.

5 People are sometimes injured.

6 The weather is nice today.

5))) **2.10** Listen to the second interview again and answer these questions.

1 When does this festival take place?

2 What's the main industry in Port Lincoln?

3 What is tied to the frozen tuna fish?

4 What's the world record for throwing the fish?

5 What other entertainments are there at the festival?

6 Work in pairs. Student A: Read text A.
Student B: Read text B. Note the answers to these questions.

1 Where does the event take place?

2 When does it take place?

3 What happens during the event?

4 What rules do participants have to follow?

5 When was it first organized?

6 Where did the idea for the festival come from?

Speaking: An interview

8 Work in pairs. Think of a festival or event that takes place in your country or region. Write some notes about it.

> The event/festival:
>
> • Where and when it takes place:
> _____
>
> • What happens:
> _____
>
> • What the participants have to do:
> _____
>
> • The history of the event/festival:
> _____
>
> • Other interesting facts:
> _____
>
> • Reasons why tourists will enjoy it:
> _____

9 Work in pairs. One person works for your region's tourist board and it is their job to promote the festival. The other person is a foreign news reporter, asking questions. Promoters: Prepare what to say about the festival. Reporters: Prepare questions to ask. Roleplay an interview about your event. Then change roles.

10 Tell the class about the festivals you discussed. Which features of the festivals will be most interesting for tourists?

Writing: Describing an event

11 Write a short description of the event you talked about for your region's website. Refer to the texts in exercise 6 for help.

(A) **WIFE CARRYING**

The wife-carrying competitions take place every July in Sonkajarvi in Finland. Husbands have to carry their wives over a special racecourse which always includes crossing water at one point. The wives are carried on their partners' backs or over their shoulders. If a husband drops his wife, then 15 seconds is added to the couple's time. The races are run with two couples at a time until one couple finally become the winners. Prizes are also given for other reasons, too, like the most entertaining couple or the best costume.

The first competitions were organized in 1992 but the sport existed many years before that. In the past, a man sometimes took a wife by running into her village and carrying her away, so this is probably where the idea came from. Jaakko Lehtonen, from the Finnish Tourist Board, says, 'The wife carrying creates a cheerful, bright and imaginative picture of Finland and we aim at using this image in marketing our country.'

(B) **LA TOMATINA**

La Tomatina is probably the largest food fight in the world. It takes place on the last Wednesday in August in the Spanish town of Bunol. On that day, around 125,000 kilograms of tomatoes are brought into the town by truck. Then a cannon* is fired and the big tomato fight begins. There are very few rules except that you must squash the tomatoes before you throw them for safety reasons. People are also encouraged to wear protective clothing. The fight ends an hour later when a cannon is fired again. After this no more tomatoes are thrown and people begin to clean the streets.

The first tomato fight was held in 1945 but no one knows how the festival began. Perhaps it was from a fight in a restaurant. Now it's a major tourist attraction for the town and attracts visitors from places as far away as Japan and Australia.

cannon: a large gun that was used in the past to fire large metal balls

7 Tell your partner about the festival you read about, using your notes. Which festival would you prefer to go to: La Tomatina or wife carrying? Why?

Interaction

1 There is one extra word in each of these sentences. Correct each sentence by crossing out the extra word.

1 I'm afraid he might to complain to the manager about the delay.

2 I just don't have enough of energy to argue about this.

3 I don't think they'll change our work timetable but it's worth for asking.

4 If your business does well, and you can open a second branch.

5 There aren't many of historical places in that part of town.

6 They'll give us our tickets when we will arrive at the theatre.

7 All the food it is prepared from fresh ingredients every day.

8 Walkers are advised to be wear good strong shoes and warm clothes.

2 Complete this text. Put the verbs in brackets in the correct tense: either present simple or *will* for future.

How can you encourage your staff to be healthier? Perhaps you think that information is the key and that if you ¹_____ (give) your staff some leaflets about health, they ²_____ (start) to lead healthier lives. Not a good idea. Staff probably know the information already and if they ³_____ (not want) to make these changes in their lifestyle, they ⁴_____ (not do) it.

Be positive rather than negative. If you ⁵_____ (charge) higher insurance for unhealthy staff, for example, some people ⁶_____ (complain). Something like a system of gift vouchers for going to the gym is a better idea. Another possibility is to offer the healthiest food in the canteen for free. You can be sure that staff ⁷_____ (eat) healthily if they ⁸_____ (know) that they are saving money.

3 Match the beginnings and endings of these sentences.

1 If they've sent the wrong items,

2 I might look for another job

3 You'll feel much healthier

4 If you talk to yourself on the train,

5 If that woman phones again,

6 I think you should go home

7 If the boss thinks the sales figures are OK,

8 You'll have to phone technical support

a tell her I'm out of the office!

b perhaps I'm worrying unnecessarily.

c if you're feeling sick.

d if you've forgotten your password.

e you should phone the company to complain.

f if I don't get a promotion soon.

g people generally think you're mad.

h if you cycle to work.

4 Complete this text. Put the verbs in brackets in the correct tense. Use the present or past, active or passive forms of the verbs in brackets.

The Laff Box is a machine that produces the sound of laughter. It ¹_____ (invent) in 1953 by a sound engineer called Charlie Douglass. Today, sounds from the Laff Box ²_____ (still add) to the soundtracks of TV comedy programmes so the viewers at home ³_____ (feel) they are laughing along with other people.

An American laugh is different to a Chinese laugh or a French laugh, so today's Laff Boxes ⁴_____ (contain) a variety of international styles. To make it more natural, sometimes TV shows ⁵_____ (film) in front of a live studio audience, and then the artificial laughter ⁶_____ (add) to the natural laughter later.

Artificial laughter ⁷_____ (know) as 'canned laughter' and some people ⁸_____ (complain) that it is annoying. But it's not a new idea. In the 4th century BC the writers of Greek comedies ⁹_____ (hire) people to laugh at their plays to get a positive audience reaction. At the age of 82, nearly 40 years after he ¹⁰_____ (invent) the machine, Charlie Douglass ¹¹_____ (give) an Emmy award for technical achievement in entertainment.

5 Complete these sentences. Choose the correct words.

1 They don't give employees *much / many* opportunities to upgrade their skills.

2 The brochure doesn't give *much / many* information about their products.

3 We'll have a late lunch because there'll be *too / too much / too many* people in the restaurant now.

4 I don't like big cars because they cause *too / too much / too many* pollution.

5 It's *too / too much / too many* cold today to eat in the garden.

6 I don't think those boxes are *enough strong / strong enough*.

6 Match each phrase 1–8 with the most suitable response a–h.

1 I'm afraid I can't come to your session this afternoon.

2 Would you like to come to supper on Friday?

3 The staff won't like this new system.

4 I don't think it's worth it.

5 I thought his talk was really good.

6 These sales figures are disappointing.

7 We could install new CCTV cameras.

8 Are you doing anything next Sunday?

a That'd be great. We'd love to.

b I don't think so. Why?

c Yes, but they're very expensive.

d No, they'll all complain,

e Not to worry.

f Yes, it was brilliant.

g Yes, they're not very good at all.

h No, it's too much effort.

7 Complete these conversations. Write one word in each gap.

1

(**A** and **B** are colleagues)

A: Could we ¹_____ a time to meet next week?

B: OK. How ²_____ Thursday?

A: Sorry, I'm afraid I'm ³_____ up on Thursday. I'm ⁴_____ a presentation in South London. Are you ⁵_____ on Friday?

B: Yes, Friday ⁶_____ good. Would ten o'clock ⁷_____ you?

A: I can't ⁸_____ the morning, I'm afraid but I'm ⁹_____ any time on Friday afternoon.

B: ¹⁰_____ about two o'clock?

A: Yes, that's fine. ¹¹_____, that's Friday afternoon at two o'clock.

B: Fine. ¹²_____ you then.

2

(**A** is a hotel guest; **B** is a receptionist)

A: Excuse me. I have a problem.

B: Really?

A: I ¹_____ that you've put internet use on my bill.

B: Isn't that correct?

A: I tried to use the internet yesterday, but I ²_____ get a connection.

B: Oh dear. That's ³_____.

A: But you've ⁴_____ me eight euros for internet use.

B: Oh, I'm so sorry. I ⁵_____ apologize.

A: I needed to send an email urgently and in the end I ⁶_____ to go the internet café in town.

B: We're ⁷_____ some problems with our computer system at the moment. I ⁸_____ remove that charge and issue you with a new bill.

A: OK. Thanks for your help.

8 Complete these sentences. Choose the correct words.

1 I'll try to go the meeting but the time is very *uncomfortable / inconvenient*.

2 They employ a very famous *chef / cooker* at that restaurant.

3 I'm afraid I have to *turn off / turn down* your kind invitation.

4 He *made / gave* a number of examples of how we could change things.

5 He was accused of *thief / theft* and dismissed from his job.

6 The food comes to 240 euros, so how much should we leave as a *tip / bill*?

9 Put each word in the box into the correct group according to its stress pattern.

> commercial courtesy priority entertainment shoplifter attraction competition merchandise correspondence fantasy redundancy consultant bureaucracy adventure participant application

Ooo	oOo	oOoo	ooOo
technical	*connection*	*receptionist*	*invitation*

10 Complete the crossword.

Across

1 The place where a film is made.

3 Shilpa Shetty is a famous one in Bollywood.

5 The person who organizes the work and money for making a film.

8 A type of film about two people who fall in love.

9 A type of film about magic or mythical creatures.

Down

1 The part of the cinema where a film is shown.

2 The person in charge of making a film.

4 The translation of the words of a foreign film printed across the screen

6 To replace the original language of a film with another language.

7 A type of film that makes you laugh.

13

A -*ing* forms
B -*ing* and -*ed* adjectives
C **Communication strategies** Compliments
D **Interaction** Entertaining guests

Politely does it

-*ing* forms

Reading: Mobile phone manners

1 Do you feel annoyed when people have loud conversations on their mobile phones on the train? In what other situations are mobiles annoying?

2 Read the article about mobile phone manners. Does it mention any of the situations you thought of?

3 Work in pairs or groups. Close your books and try to remember the cities and countries mentioned in the article. What did it say about each one?

Manners on the move

There are more than 3.3 billion mobile phone users in the world today. That's more than half the planet. Phones are ringing all the time and researchers have found that people everywhere are complaining about bad manners.

Conversations during a movie are the top complaint in Hong Kong. People in the Czech Republic can't stand phones interrupting business meetings and in Thailand they hate phones ringing in restaurants. In Japan, it's rude to make calls on trains but interestingly, using your phone to play games isn't annoying.

Researchers have also found differences in the way people handle calls. When a phone rings in a restaurant in Paris, the owner usually ignores it. In Madrid they may accept the call but then try to include everyone at the table in the conversation. In London, people often take the call but then take their phones outside to talk and they often stand near traffic. This seems a surprising habit in view of the noise and danger but apparently they don't like speaking where other people can hear.

In some cultures, people don't mind leaving voicemail messages but in others they aren't keen on them. Spanish callers prefer speaking to a human being so if you don't answer, they usually want you to call them back. Calling people back is good manners in Mumbai, too, but for different reasons. Men often ignore a call from their girlfriend but then call her back immediately so that they pay the bill. It's the polite thing to do.

Mobile phone manners may be different in different parts of the world but there's one thing that is true everywhere: people love their mobile phones and they aren't going to stop using them. In Ireland, when someone dies, traditionally people bury* a treasured possession* with them. These days it's often a mobile phone.

bury: put something under the ground, e.g. a dead body
treasured possession: something you own which is very important to you

Grammar: -ing forms

4 Read the notes on -ing forms in the table. Then look at the article again and find more examples of verbs that are followed by -ing forms.

-ing forms

1 English -ing forms can be …
   a parts of a continuous tense.
   *Phones are **ringing** all the time.*
   *People are **complaining** about bad manners.*
   b adjectives.
   *This seems a **surprising** habit.*
   *It isn't **annoying**.*
   c the subject of a sentence.
   ***Calling** back is good manners in Mumbai.*
   ***Using** your phone to play games is OK.*

2 We also use -ing forms after certain verbs. We generally use them when we're talking about things we like and dislike.
   *He **loves playing** games on his mobile phone.*
   *Some people **aren't keen on leaving** voicemail messages.*

>> For more information on -ing forms, see page 172.

5 Put these verbs in the correct order below.

can't stand   don't mind   like   not be keen on

love				hate	

6 Complete these sentences. Use the -ing form of the verbs in the box.

play   send   switch off   chat   take   use   text   hear

1 I can't stand people _____ on their mobile phones while I'm trying to sleep on the train. I don't mind people _____ because that doesn't make a noise.

2 I don't like _____ phones ring in restaurants and cinemas.

3 I enjoy _____ games on my mobile phone and I love _____ photos with it and sending them to my friends.

4 My phone came with a hands-free device but I'm not keen on _____ it in public. People think I'm talking to myself.

5 I prefer _____ text messages to calling because it's much cheaper.

6 I hate _____ my phone. I think I might be a mobile phone addict.

7 Work in pairs. Compare how you feel about the activities in exercise 6.

A: *I don't mind people chatting on their mobiles on the train.*

B: *Oh, I hate that. But I don't mind people texting because I can't hear that.*

Speaking: Annoying behaviour

8 Work in groups. Here are some other things that annoy people about modern life. Think of some more to add to the list.
- getting calls from telemarketers
- people dropping litter
- receiving spam emails
- calling a company and finding that you're talking to a machine
- having to remember lots of passwords
- people reading text messages when you're trying to talk to them

9 Which three things are the most annoying and why? Decide together on the top three. How do you deal with these things?

TALKING POINT
What are the top complaints about mobile phones in your country?

Listening: The American way

1 Does your country have a tradition of showing hospitality to strangers? What other cultures do you know that are hospitable (friendly to visitors and ready to welcome them)?

2 🔊 **2.11** Do you think Americans are hospitable? Listen to two people describing their experiences. Do they agree with you?

3 🔊 Listen again. Are these statements true (T) or false (F)?

1 At first the woman enjoyed looking round American houses.

2 At first the woman thought that Americans are conceited (too proud of how good, clever or attractive you are).

3 The woman thinks that German people are more modest (not too proud of yourself or what you have) than Americans.

4 The man thinks British furniture is smaller than American furniture.

5 The man was surprised by the guests' behaviour at an American party.

Word focus: -ing and -ed adjectives

4 Compare these sentences. Then answer the questions.

   a *He was very interesting.*

   b *He was very interested.*

Interesting and *interested* are both adjectives. Which one describes …

1 how people feel?

2 a person or thing that causes the feeling?

5 Look at the information in the table and check your answers in exercise 4. Then think of more adjectives that can end in *-ing* or *-ed*.

-ing and -ed adjectives

Interesting describes a quality something has.

   *It was an **interesting** visit.*

Interested describes a reaction to something else.

   *I was **interested** in your presentation.*

Some other adjectives also have *-ed* and *-ing* forms. For example:

embarrassing (the quality)   **embarrassed** (the reaction)

---

6 Complete these sentences. Add the correct ending to each adjective.

1 Travelling to other countries is always very interest_____ .

2 I'm sometimes surpris_____ by different foreign customs.

3 English people talk about the weather a lot, but I think it's a bor_____ topic.

4 I'm always interest_____ to see how other people live.

5 I felt really excit_____ when I went on my first trip abroad.

6 You can get into some embarrass_____ situations if you don't learn about the customs of a country before you go there.

Reading: Travellers' tales

7 Read these travellers' stories. What did they find surprising, and why?

1 A strange thing happened to me when I was visiting Dallas, Texas. I got into an elevator and another man got in at the same time. I didn't know him so I was very surprised when he started talking to me and said, 'I really like your tie.' Why did he say something like that to a stranger?

2 I went to a meeting in Seoul in Korea. We made small talk before it began and chatted about the weather and my flight. Then Ms Kim asked, 'How old are you?' I was very surprised. Isn't it impolite to ask someone's age?

3 I visited our Tokyo office for a couple of days and the team took me out to a restaurant for a meal. Takahashi asked about my family so I told him that my wife is a professional musician. Our children can both play an instrument and I'm very proud of them. He told me he was married but he didn't say much about his wife. However, I later learned that his wife is a famous writer in Japan. Why didn't he tell me?

4 Many years ago we visited a client's home in Saudi Arabia. I admired a piece of artwork on the wall and he took it down and gave it to me. How generous! I was so surprised. Of course, I didn't want to take it but he insisted, so in the end I had to. But I'm worried because I think it cost a lot of money. Did I do the right thing?

8 Read four other views of the situations in exercise 7. Match each one to the correct situations 1–4.

◯ When someone is a guest in our home, of course we try to give them everything they want. This is difficult if they want things that we don't want to give them. So, where I come from it's not always polite to admire things that are very expensive. It's similar to asking for them. As a host, I might give them to you, but I might not invite you to my home again. Times are changing though and younger people behave differently.

◯ I think I'm very lucky because my wife is very talented but I don't talk about it in public. I thought it was strange when my American colleague praised his family. We're part of our families so it sounds like we're praising ourselves if we praise them. I try to be modest about them.

◯ Where I come from, people are friendly and it's polite to say 'Hi'. I don't want to ignore anyone so I often use compliments to start conversations. I think it's a nice way to say 'hello' and welcome a stranger.

◯ Age brings wisdom and we respect older people in our culture. Age is important for practical reasons, too. It affects the seating arrangements for a meeting, who speaks first and things like that. I can't always tell how old westerners are by looking at them, so I sometimes need to ask.

Speaking: Comparing cultures

9 Discuss these questions.

1 In your culture, do people use compliments to start conversations with strangers? Do men often compliment other men on their appearance? And what about women?

2 Is it OK to tell people about the talents and accomplishments of your family, or does it sound conceited?

3 Is it ever rude to admire other people's possessions? When? Are there any questions you can't ask, like 'How much did it cost'?

4 When someone pays you a compliment, is it better to agree or to be modest and disagree?

10 Prepare to tell a story.

1 Think about a time when you visited a foreign country or entertained a foreign guest. Did anything interesting or surprising happen? For example …

- during a meal.
- when you asked for directions.
- in a taxi ride.
- on public transport.
- when you visted someone's house.
- somewhere else (when?).

2 Take a few minutes to prepare your story.

11 Work in groups. Take turns telling your stories. Listen carefully to each other's stories. Identify the interesting and surprising events.

TALKING POINT
- Do you think people were more hospitable to strangers in the past? Are traditions about hospitality disappearing in today's world?
- Do you think the growth in tourism around the world has made people less hospitable to strangers?

Speaking: Paying compliments

1 Match these compliments to the photos below. How could you reply to each one?

1 I really like it. It suits you.

2 What a lovely view!

3 Great shot!

4 That looks delicious.

5 You're so talented.

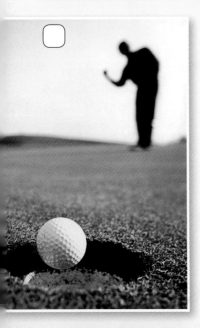

2 Use the phrases in the box to complete the compliments.

> nice jacket   your attitude to life   really kind   so helpful
> lovely coffee   wonderful photos   looks great   brilliant idea
> the way you've organized things   smells really nice

I really like …	your house.
	1 _____.
	2 _____.
What a …	fantastic party!
	3 _____.
	4 _____.
What …	beautiful pictures!
	5 _____.
	6 _____.
You're …	looking great.
	7 _____.
	8 _____.
That …	looks very pretty.
	9 _____.
	10 _____.

> **!** We use *What…* with uncountable nouns and plurals. We use *What a …* with singular countable nouns.

3 Discuss these questions.

1 How important is it for bosses to praise their employees?

2 How important is it for colleagues to pay compliments to each other?

3 What's the nicest compliment you've ever received?

Listening: A business meeting

4))) **2.12** A consultant is visiting some clients. Listen to the start of their conversation and make a note of the compliments you hear. What are they about?

5))) Listen again and complete these sentences.

Compliments and responses
A: It's nice to see you again.   **B:** 1_____ _____. You look very well.
A: I love your new 2_____.   **B:** My hairdresser 3_____ me to try a new style.
A: It really 4_____ _____.   **B:** Oh, thank you.
A: We have 5_____ a nice meeting room today.   **B:** I can't take 6_____ for that. Jeremy booked it.
A: The screen's 7_____ nice.   **B:** It's OK, but it's not very fast. It takes a long time to 8_____ _____.

6 Look at the different strategies used in the responses in exercise 5 and answer these questions.

Which one …

1 accepts the compliment?

2 repays the compliment?

3 gives an explanation?

4 downgrades the praise so it sounds less important?

5 shares the praise with other people?

7))) **2.13** You are going to hear five more extracts from the meeting. In each one, identify a) the compliment and b) the strategy the person uses to respond.

8 Think of some different ways you could reply to these compliments. Try to use different strategies.

1 Your boss has read a report you wrote. She says, 'It was excellent. You did a great job on the research.'

2 You've recently bought a new car. You give a colleague a lift home and they say, 'Wow, I love this car. It's fantastic.'

3 You invited a co-worker for dinner at your home and cooked a meal. At the end they say, 'That was wonderful. I didn't know you were such a good cook.'

4 You've just played a round of golf with some business contacts. At the end of the game one of them says, 'You played really well today.'

5 You've dressed up for a colleague's retirement party. A co-worker says, 'That outfit really suits you.'

6 You're organizing a conference. A co-worker who's helping you says, 'You're such a good person for this job. You're so efficient and pleasant to work with.'

Speaking: The compliment game

9 Take turns paying and responding to compliments with the class. One person compliments another class member who responds. Then, after they have responded, that person compliments someone else and so on.

You can compliment people on …

- their appearance (how they look or what they are wearing).
- their possessions (something they own).
- a job they did.
- their skills or abilities.
- their personality.

Writing: Passing on praise

10 Your friend gave a training session to the staff in your department yesterday. Many people have told you how good it was. Write an email to your friend.

In your email …

- tell your friend one or two of the compliments you have received about the training session.
- say something that you thought was especially good about it.
- ask if they can repeat the session for people who were absent and suggest a date.

Begin your email like this:

> Hi _____,
> I'm just writing to tell you how much people enjoyed your session yesterday. Lots of the staff said…

Reminder

Grammar reference page 172

Here are some phrases we use when we pay compliments to people about their possessions.

I really like/love ...

What a ...

That looks really ...

We use *interested, surprised, tired,* etc. to say how people feel.

We use *interesting, surprising, tiring,* etc. to describe the people and things that cause the feelings.

1 Do you know the polite things to say when you invite guests to your home? Try this quiz and find out.

Are you a good host?

1 You hear the doorbell, open the door and greet your guests. What do you say?

A *Hello! You have come!*

B *Hello! Lovely to see you!*

2 You want your guests to feel relaxed in your house. What do you say?

A *Make yourself at home.*

B *Please have the sofa.*

3 You have put food on the table and you want your guests to serve themselves and not wait for you to give it to them. What do you say?

A *Please help yourself.*

B *Take the food yourself.*

4 You want to offer your guests more food. What you do say?

A *Do have some more.*

B *Please eat more.*

5 Your guests say, 'I think we'll have to be on our way soon.' What do you reply?

A *I'll come with you to the door.*

B *Oh, do you really? How about another coffee first?*

6 At the end of the visit, your guests say, 'You must come and see us next time.' What do you say?

A *That would be lovely.*

B *Thank you. Next week would be a good time.*

2 Compare your answers with a partner. Then check your answers: Turn to File 39, page 145.

3 In your country, what do people say in the situations in the quiz in exercise 1? How similar is it to what people say in English?

Listening: Lovely to see you

4))) **2.14** Listen to Steve and Angie welcoming some guests to their home and answer these questions.

1 In what part of the house does the conversation take place?

2 What do you think the guests have brought?

3 What do their guests say about their house?

4 How does Steve respond?

5))) Listen again and complete these sentences.

1 _____ _____ you could come.

2 _____ _____ _____ your coats.

3 _____ _____ _____ to the living room.

6))) **2.15** It's now the end of the evening and their guests are getting ready to leave. Listen and answer these questions.

1 How many times do the guests suggest that they should leave?

2 What's Elaine doing tomorrow?

7))) Listen again and complete these sentences.

1 Well, I think we'll have to _____ _____ soon.

2 Anyway, I think we'll have to _____ _____ now.

8))) **2.16** Here are some things they say when they are leaving. Match pairs of sentences that go together. Then listen and check your answers.

1 Thanks for the great meal.

2 You have to come to our house next time.

3 Thanks for having us.

4 We'd love to.

5 Good to see you, too.

6 Glad you enjoyed it.

7 Thank you for coming.

8 It's always lovely to see you.

Speaking: The visit

9 Work in pairs or small groups. Prepare to act out a visit to someone's home. First, decide who will be the host(s) and who will be the guest(s). Guests: Turn to File 3, page 140. Hosts: Turn to File 29, page 144. Then read the situations below and take a few minutes to prepare what you will say.

THE ARRIVAL

Host:
Welcome your guest at the door. Take their coat and then take them through to the living room.

Guest:
Give your host a gift and compliment them on their house.

SMALL TALK BEFORE DINNER

Host:
Offer your guest a drink and try to make them feel at home.
After some small talk, announce that dinner is ready and take them through to the dining room.

Guest:
Begin conversations by commenting on some things you can see in the living room.

AT THE DINNER TABLE

Host:
Offer your guest food throughout the meal and take part in the small talk. Ask your guests questions, too – e.g. where they live, how they spend their holidays, their family.

Guest:
Compliment your host on the meal.
Use some of the things you see in the dining room to start conversations.
When it's time to leave, explain you must be going.

SAYING GOODBYE

Host:
Get your guest's coat and say how much you enjoyed seeing them. Thank them for coming.

Guest:
Thank your host for having you. Insist they must come to your home next time. Say goodbye.

10 Work in pairs or small groups and act out the visit.

11 How did the visit go? Did the guest discover the host's special talent and the three things that they can do?

Interaction

14

A Present perfect
B Present perfect vs past simple
C Communication strategies Public speaking
D Interaction Job interviews

Career moves

Present perfect

Reading: The caretakers

1 Look at the photo and discuss these questions.

1 Would you like to live in a place like this?

2 What kind of work could you do there to earn a living?

2 Read the article. What do the young couple do for a living?

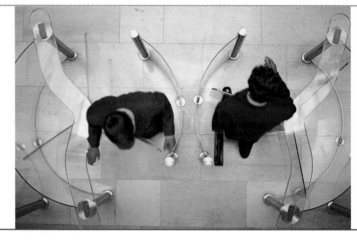

The life of your dreams

FROM TIME TO TIME most of us dream of getting away from it all and going to live on a beautiful island. The problem is that even on a beautiful island you still have to pay the bills. But Lionel and Dawn Collier, a couple from Atlanta, Georgia, have found the answer. Since 2004, they have worked as caretakers.

When the couple first met back in 2000, Lionel was a marketing consultant and Dawn had a job in public relations. But when they had their first child in 2003, they wanted a complete change of lifestyle. Lionel had some contacts in the Bahamas so he looked into the possibility of caretaking work. They got their first job a year later on Blue Cay, a private island owned by a Californian billionaire. Lionel and Dawn were responsible for the maintenance of the owner's two houses, and they also acted as hosts for the owner's friends.

Lionel and Dawn are still caretaking today. Since 2008, they've looked after an olive grove* in Greece, taking care of the property and selling the olives to local shops and oil producers. Dawn says, 'Caretaking has provided us with something we can do together, away from the stress of the corporate world. We've been lucky to look after such beautiful places.'

olive grove: an area of land where there are a lot of olive trees

3 Complete these sentences with words and phrases from the article.

1 G_____ _____ _____ _____ _____ is going somewhere to escape from your usual routine.

2 P_____ is something that you own, like land or a house.

3 If you work for a big company, you are part of the c_____ w_____.

4 Another way of saying *take care of* something (a place or a person) is: l_____ a_____.

4 Are these sentences true (T) or false (F)? Correct the ones that are wrong.

1 Lionel and Dawn were caretakers when they met.

2 Lionel knew people in the Bahamas before he went to live there.

3 On Blue Cay, Lionel and Dawn had to look after the owner's houses.

4 Lionel and Dawn live in Greece now.

5 Lionel and Dawn own a company which makes olive oil.

Grammar: Present perfect + *how long?*

5 Look at the article again and answer these questions. Then read the information in the table and check.

1 Which tense is used in paragraph 2? Why?

2 Which tenses are used in paragraph 3? Why?

Present perfect vs past simple

We use the present perfect to talk about actions that began in the past and are still continuing now.

They**'ve worked** as caretakers since 2004.

	They got their first caretaking job.		They are still caretakers.	
Past ———————		—┼———————————————		—┼——————— Future
	2004		now	

When actions are not continuing now, we use the past simple.

In 2000, Lionel **was** a management consultant and Dawn **had** a job in public relations.

They first **met** in 2000.

>> For more information on the present perfect, see page 165.

6 Look at the article again. Match these questions with the correct answers.

1	When did they meet?	**a**	Since 2004
2	When did they have their first child?	**b**	In 2003
3	When did they move to Greece?	**c**	Since 2008
4	How long have they lived in Greece?	**d**	Since 2000
5	How long have they been caretakers?	**e**	In 2008
6	How long have they been together?	**f**	In 2000

7 Complete the text. Put the verbs in brackets into the past simple or present perfect.

Chris Dolder ¹_____ (be) interested in the polar regions since he was a student. As part of his university course, he ²_____ (spend) time in the Arctic studying the effects of climate change but then he ³_____ (get) a job as a management consultant. He ⁴_____ (earn) a salary of around £75,000 but money didn't bring job satisfaction and he always ⁵_____ (dream) of doing something different.

He ⁶_____ (do) a lot of networking and ⁷_____ (send) a lot of job applications, but it ⁸_____ (take) him eight years to find his dream job. Since 2007, Chris ⁹_____ (work) as a polar expedition leader in the Antarctic.

'I'm so lucky,' he says. 'I love the beauty of the Antarctic and I love helping others to experience it. In this job, I ¹⁰_____ (act) as a guide for scientists, journalists and tourists and I ¹¹_____ (meet) some wonderful people. I ¹²_____ (not get) much satisfaction when I was a management consultant. Quality of life is the important thing.'

Speaking: How long?

8 Complete some sentences about your life and career.

1 I live … in Madrid/Warsaw/Osaka/…. alone/with …

2 I am … an engineer/a consultant/ a lawyer … married/single … interested in …

3 I work … for IBM/Sony/Petrobras/ … with tourists/journalists/ young people …

4 I have … a holiday home in … an apartment in … a BMW/a Honda/ a Peugeot …

9 Work in pairs. Share information about your lives and careers. Ask questions with *how long*.

> A: *Where do you live?*
>
> B: *In Flores.*
>
> A: *How long have you lived there?*
>
> B: *Since 1986. I moved there when I got married.*

TALKING POINT • Is there a place you've always dreamed of living? Where?

• Could you be happier earning less money but with a different kind of lifestyle? How?

1 Work in pairs. Discuss these questions.

1 Who is your oldest friend?

2 How did you meet?

3 How long have you known them?

4 When did you last see them?

5 What did you talk about?

Listening: Old friends

2))) **2.17** Listen to two friends who are meeting after a long time. How do they know each other?

3))) Who has done these things? Write J (Janet), D (Daniel), E (Ethel). Then listen again and check.

1 _____ hasn't changed.

2 _____ has always wanted to go to Sardinia.

3 _____ has worked abroad.

4 _____ has become a software engineer.

5 _____ has changed their name.

6 _____ has seen Ethel on television lots of times but didn't recognize her.

Grammar: Present perfect vs past simple

4 Read the notes in the grammar box and choose the correct words to complete the rules.

5 Think of some things you have wanted to do and some things you have done in your life. Write down these things.

1 A country you've always wanted to go to and an interesting place you've actually been to.

2 A movie you've always wanted to see and a movie you've already seen.

3 A book you've always wanted to read and a book you've actually read.

4 Someone famous you've always wanted to meet and someone interesting you've actually met.

5 Something you've always wanted to learn how to do and something you've already learnt how to do.

6 Something that sounds fun that you've always wanted to try and something that's fun that you've already tried.

Present perfect vs past simple

1 We use the present perfect to talk about situations that have continued up to now.

We've been married for five years.

2 We use the past simple for finished actions that have no connection with the present.

I was a tour guide in Sardinia. (I'm not a tour guide now.)

I met Carlo in Sardinia. (I'm not meeting him now.)

3 We also use the present perfect to describe life experiences.

I've always wanted to go to Sardinia.

I've watched her show lots of times.

Have you ever seen Selima Sanchez on TV?

Rules:

1 We use the present perfect to talk about *a definite / an indefinite* time in the past.

She's changed her name.

Have you heard from Ethel?

2 We use the past simple to refer to *a definite / an indefinite* time in the past.

When I left university, I got a job with a holiday company.

I became a software engineer.

>> **For more information on the present perfect vs past simple, see page 167.**

6 Work in pairs or small groups. Find out if your partner(s) have ever done the things on your list. Ask more questions about the things your partner(s) have done. When you start talking about a definite time, use the past simple.

A: Have you ever been to Thailand?

B: No, I haven't. Have you?

A: Yes, I've been twice.

B: Oh, where did you go exactly?

A: I went to Bangkok, Phuket and Chang Mai.

Word focus: *for* and *since*

7 Look at the examples and complete the rules. Write *for* or *since*.

---

for and since

*I haven't seen you **since** we left university.*
*We've been married **for** five years.*

Rules:

1 We use _____ to say when an activity started.

2 We use _____ to say how long an activity has continued.

3 We use _____ with a period of time and _____ with a point in time.

⚠ We use the present perfect with *since*.
***I've worked for** the same company **since** 2006.* (I started working for them in 2006 and I still work for them now.)
We can use the present perfect *or* past simple with *for*.
*He**'s had** that job **for** about two years.* (He has that job now.)
*She **worked** for a software company **for** some years.* (She has a different job now.)

8 Do we use these words and phrases with *for* or *since*? Divide them into two groups.

2008   two o'clock   five years   an hour   a month
August   three weeks   a long time   I last saw you
a moment   we left university   a few days   ages
they opened the new factory

Speaking: Updates

9 Work in pairs. Student A: Look at the information below. Student B: Turn to File 31, page 144.

Student A:
Your partner works in your head office in another country, but sometimes they visit your local office. They're going to ask you about some of your colleagues. Use the information in the photo below to answer their questions. Also find out how your partner knows your colleagues and how long they have known them. Read the notes and think about what you will say. You can invent any information you don't have.

Writing: A chance meeting

10 Imagine you met an old acquaintance yesterday. Email a friend and tell them about the meeting.

1 Begin …

Do you remember _____? I met him/her by chance at/in _____ yesterday.

2 Continue by saying …

● how he/she has changed.

● what he/she is doing now and how long he/she has done it.

● how you felt about seeing him/her again.

Frank Hollins
Left the company last year. Now works for a competitor.

Edward Jones
Wife had another baby (their sixth). On paternity leave at the moment.

Claire Parker
Promoted last April. Now the Regional Sales Director at the Hong Kong Office.

Louise Johnson
Retired last month. Bought a holiday home in the country and now lives there permanently.

Mary Slawter
Injured her back and had to have an operation. Came back to work last week.

TALKING POINT
● Have you kept in touch with any of your old school/university friends? What have they done since they left?
● Have you ever reconnected with an old friend via a social networking website? What happened?

Reading: Connecting with an audience

1 Discuss these questions.

1 Think about someone you know who is good at speaking to an audience. What makes their talks and presentations so good?

2 What mistakes do poor presenters sometimes make?

2 Read about an executive who gave presentations in Japan. What mistake did he usually make?

★ ★ ★ ★ ★ ★ ★ ★

An American executive often travelled to Japan. He didn't speak Japanese, so when he had to make presentations, he employed an interpreter. One day his regular interpreter wasn't available, so he had a new one.

The executive began his presentation, as he always did, with a joke. His jokes were popular in the US but in Japan people didn't usually laugh. But with the new interpreter it was different. Everyone in the audience laughed loudly and some people clapped and cheered. The American was delighted. After the talk, he thanked the translator and said, 'You're much better than the other guy. I've given lots of talks in Japan and audiences don't usually get my jokes. But they do when you tell them.'

Sometime later he discovered that this is what the interpreter said: 'The American is now telling a joke. It has nothing to do with his presentation and I don't know why he is doing this. But it is an American custom. Please laugh and clap when I tell you.'

★ ★ ★ ★ ★ ★ ★ ★

3 Answer these questions.

1 Why did the executive have a new interpreter?

2 How did Japanese audiences normally react to his jokes and how did they react this time?

3 Why did the executive think the audience laughed?

4 Why did the audience really laugh?

4 Here are two opinions on joke telling. Which one do you agree with most and why?

A

> Jokes are fine at the end of the workday but they're not a good way to start a business presentation. Presenters should give their audience the information they want. They shouldn't tell them jokes.

B

> Jokes are a great way to connect with an audience. If a presenter can make their audience laugh, their audience will relax and like them. Then they will listen to what they have to say.

5 Which of the presenters in photos A–C would you like to listen to? Why? Would other people you work with appreciate their presentation style? Why?/Why not?

6 Discuss some other ways you expect presenters to behave.

Is it good or bad if they …

1 look serious and don't smile very much?

2 take their jacket off, loosen their tie and roll up their shirt sleeves?

3 read their presentation from a piece of paper?

4 have lots of writing and detailed statistics in their PowerPoint slides?

5 use long words and are creative and poetic with language?

6 only accept questions from the audience at the end of their talk?

7 speak for longer than scheduled?

B

C

Listening: Starting presentations

7)) **2.18** Listen to a speaker beginning a presentation. Does he make a joke? What is he going to talk about?

8 The speaker described the structure of his presentation. Do you think this is a good way to start? Why?/Why not? What other techniques do speakers use to start talks?

9)) **2.19** Listen to the beginnings of four more presentations. Which begin with these things?

a a surprising fact or statistic ◯

b a challenging question ◯

c a short story ◯

d a quotation ◯

10 Work in pairs. What do you think the four presentations will be about?

11)) **2.20** Listen to the complete introductions and find out if you are right.

Speaking: Beginning a talk

12 Prepare the first one or two minutes of a presentation. Work in pairs and share ideas but prepare your own individual introductions.

1 Why are you giving the talk and who is the audience? You can choose one of these situations or invent another.

  a Your old school/university has asked you to give a talk about your job to its students.

  b You boss wants you to give a talk about your products/services/future plans to some visiting clients.

  c A social club has asked you to speak at their next meeting, perhaps about your hobby or a place you've visited.

2 What will your talk be about?

  a Write the title of your talk:

  _____

  b In 12 words or less, write the key message:

  _____
  _____
  _____
  _____
  _____

  c Write three topics you will cover:

  1 _____
  _____
  2 _____
  _____
  3 _____
  _____

3 Decide how to start your talk. Do you want to …

  a explain the structure of your talk?

  b tell a short story?

  c give a surprising statistic or fact?

  d ask a challenging question?

  e begin with a quotation?

4 Make notes on what you will say in your introduction.

13 Work in small groups. Take turns to stand up and introduce your talks.

Reminder

Grammar reference page 167

We use the past simple when we're referring to a definite time in the past.
I worked for a charity in Tanzania for nine months in 2007.

We use the present perfect when we're referring to an indefinite time in the past.
I've worked for three different non-profit organizations.

Reading: Volunteering jobs

1 Answer these questions.

1 Have you ever done any volunteer work in your local community? What?

2 Do you know anyone who has done volunteering work in another country? What did they do and did they enjoy it?

2 Work in pairs. You've decided to give up your jobs and spend a year or two working for a much smaller salary doing charitable work abroad. Read these job ads with your partner. Which job appeals to you most, and why?

3 Look at each job again and think about the skills people need to have to do them well. Make notes in the table.

	Skills needed	Personal qualities needed
Job 1	good communication skills, good motivator, …	sociable and friendly, …
Job 2		
Job 3		
Job 4		

4 Look at the skills and qualities in exercise 3. Which ones do you have?

5 Work in pairs. Find out what skills your partner has and learn more about what they have done. Use the questions in the table below and any other questions about work or study experience you would like to ask.

Can you give me an example of … Tell me about … Describe …	a project you've planned? a team you've worked in? a presentation you've given?
What problems have you had … What problems did you have …	and how did you deal with them?

Volunteer pathways

Join our team of dedicated volunteers and help to make the world a better place.

Use your love of sports to educate and inspire children in Africa. Sports organizers are urgently needed by schools in Ghana, Benin and Cameroon to coach and organize regional sporting events. Volunteers should have good communication skills, be fit and healthy, and enjoy working with children.

Join an international team of researchers from 28 countries and help to save the whale. Use your IT skills to compile and share research data via the web. You will be based in Salvador, Brazil, but you will also spend days at sea observing and collecting data on whale behaviour.

6 Here are some more things an interviewer could say. Complete the sentences. Match the beginnings and endings.

A

1	Tell me a little …	**a**	do you find it difficult to work with?
2	Why have you …	**b**	expecting to receive for this job?
3	What's your …	**c**	about yourself.
4	What kinds of people …	**d**	applied for this job?
5	What kind of salary are you …	**e**	to do a good job?
6	What motivates you …	**f**	greatest strength?

B

7	Have you worked …	**g**	work under pressure.
8	Can you give me an example of …	**h**	that you've been a part of.
9	Tell me about a team project …	**i**	abroad before?
10	What have you found …	**j**	your skills in your current job?
11	What have you done to improve …	**k**	a project you've managed and completed?
12	Describe a time when you had to …	**l**	most satisfying in your present job?

7 Answer these questions.

Which group of questions (A or B) is about …

1 the candidate – their personality and skills?

2 their experience?

8 Work in pairs or small groups. Discuss these questions.

1 When was your last job interview and how did it go?

2 Have you ever had to interview job candidates? If so, when and what for?

3 What's the best advice to give a friend who is going for a job interview?

4 What's the best advice to give to someone who is interviewing candidates for a job?

Speaking: A job interview

9 Work in groups of three. Give job interviews for the jobs in exercise 2. Take it in turns to be the candidate and the interviewers. Use the information below. Take a few minutes to prepare before each interview.

Candidates:
Tell the interviewers which job you are applying for. Then think about some past experiences you've had that could help you in this job and why you're the perfect candidate. You can make up information if necessary.

Interviewers:
Prepare questions to ask the candidate. You can use some of the questions in exercise 6 if you like and think of some more. While you are interviewing the candidate, give him/her a score from one to five (five is highest) for the things in the table below.

	Candidate 1	Candidate 2	My scores
Relevant experience			
Relevant skills			
Overall impression			

10 Discuss and explain the scores the interviewers gave. What impression did the candidates make on them?

Business advisors are needed to work with local artists and craftspeople in Bangladesh to advise on the design, production and sale of goods produced with local materials. Help communities increase their income through improved networking and business skills. Volunteers need to have the flexibility to work with limited resources in remote areas.

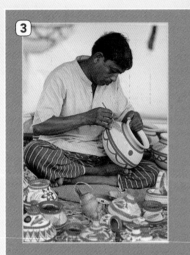

A professional volunteer is needed to help manage a chain of orphanages* in Cambodia. Use your organizational and financial skills to ensure that hundreds of children have a secure home and access to education opportunities. Volunteers should have experience of planning and managing a budget, and a genuine interest in helping children.

orphanage: a home for orphans – children whose parents have died

Interaction

15

A Past continuous
B Past simple vs past continuous
C **Communication strategies** Making excuses
D **Interaction** Storytelling

Memories

Past continuous

Reading: First impressions

1 When you meet someone for the first time, what can these things tell you about them? Which of these things make a strong impression on you? Why?

- their voice
- their handshake
- the way they stand
- the way they're dressed
- their eyes
- their smile
- whether they have a beard or not
- something else (what?)

2 Read about two people who made a powerful impression on each other when they first met. Look at the photo. Do you know who they are? Find out if you are right.

3 Find words in the article that mean the same as these phrases.

1 after a long time/in the end

2 looking at someone for a long time without moving your eyes

3 carry/communicate/express

4 Answer these questions about the article.

1 Where and when did Hillary and Bill meet?

2 What was he doing? What was she doing?

3 How long do people take to form first impressions?

4 Why do you think …

  a Bill and Hillary kept staring at each other?

  b Bill says he couldn't remember his name?

You have three seconds –
SMILE!

They first met in the law library at Yale University in 1971. She was studying and he was talking to a friend. But when their eyes met, they couldn't stop looking at each other. Eventually she got up and walked over to him. She said, 'Look, if you're going to keep staring at me, and I'm going to keep staring back, we should introduce ourselves. I'm Hillary Rodham. What's your name?' Bill Clinton says he couldn't remember his name.

First impressions are very important and researchers have found they can convey a lot of information fast. Little things like having a pleasant voice, your handshake, and how you stand are all important. But probably the most important is a smile. A smile tells us we can expect a positive response, but we have to smile back fast. Researchers say we form an impression about new acquaintances in just three seconds.

Listening: A famous partnership

5 🔊 **2.21** Look at the picture on the right. It is the birthplace of another famous partnership. Which company started here? Listen and find out.

6 🔊 Listen again and answer these questions.

1 What were Bill Hewlett and Dave Packard studying when they met?

2 When did they start the company?

3 Why were things difficult at that time?

4 How did they survive?

Grammar: Past continuous

7 Complete the question and negative forms in the table. When do we use the past continuous tense? Read the notes and find out.

Past continuous		
+	−	?
He **was talking** to a friend.	No, he ¹ _____ **studying**.	³ _____ he **studying**?
They **were studying** electrical engineering.	They ² _____ **studying** computer science.	What ⁴ _____ they **studying**?

We often use the past continuous when we're telling stories. We use it to describe the background to past events – what was going on at the time.
A lot of companies **were failing**.
She **was studying** *and he* **was talking** *to a friend.*
The past continuous sets the scene and the past simple describes the events.
They **were sitting** *in the library. Then, she got up and walked over to him.*

>> For more information on the past continuous, see page 167.

8 Match the beginnings of these sentences to the correct endings. In each sentence, identify the background and the event.

1 I liked Elaine immediately   a because it was raining.

2 I knew he was a musician   b so I showed them where it was.

3 They were looking for the lift   c because she was smiling and laughing.

4 The man wasn't wearing a suit   d because she was wearing a ring.

5 He was rushing to leave the office   e so I didn't want to interrupt her.

6 I offered him a lift   f so we didn't talk for long.

7 I thought she was married   g because he was carrying a violin case.

8 She was talking on the phone   h so I didn't think he was important.

9 Work in pairs. Practise setting the scene and describing events.
Student A: Turn to File 4, page 140.
Student B: Turn to File 30, page 144.

Speaking: A first meeting

10 Think of someone important in your life, for example, your wife, husband, partner, best friend or boss. Prepare to tell the story of how you first met. You can tell the truth or make a story up.

1 Think about the background to your meeting.

● What were you both doing at the time?

● Where were you living and working?

● What was happening at the time?

2 Think about the moment you met.

● How did you meet?

● Did you make a strong first impression on each other? Why?/Why not?

11 Work in pairs or groups. Take turns to tell your stories and ask questions.

TALKING POINT
● Should we trust our first impressions?
● Have you ever found your first impressions were wrong later?
● Do we make judgements about people we meet too quickly?

Listening: What were you doing?

1 Approximately how many calls do you make and receive on your mobile phone each day? And how many text messages do you send and receive? When is it better to call instead of texting? When is it better to text?

2 Keith was travelling on business this morning. His assistant, Toby, was manning the office. Look at a message Keith sent Toby. What does he want?

> **Toby**
> **Where are you? I called the office and your mobile but no answer. Pls phone me back ASAP. Thanks.**
> **KB**
>
> Sent from my Blackberry wireless device

3))) **2.22** Listen to their phone conversation and answer these questions.

1 What time did Keith first call? What was Toby doing?

2 What was Toby doing when Keith called the second time?

4))) Listen again and complete the missing words.

1 _____ you _____ to reach me?

2 Yes, I _____ at about ten.

3 What _____ _____ _____ in the basement?

4 I _____ _____ _____ some old files.

5 It wasn't a real fire. I think someone _____ _____ and they _____ _____ the alarm by accident.

6 Me? No, no, I _____ _____. I _____ _____ when the alarm _____ _____.

5 Later that evening Toby sent this text message to a friend. What was he really doing the first time Keith called?

> Interview went well. Thx 4 asking. They will tell me 2moro if I got the job. Got back B4 the boss so he didn't know NEthing about it.
> CU L8R

Word focus: Text messages

6 Look at the abbreviations in Toby's text message. What do they mean? (If you are not sure, try reading them out loud.)

7 Here are some more text abbreviations. What do they mean?

1 **Where r u?**

2 **2nite**

3 **no 1**

4 **n e 1**

5 **oic**

6 **gr8**

8 Read someone's thoughts about abbreviations in text messages. Underline the words that are spelt differently from standard English. How would you write them in full? Turn to File 12, page 141 to see a full version of the text.

> **Txt msg abbreviations**
> Many ppl luv txt abbreviations cuz they save time n they cn write faster. And some abbreviations are funny n make u LOL.
>
> Bt other ppl h8 m and they r no gd @ txting. So b4 u press send, u hav 2 stop n think. Cn I b cer10 the person I'm writing 2 will understand this msg? It's no gd sending msgs that no1 cn understand.

9 Discuss these questions.

1 What are the advantages and disadvantages of abbreviations in emails and text messages?

2 Do you always understand the abbreviations that other people use? When shouldn't people use them?

Grammar: Past simple vs past continuous

10 Complete the rules.

> **Past simple vs past continuous**
>
> **Rules:**
> We can use the past simple and continuous tenses to talk about interruptions.
> We use the ¹_____ tense to describe the longer action that was happening at the time.
> We use the ²_____ to describe the event that interrupted it.
>
> *I **was working** when the fire alarm **went off**. Everyone **left** the building.*
> ——|————————————————|——————————|————
> The action   The interruption   The events
> in progress   that followed

11 Complete these sentences. Put the verbs in brackets in the past simple or past continuous.

1 I _____ (work) on your invoice when my computer screen _____ (freeze).

2 The new clients _____ (arrive) just as I _____ (prepare) to leave.

3 I _____ (walk) to the coffee shop when I _____ (remember) it was closed today.

4 I _____ (drive) along the freeway when the police _____ (stop) me.

5 Your wife_____ (ring). She _____ (try) to use her credit card when she _____ (get) a message saying 'insufficient funds'.

6 I _____ (just write) to you when your message _____ (arrive).

7 He _____ (call) me when I _____ (take) a shower so I _____ (not hear) the phone.

8 A: Your eyes were closed when I _____ (come) into the office. _____ you _____ (sleep)?

  B: No. I _____ (not sleep). I _____ (rest) my eyes, that's all.

12 Work in pairs. Student A: Turn to File 15, page 141. Student B: Turn to File 21, page 142.

13 Look at the picture on page 141 again. Say what the people were doing when the boss walked in.

> **TALKING POINT** • How easy is it to know if someone is lying to you? What signs do they show?
> • Do people usually know if you are lying to them?

Speaking: Alibi

14 Work in pairs. Your boss sent you both to a conference last Friday. His instructions were very specific. Look at his email. What did he want you to do at the exhibition?

> Make sure you both:
> • attend the keynote speech.
> • try to sit next to some interesting people at lunch.
> • go to the exhibition.
>
> See if there's any new equipment we should buy. You work better as a team, so stay together at all times.
>
> I'll call you to find out how it's going.

15 The weather was beautiful last Friday so instead of going to the conference you both went to the beach. Your boss called you at 4 p.m. but you did not take the call. You need to pretend you spent the day together at the conference. Create a story about what you did and what you were doing when the boss called.

Be as detailed as possible. Your story will be your alibi (a story that proves you did not do anything wrong). It will need to match your partner's story when the boss asks questions. For example, decide things like …

• who gave the keynote speech.
• the subject of the speech.
• the questions the audience asked.
• why you didn't answer when your boss phoned you.

16 It's now Monday morning and your boss wants to hear about the conference. Choose a pair from the class to question. Send one member of the pair out of the room and ask the other one questions. They must answer every question. 'I can't remember' is not an acceptable answer.

Who gave the keynote speech?
What were they wearing?
What were you doing at 4 p.m.?

17 Call the other person back into the room and ask the same questions again. Do their stories match? If not, you can fire them both. Then choose another pair and start again.

Reading: Excuses! Excuses!

1 Read this situation. What did the writer find strange, and why?

> We arranged a 9 o'clock meeting with our Japanese supplier. He's usually very punctual, but at 9:30 there was still no sign of him. Then, just when we were getting ready to leave, we saw him running up the steps of the building. A minute later he rushed into the meeting room, very out of breath.
> 'Are you OK?' we asked.
> He said he was fine and apologized again and again. But it was strange because he never told us why he was late. Did he get lost, we wondered, or did he forget to set his alarm clock?

2 🔊 **2.23** Listen to the Japanese supplier's story. Why was he late and why did he not explain? Do you know anyone who would behave like this?

3 Read a different situation about someone else who was late. What is the writer annoyed about?

> Darren was half an hour late for work today – again. He often has to stay out late entertaining clients, so it's hard for him to get to work on time. But the trouble is he makes up silly excuses. According to Darren, when things go wrong, it's never his fault. I can't remember what his excuse was today – something about leaving his mobile phone at home and going back for it, and then locking himself out of the house. He had a long detailed story. Darren reminds me of my ex-husband – he was a good storyteller, too.

4 Do you know any people like Darren? If so, in what ways are they similar? What is the worst excuse you have ever heard for someone being late? And what is the most original excuse?

Word focus: *remember, forget* and *remind*

5 One sentence in each group is wrong. Which one is it? Read the notes and check your answers.

1
a He remembered to set his alarm clock.
b He forgot to set his alarm clock.
c He reminded to set his alarm clock.

2
a Darren forgot his mobile phone.
b Darren forgot his mobile phone at home.
c Darren left his mobile phone at home.

---

remind and forget

remind

Remind means 'make someone else remember something'. We remind other people. So after *remind* say 'who'.

She **reminded everyone** that they were running late.
Remind me to switch off my mobile phone when we go inside.

forget

In British English we use *leave* when we mention the place we forgot something.

He **forgot** his umbrella. = CORRECT
~~He forgot his umbrella in the taxi.~~ = WRONG
He **left** his umbrella in the taxi. = CORRECT

---

6 Complete these sentences with the correct form of *remember, forget* or *remind*.

1 It's been a wonderful holiday. I'll _____ it for the rest of my life.
2 Can I _____ you that smoking is not allowed in this building.
3 We mustn't _____ to switch off the computers at night.
4 It's Pat's birthday so don't _____ to send her a card.
5 I'll be there. Thanks for _____ me.
6 **A:** 'I must pay you back the two dollars you lent me.'
   B: 'Oh _____ it! It's not important.'

Listening: Apologies

7 🔊 **2.24** When we accept an apology, we often say things like *It's all right*, *Don't worry* and *Forget it*. Listen to three conversations where people apologize for things they have done. For each person answer these questions.

1 What did they do wrong?

2 What was their excuse?

3 Was their apology accepted?

8 🔊 Listen again and complete these sentences.

1

I'm sorry. The phone _____ _____ so I was _____ to answer it.

I _____ remember. _____ _____ and lock it now.

2

I wasn't thinking _____ .

I'm _____ sorry. I'm usually so careful about _____ _____ _____ .

It _____ _____ _____ , I promise.

3

I'm sorry. _____ _____ _____ _____ and I didn't hear you.

I didn't mean to _____ you.

9 🔊 Look at some things English speakers often do and say when they apologize. Then listen to the conversations again and find more examples of people doing these things.

Making excuses	
Explain they didn't mean to do it.	*It was an accident.*
Say it was just a temporary thing and not how they normally behave.	*I don't normally do that.* *I wasn't paying attention.*
Say that something else was partly responsible.	*The weather was really bad.* *The traffic was terrible.*
Offer to put things right.	*I'll sort it out.*
Make promises.	*I'll never do that again.*

Speaking: Making excuses

10 Work in pairs. Roleplay these conversations. Take turns to make excuses in these situations. You can decide whether to accept your partner's apologies or not.

1 A client left you a voicemail message four days ago and you didn't return their call. Ring them and apologize for the delay.

2 There's was a weekly team meeting yesterday afternoon but you didn't go. Tell your boss you're sorry and give an excuse.

3 You had a loud party last night that probably disturbed your neighbours. Today you must apologize.

4 Your friend lent you a book three months ago. You forgot you had it so you're only just returning it now.

5 You picked up the wrong papers at the end of a meeting and took your partner's private files as well as your own. Give them back and say you're sorry.

6 You didn't do the homework for your English class. Apologize to your teacher and explain why.

7 You weren't looking where you were going in a restaurant, and you bumped into a waiter. They were carrying food that fell onto another customer. Apologize.

8 You borrowed €50 from a friend and promised to repay them today. Explain why you can't and apologize.

Writing: An apology

11 Unfortunately, you had to miss an important meeting yesterday. Write an email to the organizer.

- Apologize
- Explain why you could not attend (invent a reason).
- Ask for a copy of the meeting minutes.

Reminder

Grammar reference
pages 166 and 167

When we're telling a story, we often use the past continuous tense to set the scene and describe the background.
We were visiting our office in Korea.

Then we use the past simple to describe the events.
One of my colleagues invited me for a meal at his home.

Reading: Muddled stories

1 Here are two stories but they are muddled up. Work in pairs. Student A: Underline the first story about the Korean dinner invitation. Student B: Underline the second story about the Japanese software engineer.

A funny thing happened to me when I was visiting Seoul. I had an interesting experience when I was working on a project with a Japanese software engineer. One of my Korean colleagues invited me to his home for a meal. I was very grateful for the opportunity to see how a Korean family lived and to meet his family. He was a brilliant programmer but sometimes he sent me emails with symbols I didn't understand. His wife was lovely and she served a fantastic meal with all kinds of wonderful dishes. So I asked, 'What do these things mean?' At the end of the evening, I thanked her and said how much I enjoyed her cooking. He explained that when he was joking he wrote happy eyes ^_^ and when he was sad he wrote crying eyes ;_;. 'Oh, I didn't cook it,' she said, 'it came from the local Chinese restaurant.' The symbols were like our smiley faces :-) and :-(. So it just goes to show how different things can be. In the west, we generally look at people's mouths to see if they're smiling. So it just goes to show that people are the same the world over. But in Japan, people look at their eyes. They all appreciate a good Chinese takeaway.

2 Check your answers with your partner. Student A: Read the first story. Student B: Listen. Does it make sense? Then, Student B: Read the second story. Student A: Listen. Does it make sense?

3 Answer these questions about the stories.

1 In the first story, what was the writer thankful for and why?

2 In the second story, what didn't the writer understand and why?

3 What did the first writer learn about the meal?

4 What did the second writer learn about Japanese smiles?

5 What conclusion did the first writer draw?

6 What conclusion did the second writer draw?

Listening: What's the ending?

4 🔊 **2.25** Listen to another story. How do you think it will end?

5 🔊 Listen again and answer these questions.

1 Why couldn't the boys ring the doorbell?

2 What did the old lady think the boys were trying to do?

3 What were they really doing?

6 Write a possible ending for the story.

So it just goes to show that _____.

7 🔊 **2.26** Listen to another story. How do you think this one will end?

8 🔊 Listen again and answer these questions.

1   What was the subject of the training course?

2   Why did the trainer speak privately to one of the people in the class?

3   Why did she tell her boss she couldn't plan projects?

9   Write a possible ending for the story.

So it just goes to show that _____.

10   Here are some possible endings to the two stories you heard. Are any similar to the endings you wrote? Which ones go with the first story and which ones go with the second? Do any work for both stories?

1   ... sometimes very nice people do bad things.

2   ... sending people on training courses doesn't always solve problems.

3   ... it's difficult to manage people if they don't enjoy their work.

4   ... first impressions are sometimes wrong.

5   ... success depends on wanting to do something, not just knowing how.

6   ... good intentions don't always lead to good results.

11   Which endings do you like best? Why?

Speaking: Telling stories

12   Prepare to tell a short story to the class.

1   First, think of the story. It should be very short (just one or two minutes). Your story could be ...

● a joke or serious.

● a story about something that happened to you or someone else.

● about travelling, a meal you had, foreign guests, meeting someone for the first time, a team project, something you learned on a training course, or it could be about something else.

2   Plan how you will begin.

A strange thing happened to me/my friend/one of my colleagues recently ...

I had an interesting experience a few years ago. I was working with ...

I heard a funny story a few days ago. It was about ...

3   Think about how you will end the story. What lesson can you draw from it?

So it just goes to show that ...

13   Take it in turns to stand up and tell your stories to the class. Listen carefully to your colleague's stories and ask questions if you don't understand anything. Whose story did you like the most and why?

A: I liked all the stories but I liked Sven's the most because it was dramatic.

B: I liked Ingrid's story the most because it was entertaining.

16

A *would*

B Second conditional

C **Communication strategies** Differences of opinion

D **Interaction** Making your case

The right choice

would

Listening: Dream jobs

1 These people have unusual jobs. The photos show them working. What do you think each person does for a living?

2 2.27 Listen to three interviews where the people describe their jobs. Were you right?

3 Here are some of the things the people said. Can you remember who said them: the chocolate taster (CT); the personal shopper (PS); the sleep director (SD) or the interviewer (I)?

1 I'd rather not say their name.

2 What would you like to change about your job?

3 I'd prefer to travel less and stay home a little more.

4 Sometimes I'd like a little more free time.

5 We wouldn't want to sell a product that wasn't tested.

6 My teenage daughter would love your job.

4 Listen again and check your answers. Then discuss these questions.

1 Imagine you could have any one of the three jobs. Which one would you rather do? Why?

2 Is there a job you wouldn't like? Why?

Grammar: *would*

5 Read the notes on *would*. Then work in pairs. Read the audio scripts on page 162 and find more examples.

would

1 We can use *would* to talk about imaginary possibilities (and impossibilities).
*What **would** you like to change about your job?*
*I **wouldn't** want to change a thing.*
*That**'d** be impossible.*

2 We often use *would* with verbs about 'liking' and 'disliking'.
***I'd like**/I **wouldn't like** a little more free time.*
***I'd want**/I **wouldn't want** to do anything else.*
***I'd love** it.*
***I'd hate** to lose it.*
***I'd rather** (**not**) say their name.*
***I'd prefer** (**not**) to travel.*

Would is often contracted to *'d*. The contraction for *would* + *not* = *wouldn't*

6 What would turn your job into a dream job? Look at these alternatives and choose the ones you would prefer.

1 a A big fat pay rise so you earn twice your current salary

b Six months paid holiday each year

2 a The fastest computer in the company – one that would never freeze or go down

b Free training in whatever you want to learn, for example, acupuncture, deep sea fishing, poker

3 a A promotion to your boss's job

b A powerful new boss who listens to you and acts on all your suggestions

4 a Being allowed to bring your pets to work

b Being allowed to bring your children to work

5 a Free company day care for your children or elderly parents

b Free membership of a luxury gym with your own personal trainer

6 a Polite and helpful colleagues

b Customers who think you're wonderful

7 a Being allowed to work from home whenever you want

b Your own large office with comfortable seating, a coffee machine, a private bathroom and wonderful view from the windows

8 a A company car with your own personal driver

b Permission to borrow the company jet to fly you and your family wherever you want, whenever you want

7 Work in pairs or small groups. Say which alternatives you would and would not prefer in exercise 6. Then ask questions about your partners' choices and find out what is important to them.

I'd prefer (not) to …

I'd rather (not) …

A: I'd rather have six months paid holiday each year.

B: But what would you do with all your free time?

A: I'd love it. I'd read a lot of books and relax. Perhaps I'd travel a bit.

B: Wouldn't you get bored?

A: Never.

Speaking: Job swap

8 Think of someone you know who has an unusual or interesting job. For example, someone you work with, a family member or friend. Work in groups. Take turns describing what they do. Would you like to have their job? Why?/Why not?

9 Imagine you could swap jobs with anyone in the world. Who would you like to swap with? Why?

Writing: Choosing alternatives

10 You are going to visit your London office next week. The people there want to know what you would prefer to do. Write an email to them.

Tell them if you would prefer to …

- fly in on Sunday and stay in a hotel, or fly in very early on Monday morning.

- stay in a hotel in the city centre or a hotel near the office.

- make your presentation with your own computer or use one they can provide.

TALKING POINT Would you want to have any of these jobs: an astronaut, a comedian, a video games tester, a magician's assistant, the president of your country? Why?/Why not?

Listening: A dilemma

1 A dilemma is a situation where it is difficult to choose between two alternative actions. Read a famous dilemma created by the Dutch social scientist Fons Trompenaars. Decide what you would do. Would your choice depend on anything? What?

> Imagine you're riding in your friend's car when he hits a pedestrian*. Your friend was driving at least 35 miles per hour in an area of the city where the maximum speed limit is 20 miles per hour. Nobody saw the accident. If you lied and said your friend was only driving at 20 miles per hour, it would save him from serious consequences. Would you lie to save your friend?
>
> *pedestrian*: someone who is walking, not driving or riding a bicycle

2))) **2.28** Listen to two people discussing the dilemma. Who would lie: the man or the woman?

Grammar: Second conditional

3))) Listen again and complete the sentences with the missing verbs. Then answer the questions.

if + past, would

1 What **would** _____ to my friend **if** I _____ the truth?

2 But **if** the pedestrian _____ , perhaps he'**d** _____ to prison.

3 But **if** the accident _____ serious, it'**d** _____ more important to tell the truth.

Look at the verb forms in the sentences.

4 What form is used after *would*? _____

5 What form is used after *if*? _____

6 Are these sentences about …
  a past time?
  b an imaginary future time?

! In second conditional structures, we sometimes use *were* instead of *was* after *if*.
If the accident **were** serious …
If the accident **was** serious …
Were is rather formal. In spoken English, people usually say *was*.

>> For more information on the second conditional, see page 171.

4 Complete these second conditional statements. Use the correct form of the verbs in the box.

tell not lie ~~be~~ have not have do support happen

1 The world would ___*be*___ a worse place if we _____ friends we could trust.

2 I can trust my friend. If something bad _____ , she would _____ the truth.

3 I can trust my friend. If I _____ a problem, he would _____ me.

4 If a friend of mine _____ something wrong, I _____ to save them.

5 Fons Trompenaars gave the dilemma about the pedestrian to people in 31 different countries. Read about his results and answer these questions.

1 How did most Americans answer the dilemma?

2 What do you think the results would be in your country? Why?

How we trust

People around the world answered the pedestrian dilemma rather differently. People in Switzerland and the USA generally placed a high value on the truth and the law. 97% and 93% said they wouldn't lie. But the figure was lower in other countries, and more people felt they should support their friend. For example, in France the figure was 73%, Japan 68%, India 54%, South Korea 37% and Venezuela 32%.

Of course everyone wants to think their friends will do the right thing and everyone one wants friends they feel they can trust. But compare these two views. They are both logical in their own way:

1 *If something bad happened, this person would tell the truth, so I can trust them.*

2 *If something bad happened, this person would support me, so I can trust them.*

6 Look at some more dilemmas. Write sentences about what you would do in each situation.

1 Your boss wants you to call a competitor and pretend to be a potential customer in order to get information about their products.

  If my boss asked me to do this, I wouldn't because …

  If this happened to me, I'd make the call because …

2 A supplier wants to know where their cheque is. Your boss has told you to say it's in the post but you know that's not true.

3 You're a food critic for a newspaper and your best friend owns a restaurant. They want you to write a very favourable review. You think the food is OK but nothing special.

4 You're a student on an MBA course. One of your classmates pays someone he found on the internet to write his homework assignments. He asked you not to tell the teacher.

5 You helped your son to do his school science project and he didn't tell his teacher. If the teacher asks 'Did he do it all himself?' he wants you to say 'Yes'.

6 You need your husband/wife's signature urgently on a document. They're travelling on business. They say, 'Just forge* it and sign the document in my name.'

forge: produce a signature, document or picture and pretend that someone else produced it

7 Compare your answers with a partner. Would your decisions depend on anything? If so, what?

Speaking: How well do you know me?

8 How well do you know your colleagues in this class? Play a game and find out. First, read some questions and make a note of your answers in the table.

	Yes	No	It depends (on what?)
1 You've sold your house. Hooray! But before you move, the roof starts leaking*. Would you repair it?			
2 You're alone in your boss's office one day when you see a private file on their desk. It has information about you in it. Would you take a look?			
3 You're in a hurry and there's only one space in the car park. It's for disabled* people. Would you park there?			
4 You accidentally deleted an important file from your colleague's computer. There is no way he can find out who did it. Would you tell him it was you?			
5 You run a video store. One day you catch a fifteen-year-old boy shoplifting. He says it's the first time he's done it. Would you call the police?			
6 You're a famous athlete. A manufacturer offers you $50,000 to appear in advertisements saying you drink their cola. You don't like their cola. Would you agree?			
7 Your friend has a CD that you love and he offers to make you a copy. It's illegal to copy CDs and all the royalties* from this one go to charity. Would you say 'yes'?			

leaking: having a hole that allows water to come in

disabled: someone who is disabled can't used part of their body in the way that most people can

royalties: payments that are usually made to the writer of a piece of music

9 Work in groups. Guess how some other students in your group will answer the same questions. Write the student's name and the answer you think they will give in the table below.

Name	Question number	Yes	No	It depends
	1			
	2			
	3			
	4			
	5			
	6			
	7			

10 Ask the questions in exercise 8 and find out if you are right. If you think someone is lying, you can ask more questions to check. The person who guesses the most correct answers wins the game.

TALKING POINT

Are there any situations in which you might lie to …

a your boss?

b your husband or wife?

c your English teacher?

If so, what are they?

Word focus: *say* and *tell*

1 Do you ever have to give people job references? Read this dilemma and discuss what you would do in this situation.

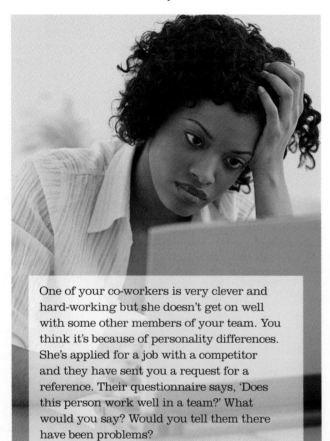

One of your co-workers is very clever and hard-working but she doesn't get on well with some other members of your team. You think it's because of personality differences. She's applied for a job with a competitor and they have sent you a request for a reference. Their questionnaire says, 'Does this person work well in a team?' What would you say? Would you tell them there have been problems?

2 Look at some situations where we use the verbs *say* and *tell* and complete the rules.

say and tell

There are lots of situations where we can use the verb *say* <u>or</u> *tell*.	I'd **say** there have been problems. I'd **tell** him there have been problems.
We generally use *say* with the words people use.	He **said** 'Thank you'.
We often use *tell* when people give information or instructions.	She **told** me to fill in the questionnaire. **Tell** us what she's like.

Rules:
1 We _____ someone something.
2 We _____ something (to someone).

Special cases:

There are some special expressions with *tell* that are different.	Don't **tell lies. Tell the truth.** I can't **tell the difference** between Coke and Pepsi.

3 Complete these sentences with the correct form of *say* or *tell*.

1 We _____ 'Good morning' to each other but we didn't shake hands.

2 Ask at reception. They'll _____ you where the meeting room is.

3 Matthew _____ he might call back later.

4 She _____ us she plans to catch the 8:30 train.

5 Can you _____ me how to get to the city centre?

6 Could you _____ me when the next train leaves?

7 I'm sorry. I didn't hear you. What did you _____?

8 In France, people usually _____ 'Bon appétit' before they start eating a meal. Do people from your country usually _____ anything?

9 Did Jason _____ you what his new email address is?

10 Don't believe her. She's _____ lies again.

Listening: A disagreement

4 🔊 **2.29** Listen to the owners of a small training organization discussing a scheduling problem. What is the problem? What do they disagree about?

5 🔊 Listen again and complete these sentences.

1 I'd like to talk to them and explain. _____ _____ _____ _____ reschedule one of the courses … OK?

2 I _____ _____ _____ wait a little while.

3 No, I think _____ _____ _____ _____ now. They need to reorganize their schedules.

4 _____ _____ _____ _____ we don't want them to think we can't handle their business.

5 I _____ _____ _____ _____ and see if they cancel first.

6 It's too risky. _____ _____ _____ ask them to reschedule now.

6 Look at the phrases in exercise 5. Which ones sound most forceful?

Disagreements

7 Read how English speakers handle disagreements at different stages of a discussion. Then look at expressions a–h. Which ones are more direct and forceful? Would you expect to hear the forceful expressions at the start of a disagreement or later?

Disagreements

People are often slow to say they disagree. They might …

- hesitate before they begin. → *Well, erm …*
- claim they partly agree. → *Yes, but …*
- ask challenging questions. → *Do we want to tell them that?*
- apologize. → *I'm afraid they need to know.*

When the disagreement is clear, they become more direct and forceful.

No, I (don't) think …
What I'm saying is …

---

a *We have to …*
b *We could try to …*
c *I thought we might …*
d *We have no choice.*
e *I'd like to …*
f *No, I (don't) think we should …*
g *Do you want to … ?*
h *We'd better (not) …*

> **!** *We'd better …* is the contracted form of *we had better* and we use it to say what we think we should do. After *We'd better …* we don't use *to*.
>
> **We'd better tell them now.** NOT ~~We'd better to tell them now.~~

Speaking: Finding solutions

8 Work in pairs. Read these situations and roleplay the disagreements. Begin gently and then become more direct and forceful. Try to agree on a solution you both feel is right.

Situation 1
One of your employees has lost a laptop containing sensitive data about your employees and customers. If it falls into the wrong hands, it could be used by criminals to steal people's identities. You need to decide what to do.
Student A: Turn to File 32, page 145.
Student B: Turn to File 5, page 140.

Situation 2
Your company has made an error. You sent one of your customers a price estimate for a job that was 25 per cent above your standard rates. Although the estimate was high, your customer accepted it. You need to decide what action to take.
Student A: Turn to File 32, page 145.
Student B: Turn to File 5, page 140.

Reminder

Grammar reference page 171

We often use *would* to talk about imaginary situations.

What would you do?

It'd depend.

I wouldn't want to break the rules.

We form second conditional sentences with *if* and *would*.

if + past, *would* + present

If something bad happened, I'd feel terrible.

Reading and speaking: A rescue dilemma

1 Work in groups. You are going to read a rescue story and make some decisions. Read the situations and discuss what to do.

The girl is here.

90 m

① You're a volunteer coastguard* and one evening you receive a call for help. A young teenage girl is stuck on a cliff*. The rocks under her feet have fallen away and she is hanging on by her hands. She's very frightened. You have a rope and other rescue equipment in your truck but it would take five or ten minutes to get it. It's very windy and you think she could fall any minute. A helicopter is coming but it won't arrive for half an hour.

coastguard: a person who helps boats and swimmers that are in danger

cliff: a high piece of land with a very steep side, usually next to the sea

❯❯ What would you do and why? Discuss and agree. Then go to **7**.

② What are you doing reading this? Should you be reading **7**?

③ The Coastguard Organization said it was glad nobody died and it launched an investigation into the rescue. It found that Paul broke the organization's safety rules because he didn't go back to his truck to get ropes and equipment before he climbed down the cliff.

❯❯ If you were Paul's boss, what would you do now and why? Discuss and agree. Then go to **8**.

④ Paul resigned from his job and then gave an interview on a BBC radio show. 'I understand I broke a rule but I felt I had to,' he said. 'There's no way I'm going to stand back and watch a 13-year-old girl fall off a cliff.'

❯❯ Imagine you work for the Coastguard Organization again. What would you do now and what would you say to the press*? Discuss and agree. Then go to **6**.

press: newspapers, magazines and other media

5 The Coastguard Organization is a government agency. Its goal is to prevent the loss of lives in accidents, and safety is a priority. Imagine you work for the organization and Paul Waugh has been one of your volunteers for 13 years. When he rescues Faye Harrison, you receive lots of calls from television stations and newspapers. They want to know what you think about Paul and the rescue.

➤➤ What would you say to the press and why? Discuss and agree. Then go to **3**.

6 The Coastguard Organization thanked Paul for his years of service but said it wasn't looking for dead heroes. It received a lot of negative publicity* and many people were angry. This is the end of the story. Do you think people were right to be angry? What went wrong here?

negative publicity: bad attention from newspapers and television

Paul Waugh, a 44-year-old coastguard in northwest England, actually faced this problem. He decided to climb down the cliff to rescue the girl. He managed to hold onto 13-year-old Faye Harrison for 30 minutes **7** until a helicopter arrived and carried her to safety. They both survived.

➤➤ Now go to **5** and read about the Coastguard Organization that Paul worked for.

8 The Coastguard Organization reprimanded* Paul because he broke the rules. They said climbing down the cliff without equipment was the wrong thing to do. Paul disagreed.

➤➤ If you were in Paul's situation, what would you do and why? Discuss and agree. Then go to **4**.

reprimand: tell someone officially that they did something very wrong

Listening: Reactions

2)) **2.30** Listen to six people's reactions when Paul resigned. How many of them thought Paul was wrong?

3)) Listen again and complete these sentences.

1 If risking your life is wrong, then why do we have coastguards? Rules are important but in a life and death situation you have to _____ the _____ out of the _____.

2 If a member of the public climbed down a cliff and rescued someone, _____ _____ _____ _____ _____. Why was Paul Waugh reprimanded? It's not _____.

3 Perhaps we don't know _____ _____ _____. It _____ _____ _____. Why did they reprimand Paul when he brought so much positive publicity to the coastguards?

4 I think the Coastguard Organization was right. Paul was lucky to survive. If other coastguards _____ _____ _____, more people _____ _____.

5 I think Paul Waugh just wanted _____. Why did he go on a radio show? Why _____ _____ _____ _____?

6 Paul's managers are crazy. _____ _____ _____ _____ _____ their child was hanging from a cliff? Go and get their rulebooks?

Speaking: Who do you agree with?

4 How far do you agree with the six opinions in exercise 3? Mark your position on these lines.

Opinion 1
Agree   Not sure   Disagree

Opinion 2
Agree   Not sure   Disagree

Opinion 3
Agree   Not sure   Disagree

Opinion 4
Agree   Not sure   Disagree

Opinion 5
Agree   Not sure   Disagree

Opinion 6
Agree   Not sure   Disagree

5 Find out what other students in the class think and why. Compare and explain your views.

6 Discuss these questions.

1 Could there be a situation when it's important to break the rules in your organization? When and why?

2 What things do you need to do to be a 'hero' in your job?

Interaction

Review 13-16

1 Complete this text. Put the verbs in brackets in the correct tense: either past simple or present perfect.

Paul Walshe is a 17-year-old entrepreneur who owns his own food company, with his family, called Kitchen Dreams. He ¹_____ (run) this business for two years.

Paul suffers from dyslexia so he ²_____ (have) learning difficulties at school and ³_____ (leave) at the age of 14 so that he ⁴_____ (can) have special lessons at home. At this time he ⁵_____ (start) helping his family in the kitchen and ⁶_____ (discover) a talent for inventing new recipes.

Paul ⁷_____ (set) up Kitchen Dreams two years ago and since then the company ⁸_____ (grow) very quickly. Last year he ⁹_____ (move) to larger premises and now he ¹⁰_____ (win) a contract to supply a major supermarket chain.

His mother says, 'Paul is a hard worker and he ¹¹_____ (put) a lot of effort into the company. We ¹²_____ (not take) on any extra staff yet but we'll have to if it keeps growing like this.'

2 Complete this text. Put the verbs in the box in the correct tense: either past simple or past continuous. You will need to put eight in the past simple and four in the past continuous.

drink stand live ride phone hear offer lose
receive write see decide

I FOUND YOUR CAMERA

Declan Campbell was on a once-in-a-lifetime trip to visit his family in the USA. Unfortunately, on the last day of his holiday, he ¹_____ his camera with all his photos.

A few days later a man called John Bowker ²_____ in a taxi in Los Angeles when he ³_____ a digital camera on the seat. He ⁴_____ to try to find the owner.

There were lots of photos in the camera and two videos of adults and children. In some pictures, they ⁵_____ near famous sites in Los Angeles and New York. On the video, John ⁶_____ Irish accents. The owner of the camera was from Ireland!

In one of the photos, the group ⁷_____ coffee outside a bar. John could see the name of the bar clearly. He ⁸_____ the bar in New York to speak to the owner and, yes, the owner could remember an Irish family. In fact, he even knew one of the men in the group. He was a member of Declan's family but ⁹_____ in New York at the time. Soon John ¹⁰_____ an email from this man. He ¹¹_____ to send the camera to Declan. Declan was delighted and ¹²_____ to John to say, 'It's nice to know there are such honest people in the world.'

3 Complete these sentences. Put the verbs in brackets into the correct form to make second conditional sentences.

1 If I _____ (not have) my PA, I don't know how I _____ (manage).

2 If your boss _____ (offer) you early retirement, _____ you _____ (take) it?

3 I _____ (give) her the job if she _____ (be) better qualified.

4 I _____ (not lend) you the money even if I _____ (have) it.

5 If you _____ (run) into a parked car, _____ you _____ (leave) a note on the windscreen?

6 What _____ you _____ (say) if someone _____ (phone) you and _____ (ask) for a reference?

4 In each sentence one of the words is in the wrong form. Find the incorrect word in each sentence and correct it.

1 I couldn't understand the lecture so I felt very boring.

2 I've knew my friend Candy for ten years.

3 I don't mind wait for a few minutes.

4 Could you tell me what you do for a live?

5 Our tour guide arrived approximate 20 minutes late.

6 I can't stand people talk on their phones in restaurants.

7 She worked as a voluntary in the local hospital.

8 I don't think he was telling me the true.

9 We respect older people in our culture because we believe that age brings wise.

10 I don't like making these cuts but we don't have much choose.

5 Complete these sentences. Choose the correct word.

1 Could you *remind / remember* me to send that fax today?

2 Oh, dear. It's raining and I've *forgotten / left* my umbrella in the office.

3 She *said / told* me that she wanted to leave her job.

4 She said no at first but *generally / eventually* she agreed.

5 I'd *prefer / rather* work fewer hours and earn less.

6 He's very *modest / conceited* and doesn't like talking about his achievements.

7 House prices are falling so don't put your money into *events / property* at the moment.

8 I can never *say / tell* the difference between tap water and mineral water.

9 It's important for managers to *give / tell* praise to their employees.

10 He decided that he wanted to *dismiss / resign* from his job.

6 Match each phrase 1–9 with the most suitable response a–i.

1 Who told you that?

2 It's lovely to see you.

3 What a great idea!

4 What a lovely ring!

5 I'm so sorry!

6 You really should be more careful.

7 Thank you for a lovely evening.

8 I think we'll have to make a move soon.

9 Did you know the CEO has resigned?

a Don't worry. Forget it!

b Thank you. It was an anniversary present.

c It won't happen again.

d Glad you enjoyed it.

e I can't take credit for it. Mary suggested it.

f How about another coffee first?

g You're kidding me!

h You, too.

i I'd rather not say.

7 Complete this dialogue. Write one word in each gap.

A: Did you know that Celia's laptop was stolen from her car last night?

B: Oh, no!

A: It's very serious. Some of those files contain details of customer's accounts. We'd ¹_____ write to the customers at once and tell them.

B: Do we ²_____ to tell the customers yet?

A: I'm afraid we have no ³_____ . If criminals got hold of that information, they ⁴_____ use it for identity fraud.

B: I thought we ⁵_____ wait and see if the police find it.

A: But what ⁶_____ they don't?

B: What I'm ⁷_____ is, we don't want customers to think we're careless with their data. We ⁸_____ wait just one or two days.

A: No it's too ⁹_____ . We ¹⁰_____ to let customers know now.

8 Complete these sentences. Choose the correct prepositions after the verbs.

1 Someone set *off* / *on* / *in* the fire alarm by accident this morning.

2 I have to look *through* / *down* / *after* my sister's cat while she's on holiday.

3 Tony makes *up* / *out* / *off* the most amazing excuses for being late.

4 Would you like to have a look *about* / *around* / *across* the building?

5 Leave this problem with me and I'll try to sort it *out* / *off* / *away*.

6 People say that the company are going to lay *out* / *off* / *down* about 200 staff.

9 Write each collocation with the verb *make* in the correct place in the word diagram.

an excuse   a cake   changes   a suggestion   a decision   a joke
supper   a copy   a mistake

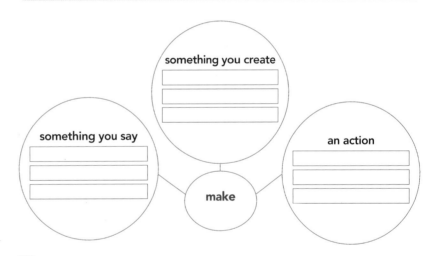

something you create

something you say

an action

make

10 Write each collocation with the verb *do* in the correct place in the word diagram.

homework   a survey   your best   well   an experiment   paperwork
a good job   research   overtime

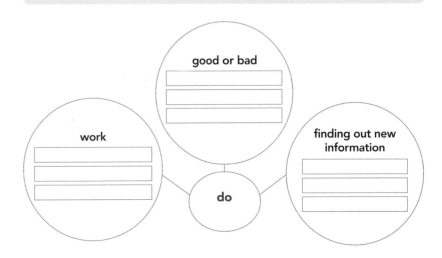

good or bad

work

finding out new information

do

File 1

Problem 3

Student A:

You think Student C should resign. If their employer has financial problems, it isn't worth waiting to see if things improve. They need to find a new job now. They should take the money and run! Take a few minutes to prepare your arguments, then give Student C your advice. Tell them why they should resign.

Student B:

Many companies are having financial problems these days and it's not easy to find a good job. You think Student A should stay with their current company and work hard. Perhaps they can help to turn things around. Take a few minutes to prepare your arguments, then give Student C your advice. Tell them why they should stay.

File 2

Student A:

In this conversation you must sit very still. Keep your hands on your lap and don't move. Don't speak unless someone asks you a question directly.

File 3

Guest:
Your host has an unusual talent that you don't know about. Make small talk throughout the evening and comment on the things you see in the hall, living room and dining room. Try to discover what their special talent is and discover three things they can do.

File 4

Student A:

1 Here are the backgrounds to some past events. Read each one aloud to your partner. Your partner will then read the event that followed. Listen carefully. Does it make sense?

1 They were speaking in Italian so …

2 The woman was looking at the subway map so …

3 He wasn't moving at all so …

4 She was sitting at the head of the table so …

5 The man wasn't wearing a badge so …

6 He was reading a medical journal so …

7 He was standing under the clock holding some flowers so …

2 Here are some past events. You partner will read what was going on when they happened. Each time, choose the best event and read it to your partner.

A … I showed them the way.

B … she didn't want to go out and meet anyone.

C … I thought he was the electrician.

D … I knew the news was good.

E … I asked if he was bored.

F … I knew they didn't work here.

G … I asked him to stop.

File 5

Situation 1
Student B:

This is your starting position, but you can change it if your partner makes a good case. Take a few minutes to prepare what to say before you start.

> You'd like to wait a week before you tell anyone about this laptop theft. (Perhaps the police will find the laptop.) Your company can't afford to cover all the potential losses, so you'd like to put a limit on refunds.

Situation 2
Student B:

This is your starting position, but you can change it if your partner makes a good case. Take a few minutes to prepare what to say before you start.

> This isn't right. The customer might discover that you overcharged them later. You want to punish the employee who made the error and apologize to the customer. You'd like to charge the standard rate but with a ten per cent discount because of the mistake.

File 6

Question	Points
1	a = 1 b = 2 c = 3
2	a = 3 b = 2 c = 1
3	a = 3 b = 1 c = 2
4	a = 2 b = 3 c = 1
5	a = 1 b = 2 c = 3
6	a = 3 b = 2 c = 1
7	a = 3 b = 1 c = 2
8	a = 1 b = 3 c = 2

Results:

18–24 Wow! You really know how to connect with people. You work at your relationships and your social network grows by the day.

13–17 You understand that strong social and business relationships are important to your success. You just need to work a little more to take your relationships to the next level.

8–12 You don't make much effort to network and stay in touch with people. But people usually do business with people they know and like, so why not try to network more?

File 7

Student C:

In this conversation you must talk as much as possible. Don't wait for your turn to speak. Speak very loudly and interrupt a lot.

File 8

FYI	For your information
Re	Regarding/about
ASAP	As soon as possible
FAQs	Frequently asked questions
Ref. No.	Reference number
P.S.	Post script

File 9

In some cultures it's polite to start an email with a greeting like *Hi* or *Hello*, and end with a friendly closing. But this isn't always necessary in English. Research shows that British and American native speakers often begin the emails they write with no greeting. The most common closing is *Thanks*, but they end more than half their emails with no closing. They just write their name or initials.

File 10

Student B:
Call one:
Student A asked you to send them a potential client's email address last week and you forgot. Student A calls you when you're in a meeting and you have no time. Tell them you'll call them back later.

Call two:
Call student A back, apologize and give them the email address:
j_heath-taylor@clearmargins.com

File 11

Product B: The Q-top

Problem that it solves: how to keep a cucumber or a lemon fresh after you cut it.

Product details: a top made of silicone, about 12 cm long. You put it on the end of your half cucumber or half lemon. Retail price: £4.99 or about €6.50.

File 12

Text message abbreviations

Many people love text abbreviations because they save time and they can write faster. And some abbreviations are funny and make you laugh out loud.

But other people hate them and they are no good at texting. So before you press send, you have to stop and think. Can I be certain the person I'm writing to will understand this message? It's no good sending messages that no one can understand.

File 13

Student B:
Look at the information below. Ask your partner questions and complete the table.

A: *How heavy is it?*
B: *11.79 kg*

Max speed	
Weight	11.79 kg
Materials	
Colour	Silver and yellow
Seating capacity	
Height	1.22 m
Width	
Length	1.83 m
Power	
Price	$499.95

File 14

Customer 1:
You are going to call Cool Presents and place an order. Look at the information below.
1 You want a new pair of sunglasses with a built-in radio. The last pair you bought cost €19.
2 You saw a black pen-style digital camera on the website a few weeks ago for $39.95 and now you'd like to buy one as a birthday present for your friend. Do they have any green ones? (Your friend loves green).
3 Check the prices before you place your orders. Take a few minutes to think about what you will say and then call.

File 15

Student A:

1 Tell your partner what is happening in this picture. They have a similar picture but there are six differences. Find and circle the differences.

2 Why are the pictures different?

File 16

Product A: The flower quiver

The problem that it solves: how to carry a bunch of flowers when you have other shopping bags with you.

Product details: a plastic cone, about 100 cm long. The flowers go inside and you carry it over your shoulder. Retail price: you can decide how much to charge for it.

File 17

Student B:

1 You work in a car showroom. Student A is a potential customer. Try to persuade Student A to buy a car. Make sure you offer a good price. Take five minutes to plan what you're going to say. Then begin with: I see you like this Volvo. It's my favourite, too …

2 You need a new jacket and it must be fashionable, good quality and you also want a good deal. You go to the department store where Student A works as a salesperson. Take five minutes to think of questions to ask Student A.

File 18

Read the situations below. Your partner should say what they will do.

> A: *Your shirts are dirty.*
> B: *I'll take them to the cleaners.*

Student A:

1 Your accountant wants your tax forms.

2 The car windscreen's dirty.

3 I have a headache.

4 We need some more milk.

5 The supplier delivered the wrong parts.

6 I'm hungry.

7 My suitcase is heavy.

8 I don't want to go to the party alone.

9 You left your umbrella in the restaurant.

10 You have 3,956 emails in your inbox.

File 19

Customer 2:
You are going to call Cool Presents and place an order. Look at the information below.

1 Your friend bought a mouse pad with a built-in calculator for €89 last month. You want one, too.

2 You're interested in buying a digital photo wallet but you only want to store about ten pictures. A few weeks ago you saw one advertised on the Creative Gifts website for €59.

3 Check the prices before you place your orders. Take a few minutes to think about what you will say and then call.

File 20

Student A:
You are going to act out three different calls with Gyan, Judith's virtual assistant. Make a note of the arrangements you make. Before taking each call, spend a minute preparing what to say.

Call one:
You're the receptionist at 'The Big Smile', Judith's dentist's surgery. All your dentists are booked up during regular office hours this week. You can schedule an 8 a.m. appointment but only if it's urgent.
When Gyan calls, answer the phone by saying: '*Big Smile Dentist Surgery.*'

Call two:
You work for Salento's restaurant. You have tables free at any time on Thursday but you're busy on Friday. You can only accept bookings after 8 p.m.
When Gyan calls, answer the phone by saying: '*Salento's restaurant.*'

Call three:
You're Judith's son Timmy and you need some help with your school science project. You're busy after school on Thursday but free on Friday evening.
When Gyan calls, answer the phone by saying: '*Hi, Timmy Harwood.*'

File 21

Student B:

1 Tell your partner what is happening in this picture. They have a similar picture but there are six differences. Find and circle the differences.

2 Why are the pictures different?

File 22

One of the dragons promised to invest in the Beanock.

File 23

Guest:
You've been staying at the Arcadium Hotel for a couple of days. You like the hotel, but you've had some problems. Here's your bill. Take a few minutes to plan what you will say. Be pleasant and explain what's wrong to the manager.

Breakfast – You thought breakfast was included in the room rate.

Internet – You spent an hour trying, but you couldn't connect to the internet.

In-room movie – You clicked on the in-room movie by mistake. It only played for 30 seconds before you turned it off.

Laundry – This is too much! You only gave them one shirt to clean.

Health club – The hotel gym has three exercise bicycles but only one of them worked. You had to wait 30 minutes to use it this morning.

TOTAL – This total isn't correct.

Arcadium Hotel
Shepherds Bush
MJ1 40J
London, England
Tel: 44 (0) 123 456 7833

ARCADIUM

Room 323
Room Rate £180

Date	Description	Charges
24/2	Room charge	£180
24/2	Health club	£20
24/2	Breakfast	£25
24/2	Laundry	£280
24/2	Internet	£5
25/2	Room charge	£180
25/2	Health club	£20
25/2	Breakfast	£25
25/2	In-room movie	£5
25/2	Room service	£35
	SUBTOTAL	£495
	Taxes	£94
	TOTAL	£789

File 24

Student B:
Read the story about the day that Paul Potts' life changed. Then answer your partner's questions. Explain any words your partner doesn't know.

It was audition* day and the judges of the TV talent show felt tired. There were singers, dancers, fire eaters and comedians* but nobody was very good. Then Paul Potts walked onto the stage. He looked shy and nervous. He didn't have a tie. His suit cost £35 and he had a broken tooth. He told the judges he was a mobile phone salesman. 'I'm going to sing opera,' he said. The judges sighed*. They didn't expect his audition to be good.

Then Paul began singing and everything changed. The audience stood up and clapped and cheered because he had an amazing voice. The video of his performance appeared on YouTube and millions of people watched it. He won a place in the semi-final, and the final, and then he won the competition. He received around two million votes from viewers. Paul won £100,000, and a recording contract. Later that year he performed in front of the Queen. Paul's first CD was a number one hit in 13 countries and today he's a successful opera star.

audition: A short performance to test whether someone like an actor or singer is good

comedians: People who tell jokes and try to make an audience laugh

sighed: Breathed out loudly because they were tired or bored

File 25

Student B:
In this conversation you must use a lot of hand gestures. Try to sound very emotional and passionate about the things you say.

File 26

Conversational style	Sport
1 Highly considerate	Bowling
2 Highly engaged	Rugby
3 A mixture	Basketball

File 27

Student A:
You're Terry. Ivan is your best friend and it's his birthday on Saturday. You have arranged a surprise birthday party for him and you don't want to tell him about it. You can invite him to do anything you want – play squash, see a movie, go to the theatre, etc. but you must get him to Caroline's flat at 7 p.m. on Saturday. All his friends will be there, and his sister from Australia, so don't take 'no' for an answer.

Make notes about what you will say. Then make the call to Ivan.

File 28

Product C: The Beanock

Problem that it solves: the need to move heavy furniture when you want to clean the floor.

Product details: a beanbag that hangs from the ceiling on metal chains. Two sizes: 2 m long and 1.75 m wide; or 1.75 m long and 1 m wide. Retail price: £795 (large) or £350 (small).

File 29

Host:
Your guest doesn't know it but you have a special talent. You can do magic tricks and you often give shows to entertain children.

You use the hat in the hall in your show. You pull rabbits out of it.

You can perform tricks with the cards in the living room.

You use the sword on the wall in the dining room in your show. You swallow it.

If your guest asks about these things, you can tell them about your talent and what you do with these things. If not, keep quiet. If the guests ask about anything else, you can make up information.

File 30

Student B:

1 Here are some past events. You partner will read what was going on when they happened. Each time, choose the best event and read it to your partner.

A … I didn't know his name.

B … I knew he was my date.

C … we were sure they were from Italy.

D … I knew she was the CEO.

E … he asked, 'Are you lost?'

F … I thought he was a doctor.

G … she thought he was asleep.

2 Here are the backgrounds to some past events. Read each one aloud to your partner. Your partner will then read the event that followed. Listen carefully. Does it make sense?

1 He was carrying some tools so …

2 They weren't wearing security badges so …

3 Louise was feeling very tired so …

4 They were smiling so …

5 He was staring at me so …

6 They were looking for the exit so …

7 He was looking at his watch so …

File 31

Student B:
You work in your company's head office. You've visited your partner's regional offices three times over the last five years, so you've met and worked with some of your partner's colleagues. You want to know how they are and what's happened to them.

Read the notes below and think about what you will say. You can invent any information you don't have.

Frank Hollins
Met him once two years ago. Very helpful – gave you a lift to the airport.

Edward Jones
Very energetic. Gave you a long tour of the factory on your last visit.

Claire Parker
Only met her a couple of times – interesting person – very busy. You've heard she's moved.

Louise Johnson
Known her for years. Met her family when she invited you to her house.

Mary Slawter
Worked together on lots of projects. Haven't heard from her for ages.

File 32

Situation 1

This is your starting position but you can change it if your partner makes a good case. Take a few minutes to prepare what to say before you start.

> **Student A:**
> You'd like to fire the employee who lost the laptop. You'd like to tell all your customers and employees immediately. If anyone suffers a loss because of this, you'd like to refund them in full.

Situation 2

This is your starting position but you can change it if your partner makes a good case. Take a few minutes to prepare what to say before you start.

> **Student A:**
> There's no problem here. The customer accepted the price estimate so you should do nothing and charge the price you quoted. Perhaps you should give the employee who made this error a bonus.

File 33

The Hydrofoil Water Scooter has no engines. You travel across the water by jumping up and down.

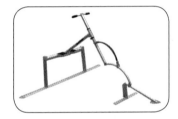

File 34

Student D:
In this conversation you must speak very slowly. If someone asks you a question, pause and think for a moment before you answer. Do not make eye contact.

File 35

Problem 1

Student B:
You think MBA courses are too expensive and they're not worth it. The extra money Student A will earn if they have an MBA will be less than the cost of the course. Take a few minutes to prepare your arguments, then give Student A your advice. Tell them why they shouldn't do an MBA.

Student C:
You think education is the best investment anyone can make in life. If you have a good education, you can earn more and lead a more interesting life. Take a minute or two to prepare your arguments, then give Student A your advice. Tell them why they should do an MBA.

File 36

Average numbers of steps per day

Postmen/women:	18,904	Lawyers:	5,062
Nurses:	8,648	Teachers:	4,726
Police officers:	5,336	Secretaries:	4,327

File 37

> **Student B:**
> You're Ivan and it's your birthday on Saturday. You've been a bit depressed because you don't like the idea of getting older and you want to get away from it all for a while. So you're giving yourself a special birthday present this year: a weekend in the country. You've booked a room in a five star hotel and bought your train tickets. You're leaving on Friday night and coming home on Sunday afternoon. It was expensive but it'll be worth it.
>
> Your friend Terry is going to call you and invite you out. Prepare for the call. Make notes about what you will say first.

File 38

Problem 2

Student A:
You think Student B and their husband/wife should continue working. They will need the money they earn to pay for their child's education later. Take a few minutes to prepare your arguments, then give Student B your advice. Tell them why they and their husband/wife should both continue working.

Student C:
You think children need the attention of their parents. It's better for a child to grow up in a home with very little money than a home where both parents work. Take a few minutes to prepare your arguments, then give Student B your advice. Tell them why they or their husband/wife should stop work.

File 39

1 B   **2** A   **3** A   **4** A   **5** B   **6** A

File 40

Student A:
Read the story about Paul Potts' early life. Then answer your partner's questions. Explain any words your partner doesn't know.

> Paul grew up in Bristol in South West England. His father was a bus driver and his mother worked in a supermarket. He had a difficult time at school because other children bullied* him and he didn't have much confidence. But he loved singing and joined music clubs at school. He graduated from university in 1993 but he had difficulty finding a good job. He got a job in a supermarket, putting things on shelves. He saved every penny he could and bought singing lessons. He sent recordings of his voice to talent agents, but he didn't get one reply. Illness was also problem for Paul. He developed a tumour* and had to spend time in hospital. Another time he was off work for nine months because he had a bad traffic accident. Paul and his wife had very little money and lots of credit card debts. Then in 2007 he decided to audition for a talent show …
>
> *bullied*: frightened or hurt someone who is smaller and weaker
>
> *confidence*: belief in your ability to do things well
>
> *tumour*: a mass of diseased cells in your body

1A, Pages 4 and 5, Exercises 4 and 5

1

A = Man, C = Christine

A: I need to do more exercise.

C: Really?

A: Yes. I'm trying to lose weight. How do you keep fit?

C: I go running with a friend.

A: Oh, I like running.

C: We usually go on Tuesdays and Saturdays.

A: Saturdays?

C: Yes. Do you want to come with us?

A: How far do you run?

C: About fifteen miles.

A: Oh … That's a long way.

C: My friend's training for the London marathon.

A: Wow!

2

A = Man, G = Gudrun

A: Do you have any contact with the Indian offices?

G: Yes, we work with them all the time.

A: Oh, because we're working on a sales training project for some clients in Mumbai.

G: Uhuh.

A: And we need to deliver a training programme.

G: How do you want to deliver it – over the web?

A: Yes.

G: Then you need to talk to Sameer Advani. He's responsible for web training.

A: Is he based in Mumbai?

G: No, Bangalore, but he travels a lot. He's working in Delhi at the moment.

3

A = Woman, R = Rob

A: Are you still here?

R: Yes, my car's at the service station. I'm waiting for them to call me.

A: Oh, I see. Which service station do you use?

R: I go to a place in Cherry Hill.

A: Is it good?

R: Yeah, excellent. It only costs fifty dollars for an oil change.

A: I need to find a new service station.

R: Do you want the address?

A: Yes, thanks.

R: Ask for Chuck. He's the owner.

A: OK.

R: And pay cash. I always pay cash. Chuck likes that.

A: OK.

R: Don't pay by credit card.

1C, Page 8, Exercises 5 and 6

1

N = Noburo Nakamura, R = Receptionist

N: Hi. I'm here to see Anne Baker.

R: May I have your name, please?

N: Yes, it's Noburo Nakamura.

R: OK, just a second, please … OK, Mr. Nakamura. Have a seat. Anne will be down in a moment.

N: Thanks.

2

A = Woman, B = Man

A: Sorry to trouble you but I've got a problem.

B: What's that?

A: My son's sick. His school just called me.

B: Do they want you to pick him up?

A: Yes, I need to leave now. Could you cover for me?

B: Yes, of course.

A: Thanks very much.

3

A = Woman, B = Man

A: Are they for me?

B: Yes, three boxes. Where do you want them?

A: Over by my desk, please.

B: OK, can you sign here, please?

A: Certainly.

4

A = Woman, B = Man

A: Excuse me.

B: Yes?

A: I need to take some stuff up to the third floor.

B: Oh, do you need some help?

A: No, it's all right thanks but there's a trolley over there. Do you mind if I borrow it?

B: Not at all.

A: Thank you.

B: But could you bring it back?

A: Yeah, no problem.

1D, Page 10, Exercises 2 and 3

J = Julia, L = Lucy, P = Paul

J: Lucy!

L: Julia! Lovely to see you. Do you know, Paul?

J: No.

L: Oh, let me introduce you. Julia, this is Paul – one of my neighbours.

J: Nice to meet you, Paul.

P: And you.

L: Julia's my cousin. Our mothers are sisters.

P: Oh, really?

J: Yes. Do you live in the same building as Lucy, Paul?

P: Yes, I'm just renting a flat there while I finish my MBA.

J: So you're an MBA student?

P: Yes. I finish this summer.

L: Paul's looking for a job.

P: What do you do, Julia?

J: I'm a financial analyst.

L: Julia works very hard – never stops. I think she's a workaholic.

J: Oh, I'm not. But I think I need a holiday.

L: I want to go to Paris for a few days. Do you want to come with me?

J: Oh, yes! That's a great idea.

L: Terrific!

J: But not this month. … We're very busy at work at the moment.

L: Another international project?

J: Yes.

P: Oh, what's that?

J: We're working on a deal with some people from Argentina.

P: Where in Argentina?

J: Buenos Aires, but they're in London this week. It's a problem, actually.

P: Why's that?

J: I'm trying to find someone who can translate for us. The person who speaks Spanish is off sick.

L: Paul speaks Spanish.

J: No! Do you really?

P: Yes. My father's from Madrid.

J: Are you free tomorrow?

P: Yes. Can I help?

J: Oh yes …

P: That's great.

J: I'm so pleased we met. Look here's my business card …

2A, Page 12, Exercise 2

A = Man, **C** = Chris Orth

A: Tech support. Can I have your employee number, please?

C: Yes, it's 240721, and my name's Chris Orth.

A: Thanks, Chris. How can I help you?

C: I'm having trouble with my computer.

A: With your laptop or desktop computer?

C: My desktop. It's running very slowly.

A: OK, I'll send someone over to take a look.

C: How soon can they be here?

A: I'll find out and let you know.

C: Can you call me back on my mobile?

A: Yes, no problem.

C: That's great. Thanks a lot.

A: You're welcome.

2C, Page 16, Exercise 5

J = Jean Pierre Moreau, **R** = Rosemary

J: Jean Pierre Moreau.

R: Hi, it's Rosemary.

J: Hi, Rosemary. Look, can I call you back?

R: Oh, sorry, is this a bad time?

J: Yes, I'm in the middle of something.

R: No problem.

J: Thanks. Bye.

2C, Page 17, Exercises 7 and 8

J = Jean Pierre Moreau, **R** = Rosemary

R: Rosemary Clark.

J: Hi, it's Jean Pierre.

R: Oh, Jean Pierre. Thanks for getting back to me.

J: Sorry I couldn't speak earlier.

R: Oh, that's OK. Jean Pierre, I'm sorry to trouble you but I need an email address for Steve Parks.

J: Ah. I have it here. It's Steve Parks … Have you got a pen?

R: Yes.

J: It's SteveParks84 at gmail dot com.

R: SteveParks, is that all one word?

J: Yes.

R: Eight oh four?

J: No, eighty-four.

R: Sorry, eighty-four?

J: Yes.

R: At gmail dot com.

J: That's right.

R: Sorry?

J: I said that's right.

R: Oh, good.

2D, Page 18, Exercise 2

Bridget? It's Ana … I'm at the airport, London Heathrow. But Bridget, I have a problem … My bag didn't arrive … They say it's in Miami. They'll send it on the next plane … I'll get it tomorrow but my driving licence is in the bag. I can't hire a car to get to your house … Oh, that's very kind of you. I'm so sorry to trouble you … I'm at terminal 3. How long will it take you to get here? … OK. I'll wait outside in half an hour. Bridget, thank you so much … I'm looking forward to seeing you, too. See you soon.

2D, Page 18, Exercise 4

A = Ana, **B** = Bridget

A: Bridget? It's Ana.

B: Hi, Ana. Where are you?

A: I'm at the airport, London Heathrow. But Bridget, I have a problem.

B: What's that?

A: My bag didn't arrive.

B: Oh no! Where is it?

A: They say it's in Miami. They'll send it on the next plane.

B: When will it arrive?

A: I'll get it tomorrow but my driving licence is in the bag. I can't hire a car to get to your house.

B: Don't worry. I'll come and get you.

A: Oh, that's very kind of you. I'm so sorry to trouble you.

B: It's no problem. Where exactly are you?

A: I'm at terminal 3. How long will it take you to get here?

B: Only thirty or forty minutes.

A: OK. I'll wait outside in half an hour. Bridget, thank you so much.

B: Don't mention it. I'm looking forward to seeing you.

A: I'm looking forward to seeing you, too. See you soon.

3B, Page 22, Exercises 3 and 5

I = Interviewer, **A** = Adam Pritchard

I: Adam, did you go to business school?

A: No, I left school when I was sixteen and I went travelling.

I: So when did you set up your first company?

A: When I was about twenty-four. I started a company to sell cars.

I: How did it go?

A: Oh, it was a disaster. I invested about 30,000 pounds but I didn't sell any cars – not one.

I: Oh dear! Why not?

A: I really didn't know much about cars.

I: Really?

A: Yeah, and I had no contacts in the car market.

I: So what did you do after that?

A: I went back to school and trained as a stockbroker.

I: That's a difficult job. Did you pass the exams?

A: Yes, but I couldn't find a job.

I: So what happened next?

A: I had an idea for another company. I set up a telephone counselling service and we gave advice to people over the phone.

I: Was that successful?

A: No. I lost 50,000 pounds in four months and I had to sell my home.

I: That's terrible.

A: Yeah, but those two failures taught me a lot, I think.

I: Where did you get the idea for Pomegreat?

A: A friend called me from Pakistan and said I had to come and try this fantastic juice. I got on a plane, tried the juice and loved it. I wanted to sell it in the UK.

I: Did it take you long to set up the company?

A: Yes, it did. I spent a year researching the fruit juice market. And I met and talked to a lot of people first.

I: And Pomegreat is a big success. What was your turnover last year?

A: 10 million pounds. We had some problems in the beginning, but yes, we're doing very well now.

3C, pages 24 and 25, Exercises 2, 3, 4 and 6

1

A = Man, **B** = Woman

A: Tired?

B: Yes, a bit, I went to a party last night.

A: That's nice. Did you have a good time?

B: Not really. I had to leave early.

A: That's a pity.

B: Yes, I had a bad headache.

A: You poor thing. Are you better now?

B: Yes, I'm fine, thanks.

2

A = Man, **B** = Woman

A: Where's Louisa today?

B: Didn't you hear? Someone drove into her car this morning.

A: Are you serious?

B: Yes, really.

A: That's terrible! Is she OK?

B: Yes. She wasn't hurt but her Honda's badly damaged.

A: Oh no! It's a new car.

B: I know. It's awful.

A: Poor Louisa.

B: Yes, but at least …

3

A = Man, **B** = Woman

A: Did you go to the sales presentation?

B: No, I couldn't go.

A: That's a shame. It was very interesting.

B: Yeah, I wanted to go.

A: Too much work, huh?

B: No, I had to take my daughter to the hospital.

A: Oh, nothing serious I hope?

B: No, she just needed some tests …

4

A = Woman, **B** = Man

A: So what happened yesterday?

B: The interview went very well.

A: Good!

B: In fact, they offered me the job.

A: Wow! That's terrific! Congratulations!

B: Thank you.

A: Fantastic!

B: Yes, I'm really excited about it.

A: Yes, I can imagine. So when do you start?

B: Next week. I can't wait.

5

A = Woman, **B** = Man

A: Did you do anything nice this weekend?

B: We went to Brighton.

A: That's nice. Brighton's a fantastic city.

B: But we couldn't find anywhere to park.

A: Really? Did you try the multi-storey?

B: Yes. All the car parks were full.

A: That's a nuisance.

B: We spent two hours looking. It was very frustrating.

A: I can imagine.

B: Then we found a spot in a back street.

A: Oh good.

B: So we went shopping and when we came back, we had a parking ticket!

A: Oh dear.

B: A fifty pound parking fine!

3D, Page 26, Exercises 3 and 5

A = Man, M = Monika Nowak

A: What was your biggest mistake at work?

M: I think it was when I worked at a paper-making plant. I was in charge of a project to speed up production but I slowed it down instead.

A: Oh no. What happened?

M: Well, we needed to improve the efficiency of our machines. There were lots of new technologies on the market. I read the sales brochures and they all looked great.

A: How much did they cost?

M: Oh, not a lot. It wasn't a big investment so my project plan looked excellent. We could install the different technologies in three months and increase production by five per cent.

A: So what went wrong?

M: Well, we installed the first technology on every machine in the plant.

A: Did it take long?

M: No, we did it overnight. But the next day we had a big problem. Every machine shut down.

A: Oh no.

M: The technology didn't work.

A: All the machines stopped working?

M: Yes, the plant manager went crazy.

A: So what did you do?

M: I learnt my lesson. I threw away my project plan and I started testing. I ran tests on all the new technologies one by one.

A: And how did it go?

M: Well, we learnt a lot. Some didn't work.

A: Ah …

M: And some worked really well – much better than we expected. We installed the best ones – but one machine at a time.

A: How long did it take?

M: A year.

A: But did you achieve your targets?

M: Well, we missed the deadline. But nobody cared because the results were so good. We exceeded the targets. Production went up by fifteen per cent.

A: Not five?

M: No, fifteen.

A: Fantastic!

4B, Page 30, Exercises 3, 4, 5 and 6

1

We can't give expensive gifts to customers because it's against the law here. But we often give them small promotional items with our company name and logo – things like pens and sweatshirts. I took some sweatshirts to Europe last month. I thought I could give them to customers but our agent said our company name and logo was too big. He told me to take them home again because they weren't fashionable. I gave them to the woman who cleaned my hotel room instead. She gave me the biggest smile you ever saw.

2

We wanted to give our business partners in Korea a very special gift to celebrate our tenth anniversary. We contacted a glass factory in our town and asked them to make a glass vase – just for us. Well, they did and it was beautiful. I didn't want it to break, so I carried it in my hand luggage. It was one of the worst journeys of my life. I had to carry the vase through three different airports and it was really heavy. But it was the ideal gift because it was high quality and it came from our city.

3

When I retired, the company gave me a gold watch and my co-workers gave me some golf clubs. They were very generous. But the best gift I had came from my friends in the post room and it's a game. It's like Monopoly but you don't buy streets and houses. You buy James Bond films instead. It was the least expensive gift but it's the one I enjoy the most. They knew I was a James Bond fan.

4

I gave a keynote speech at a conference in Singapore. The conference organizers paid for my airfare, but that was all. I didn't care because the most important people in my field were there and I loved Singapore. And on the last day of the conference, the organizers gave me a silver necklace. I didn't expect it so it was a wonderful surprise. It's the prettiest necklace I own.

5

The most unusual gift we received for Christmas was a picture of a goat – yes, really, a goat! My sister thinks Christmas is too commercial so this year she didn't buy gifts. She gave money to charity instead. The charity gives goats to families in Africa and she sent us a picture of the goat she paid for. My wife wasn't pleased. She thinks my sister-in-law is lazy and she didn't want to go shopping. But I liked it. It was nicer than last year's present. She usually gives me socks.

4C, Page 32, Exercises 3 and 4

1

A = Woman 1, B = Woman 2

A: Is it OK? I didn't know what colour to get.
B: Yellow is perfect! It's just what I wanted. I love it.
A: Oh, I'm so glad. Does it fit?

2

A = Man, B = Woman

A: That was a great presentation. Well done!

B: I was very nervous and I think I spoke too fast, but it's very kind of you to say so.

A: No, no, not at all. It was really very good.

3

A = Man 1, B = Man 2

A: It's a cheque – to help with the school bills.

B: Are you sure that's all right? I'll pay you back as soon as I can. Thank you so much!

A: Don't mention it. We're happy we can help.

4

A = Woman, B = Man

A: It's raining out. Let me give you a lift.

B: Oh, wow! You're a lifesaver.

A: No problem. I'm going your way, anyway.

5

A = Woman, B = Man

A: Come and blow out the candles. We've made you a birthday cake.

B: Oh, it's lovely, but you didn't have to go to all this trouble.

A: You're welcome. Now take a deep breath …

5B, Page 41, Exercises 9 and 11

1

Children do a lot of memorizing in school. They have to remember lots of facts and figures. But that won't be important in the future. In fact, it's already less important now. With the internet, we just have to do a search and we can find all the facts we want. So who needs a good memory?

2

You need good technical skills to work in information technology today, and that will be true in the future as well. But in the future, employers will want IT workers with other skills, too – skills like project management or marketing. So good technical skills will be less important and the extra skills will be more important.

3

English will still be an important language in the future but it won't be the most important. In education it will, because many universities will switch to teaching all their classes in English. But in business it'll be different. International companies won't just want people who can speak English. They'll look for people who can speak a third language as well. And the most important one will be Chinese.

5C, Page 42, Exercises 2 and 3

A = Man, B = Woman

A: I'm really hungry.

B: Yes, me, too.

A: Um … Did you buy some chocolate earlier?

B: Yes, I bought three big bars.

A: Are they in your bag?

B: Yes.

A: Then … can I have some?

B: Oh! You mean you want some?!

A: Yes, thanks!

B: Here you are.

A: Great.

5C, Page 42, Exercises 5 and 6

1

A = Woman, B = Man

A: Are you making coffee?

B: Yes. Do you want me to make some for you, too?

A: Oh, that'd be great. Thanks.

B: Not at all.

2

A = Man, B = Woman

A: Those biscuits look nice.

B: Would you like one? Please help yourself.

A: Oh, thanks very much.

B: You're welcome.

3

A = Woman, B = Man

A: Is that the latest address list?

B: Yes. Do you want a copy?

A: That'd be great. Can you email it?

B: No problem.

4

A = Woman, B = Man

A: Are you busy?

B: No. What's the problem?

A: I can't get the printer to work.

B: Would you like me to take a look?

A: Yes, please!

6A, Page 47, Exercise 6

I'm delighted to tell you that we now produce a mini version of the Loc8tor, known as the Loc8tor Lite. It's just eight point six centimetres long and five point four centimetres wide, so about the size of a credit card, and it weighs just twenty grams. The tags are smaller, too, just three point five centimetres by one point nine five. So it's small enough to keep in your wallet but it can locate objects up to a hundred and twenty-two metres away. It currently retails at forty-nine ninety-nine and it comes with two tags. And of course, you can always order more, as with the standard Loc8tor. To order, simply log on to our website or call our free phone line: one eight seven oh, triple one, double seven, double seven. And remember, don't lose it, locate it.

6B, Page 48, Exercise 5

1

I'd like to know its dimensions. How big is it?

2

How fast can it go when it's travelling on the surface of the water?

3

I know it goes underwater but how deep does it go?

4

How powerful are the engines?

5

How much does it cost and what does the price include? Does it come with a five-year warranty?

6

I'm surprised it doesn't sink to the bottom of the sea. How much does it weigh?

7

How far can it travel underwater? And how long does the air last?

6C, Page 51, Exercises 6 and 7

A

A = Customer, **B** = Salesman

A: Has this computer got a sixty-four-bit operating system?

B: Yes it has. I can see you know a lot about computers.

A: I know a little, yes. I'm a graphics designer.

B: Really? Then you'll understand how good the graphics are on this.

A: Yes, it's also got two gigabytes of video RAM.

B: You really know a lot about it. Would you like to buy it now?

A: Yes, OK.

B: I'll carry it for you.

A: Thanks.

B: No trouble at all. It's really nice talking to someone who's an expert on these things.

B

M = Marissa, **T** = Tom

M: Hello?

T: Hi, Marissa? It's Tom at Telebargains.

M: Oh, hi, Tom.

T: I'm calling about the television you asked about. Are you still interested?

M: Yes, perhaps.

T: I checked with our warehouse and they have one more in stock.

M: Really?

T: Yes, but only one – it's the last one.

M: Oh.

T: So we need to act fast because it's now or never. Do you want it?

M: Oh, I want it. What do I need to do?

C

A = Saleswoman, **B** = Customer

A: I see you like this mirror. It's my favourite, too.

B: Yes.

A: Beautiful, isn't it?

B: Yes, we're just not sure …

A: Where are you going to hang it?

B: Well, perhaps in the sitting room.

A: Above the fireplace?

B: Yes, I think so.

A: Oh, it's going to look lovely above your fireplace.

B: That's true.

A: And it'll brighten up your room, too. What are your friends going to say when they see it?

D

A = Saleswoman, **B** = Customer 1, **C** = Customer 2

A: So do you want me to book it for you?

B: Yes, please.

C: Absolutely.

A: No problem.

C: A week in Hawaii. I can't wait.

B: And only five hundred pounds each – what a deal!

C: Yeah!

B: Palm trees, beaches, sunshine …

C: It's going to be fabulous.

A: OK, now the total comes to just under seventeen hundred pounds.

B: Seventeen hundred?

A: Yes, it includes airport taxes, hotel transfers, and insurance.

C: Oh.

A: Seventeen hundred covers everything.

B: … OK, then.

C: Do you need our credit card number?

E

A = Salesman, **B** = Customer

A: This telephone has a clock, a camera and the internet. What do you think?

B: It's interesting.

A: It's better looking, better built and more reliable than other models.

B: Yes, perhaps.

A: It comes with a spare battery, a charger and a twelve-month warranty.

B: OK. I'll take it.

F

OK, ladies and gentlemen, there are three towels here. Normally these towels cost twenty pounds each – that's sixty pounds for three towels. But I'm not going to charge you sixty pounds. And I'm not going to charge you fifty pounds. I'm not even going to charge you forty pounds. I'm feeling very generous today, so I'm only going to charge thirty pounds! Yes – thirty pounds. And hold onto your money, don't pay me yet, because I'm going to add an extra towel here. Yes, four towels – four towels for only thirty pounds!

6D, Page 53, Exercises 5 and 6

Good morning. It's nice to meet you all. I'm Andrew Gordon and today I'd like to show you a very simple but very clever product: Stabletable. Picture this scene. You're meeting some friends in a bar or restaurant. You see an empty table and sit down and it's immediately clear that you've got a problem. You're the unlucky group who are sitting at the wobbly table. Here's what you need: Stabletable. You can put this adjustable device under the legs of any wobbly item and make it exactly the right height to stop the wobbling. It's an ideal gift for anyone who likes going to bars and restaurants – simple, practical and fun.

Stabletable comes in a range of colours — blue, green, orange – so everyone can choose their favourite. It retails at under two pounds and you can order it from our hotline on 01908 277313. It's also available on our website at www.stabletable.co.uk. Remember, with Stabletable you'll never need to sit at a wobbly table again.

Now, does anyone have any questions?

7B, Page 56, Exercises 4 and 5

I = Interviewer, **B** = Employee 1, **C** = Employee 2

I: So, tell me how the system works at Best Buy. Can you set your own schedules?

B: Yes, we all have targets we have to reach – deadlines we must meet. But we don't have to go to the office if we don't need to.

C: I can work better at home – no interruptions.

I: So, can you work from home any time you want?

C: Yeah.

A: Do you need to ask for permission from your manager first?

B: No, we don't.

I: Do you have to go into the office for meetings?

B: No, every meeting is optional.

C: We can attend meetings if we want but we don't have to. Meetings can waste a lot of time so we try not to have too many.

B: We have a lot of conference calls now.

C: Yes, we have laptops and Blackberries so we can carry our office around with us.

I: So, there are no rules about the hours you work?

C: Well, there's one.

I: What's that?

C: We're not allowed to talk about the hours anybody works.

B: That's right. People shouldn't feel guilty if they take an afternoon off.

I: I see. So, should all companies allow their employees to work from home?

B: Well, not everyone likes it.

C: Some managers think we should be in the office, so they can see we're working.

I: Mmm.

B: And they think we can't exchange ideas as well.

I: Uhuh.

C: And my wife doesn't like it much.

I: Why's that?

C: I work in an international team with people in different time zones. They often call me at night. There's no separation between work and personal time any more.

B: Right. My husband complains about it, too. He says I can't relax because I bring the office home with me.

7C, Page 58, Exercises 2 and 3

A = Woman, **S** = Sam

A: Sam. I need your help …

S: Sure, what's up?

A: I'm scheduling a meeting and I don't know what to do.

S: Oh, it's easy. First, you want to open up your Meeting Manager program.

A: OK.

S: Then select the date.

A: Uhuh.

S: After that, choose a room … That's right. Now select a time. That's great. Now click 'enter'. Good. … Oh, that's strange.

A: Nothing's happening.

S: Hang on … Let's slow down … OK, go back and try doing it again.

A: OK.

S: Try not to click too fast.

A: No, it still doesn't work.

S: Ah, I see the problem. We have to type the cost centre number in the box on the left.

A: But I don't have a cost centre number.

S: You don't?

A: No.

S: Then you need to ask your manager to give you one.

A: Oh, I see. I just need to get a number.

S: That's right.

A: Thanks, Sam. That's what I needed to know.

S: You're welcome. Just let me know if you need any more help.

8A, Pages 62 and 63, Exercises 5 and 6

1

A = Woman 1, **B** = Woman 2

A: We had one when our children were young. But this one's much bigger and heavier.

B: Oh, yes. Everything's changed now. Have you seen inside?

A: No.

B: The controls are wonderful. They look like something from the space shuttle.

A: The one we had didn't even have a cup holder.

2

A = Woman, **B** = Man

A: I love it! You can carry it in your shirt pocket.

B: Yes. That's why I chose it.

A: It's so small.

B: Yes, but you should see the instruction manual it came with. It has more than five hundred pages.

A: Oh, dear.

B: I haven't read it but I need to. There must be a button that says 'automatic' somewhere.

A: It's too complicated.

B: Yes, I just want to point and click.

3

A = Man 1, **B** = Man 2

A: I like the design.

B: Yes, and it has all kinds of features.

A: Does it have a camera?

B: Yes, it can take pictures, download emails, wake me up in the morning and beat me at chess.

A: Amazing.

B: But I've had problems making calls. The volume comes and goes.

A: That's a problem because that's why you bought it.

B: That's right.

4

A = Woman 1, **B** = Woman 2

A: I need a new one of these.

B: This one's great. We've had it for about a month.

A: Has it been reliable?

B: Yes, and really useful. It scans, shrinks, faxes and copies.

A: The only thing it can't do is make coffee.

B: That's right. You still have to do that yourself.

8C, Page 67, Exercises 5 and 6

A = Man 1, **B** = Woman, **C** = Man 2

A: Those young people are there again.

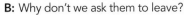

B: Why don't we ask them to leave?

C: I don't think that's a good idea. They look a bit threatening.

A: We don't want any trouble.

B: How about calling the police?

C: Yes, but they're not doing anything wrong.

A: They're allowed to stand there. It's a public space.

B: Well, we need to do something because our customers don't like walking by them.

A: We're not the only people with this problem. Could we speak to our neighbours about it?

C: There aren't enough places for young people to go in this town.

A: Yes.

C: They have nothing to do so they hang about.

B: What if we install a device that makes a high-frequency noise?

C: How does it work?

B: It's a noise that only young people can hear. It's not pleasant, so when they hear it they walk away.

A: And older people can't hear this noise?

B: No. Only people under twenty can hear it.

C: Let's look into it.

B: OK, I'll find out more about it.

A: Or we could install speakers in the doorway and play classical music.

C: That's a great idea. Most young people don't like Mozart.

8D, Page 69, Exercise 8

Hello, everyone. I'm glad to hear we've got some good creative teams ready to work. Now here's your task. We're launching a new product and we want you to create a marketing plan. The product is a perfume. It smells of … well, I'm not sure … something like roses, I think. The target market is women over forty. It's a competitive market and we're aiming at the high end. These women are wealthy – they have very large incomes.

OK, so that's it. Look at your brief and be creative. We need you to come up with some really good ideas for this.

8D, Page 69, Exercise 10

OK, everyone. Good work so far, but I have some more information for you. Management has made a small change to the brief. The thing is that the perfume has a young fresh smell so we need to change the target market. You're now aiming at young women, aged eighteen to twenty-five. These women won't have quite so much money, so I want you to rethink your ideas. Young women, at the beginning of their careers. OK. Get to work.

8D, Page 69, Exercise 12

Hi, it's me again. I have some news about that perfume campaign you're working on. The market tests have arrived and they're, well … they're surprising. The focus groups say it has a masculine smell – so the plan has changed. Instead of a perfume, it's going to be an aftershave lotion. Your target market is now men, aged eighteen to eighty. Please review your marketing plans. Thank you.

9B, Page 75, Exercise 7

1

P = Paul Jones, **G** = Gyan Malik

P: Paul Jones

G: Hi, Paul. This is Gyan Malik, Judith's personal assistant.

P: Oh, hi, Gyan.

G: Paul, Judith would like to schedule a meeting with you to talk about her investment portfolio.

P: Oh, good. Does she want me to come to her office?

G: Yes, please.

P: No problem. When's she free?

G: Does Thursday at three suit you?

P: Three doesn't work but four looks good.

G: Four's fine. So that's four o'clock on Thursday the twentieth, then.

P: Great. Thanks, Gyan.

G: You're welcome. Thank you.

2

R = Receptionist, **G** = Gyan Malik

R: Hillman Medical Centre.

G: Good morning. This is Gyan Malik and I'd like to make an appointment for Judith Harwood with Dr Goldberg as soon as possible.

R: Dr Goldberg's booked up this week. How about next week?

G: Oh, dear. It's quite urgent.

R: Judith Harwood …

G: Uhuh.

R: OK … erm, hang on … Can Mrs Harwood make Thursday at four?

G: Is that the only time available?

R: Yes. We just had a cancellation.

G: Then that's fine. So that's four o'clock on Thursday with Dr Goldberg, then.

R: Yes, that's right.

G: Thank you.

9B, Page 75, Exercise 8

P = Paul Jones, **G** = Gyan Malik

P: Paul Jones.

G: Paul, it's Gyan again. I'm afraid something's come up and Judith can't meet you on the twentieth.

P: Ah. Do you want to schedule another time, then?

G: Yes, please. Are you free at the same time on Friday the twenty-first?

P: Yeah, Friday's open. So that's Friday at four at Judith's office, then.

G: Good. Thanks. I'm sorry to mess you around like this.

P: Hey, it's no problem. I'm glad to help.

G: I'll email you to confirm, and thank you for being so flexible.

P: You're welcome. Take care.

G: Bye.

9C, Page 76, Exercise 3

A

We had a very nice conversation. When I said goodbye, I wanted to be polite so I said, 'You must come and see me when you're in Birmingham.' We didn't know each other very well so I was a bit shocked when he asked for my address.

B

I want to be helpful to foreign visitors. It's not polite to disappoint people, so if they ask for information, I have to give them some. It's polite to do that where I come from.

C

I hesitated and said it was inconvenient. In my language, that means 'no' and it's not very polite to ask why. I was surprised when she didn't accept my answer.

D

I always try to deal with callers politely and efficiently. It's not my fault that my boss is away, so why should I say sorry? Leaving a message is the logical solution.

E

In my country we have to show we are unhappy when our friends turn us down. Of course we understand when people can't come but it's polite to insist. It shows we care about our relationship. That's why I don't say 'no' to invitations. I usually say 'I'll try to come', even when I know I can't.

F

Where I come from people are very hospitable. We like to make our guests feel welcome. But polite guests don't want to trouble their hosts, so they often say no when we offer food. A good host serves something anyway, to be sure their guests feel welcome. They can leave it if they don't want it.

9C, Page 76, Exercises 6 and 8

T = Tim, **B** = Man

T: I just wondered … erm … are you doing anything this weekend?

B: I don't think so. Why, Tim?

T: We're having a barbecue in our back garden on Saturday – just a small party. I thought, well, would you like to come?

B: Oh, it's very kind of you to invite us. I'll tell Barbara but she hasn't been well.

T: Oh, I'm sorry. I didn't know.

B: Yes, it's just a cold but I'm afraid she's not well enough for a party.

T: Oh, that's a shame. I hope she feels better soon.

B: Thank you for thinking of us.

T: Not at all.

B: We'd love to come another time.

9C, Page 76, Exercises 7 and 8

T = Tim, **B** = Man, **C** = Woman

T: What are you doing on Saturday?

B: Nothing. Why?

T: We're having a barbecue. Do you want to come?

B: That'd be great! We'd love to!

C: But we're visiting my mother on Saturday.

B: Oh, I forgot.

C: I'm sorry, Tim. It'd be lovely but we're already booked.

T: Not to worry.

B: Can't we see your mother next weekend instead?

C: No! Let's get together some other time, Tim.

T: That's all right with me.

C: How about the weekend after next instead?

9D, Page 79, Exercises 6 and 7

C = Caroline, **T** = Terry

C: Hello.

T: Hi, Caroline, it's Terry. How's it going?

C: Oh, Terry. It's fine. Thirty people are coming and there might be more.

T: That's great. So, what's happening?

C: Well, Jane and Robert are in charge of the food. They're coming round on Saturday morning to prepare it.

T: Good.

C: Mara's bringing some balloons and things that we can put round my flat. James might bring his video camera as well.

T: Great.

C: What time are you bringing Ivan here?

T: I don't know yet. I'm going to phone him tomorrow. I might invite him to play squash. He likes squash.

C: I hope he's not doing anything else on Saturday evening. He could say 'no'.

T: Don't worry. I won't take 'no' for an answer.

C: Can you bring him here at seven? He mustn't suspect anything.

T: That's no problem. I could say I left my squash racquet at your flat.

C: Oh, I nearly forgot. Ivan's sister's flying in from Australia.

T: Wow! That's brilliant!

C: She's arriving on Saturday morning. Claudia's picking her up at the airport.

T: And Ivan doesn't know?

C: No. The last time they saw each other was three years ago.

T: That's fantastic!

C: It's going to be a wonderful surprise.

10A, Page 80, Exercises 5 and 6

A = Man, **B** = Woman

A: I'm not sure about the area.

B: Oh, it's changed a lot in the last five years. New people have moved in and a lot of new businesses as well.

A: Yes, but is it a bit dangerous?

B: There isn't much crime now. There was five years ago but it's safer these days. I walk around here late at night and it doesn't worry me.

A: And there isn't much to do. There are lots of shops but there isn't much nightlife.

B: Oh, but that's changing, too. New restaurants have opened in the main square. I expect some will open in this street soon as well.

A: I suppose so.

B: And remember, there are really good transport links. Lots of buses go down this street.

A: And the station isn't far.

5

B: Exactly. If you want entertainment, it's really easy to go downtown.

A: That's true.

B: This is going to be one of the top areas to live in five or ten years. Now's a great time to buy.

A: Yes?

B: This house will probably double in price in five or six years.

A: Oh.

10B, Page 82, Exercises 5 and 6

A = Woman, **B** = Man

A: OK, so these choirs make a list of complaints and then they turn them into a song.

B: That's right.

A: A list of complaints – isn't that a boring and depressing thing?

B: Oh, not at all. Everyone has fun writing them.

A: So, what kinds of things do people complain about?

B: Well, roads and traffic are common ones.

A: Like 'There's too much traffic on I95 in the mornings'?

B: Yes, that kind of thing.

A: And there are too many red lights and not enough green ones.

B: Exactly. And public transport – so in St Petersburg they sing about the poor bus service on route nine to Vasilievsky.

A: Ha! That's great. What else?

B: Well, another common complaint is not having enough free time.

A: What? Like, 'My vacations are too short'?

B: Yes, or 'Why are there only twenty-four hours in a day?'

A: Or 'There are too many Mondays and not enough Sundays'.

B: You've got the idea.

A: Yes, I'm starting to enjoy this.

B: Are you ready to join a choir?

A: I'd love to but my voice isn't good enough.

B: That's no problem. You can just say the words.

10B, Page 83, Exercise 10

[Extract from Birmingham complaints choir's song]

10C, Page 84, Exercises 6 and 7

A = Woman, **B** = Man

A: Sylvan Bus Company. Good morning.

B: Good morning. I have a problem.

A: Oh, how can I help you?

B: I tried to book some bus tickets on your internet site. I entered all my details and clicked 'confirm' and then nothing happened.

A: Nothing?

B: No, the screen froze.

A: Oh, that's frustrating for you. I'm so sorry about that. But I can take your booking.

B: No, no. You don't understand. So then I called your office and spoke to someone and they booked the tickets for me.

A: Good.

B: But I've just checked my credit card bill and you've charged me twice!

A: Twice?

B: Yes. You've charged me too much!

A: Oh dear. I do apologize. We're having some problems with our computer system.

B: I asked the person I spoke to before to check. I don't want to pay for two bookings.

A: No, of course not. We're really very sorry about this but I can delete that charge and refund your credit card. Can I have your name and the booking reference number?

…

B: So you've deleted the charge?

A: Yes, I've refunded you in full. And I do apologize again for the error.

B: Well, it was very annoying but thank you for your help.

A: That's fine. We're installing new software which will solve this problem.

B: Good.

A: Are you satisfied with this solution and the service today?

B: Well, yes. You've been very helpful, thank you.

A: It was a pleasure and we hope you'll book with us again.

B: Thanks very much.

A: Thank you.

B: Bye.

A: Goodbye.

10D, Page 87, Exercises 3, 5, 6 and 7

1

A = Woman, **B** = Man

A: What's the population?

B: Eleven.

A: You mean only eleven people live there?

B: Yes, it's very small. It's only about three kilometres long and it's privately owned. It belongs to Robert Devereux.

A: So he owns the whole island?

B: Yes, he bought it in nineteen ninety-five for about one point three million pounds.

A: Can anyone stay there?

B: Yes. There are five cottages that people can rent or there's a house.

A: Are there any historical buildings?

B: Well, there's an old castle but it's fallen down. And there aren't any shops – or cars or bicycles.

A: Really?

B: Yes, they're not allowed. But there are rowing boats – they're provided free.

A: It sounds very peaceful but I don't think my two teenage daughters would like it.

2

A = Man 1, **B** = Woman, **C** = Man 2

A: Is it easy to find?

B: No, there aren't any signs outside because it's top secret.

C: And you need a password to get in.

A: What's the password?

B: Oh … We can't tell you that.

A: So how can I get in?

C: There's a room at the entrance with a person sitting at a desk. They'll let you in if you do a trick or something.

A: What kind of trick?

B: Oh I don't know … Dance like a chicken.

C: Or act like a monkey – they'll tell you what to do.

A: And they'll tell me the password?

C: Yes, and then the bookcase slides open and the doorway is behind it.

A: That's great.

B: And when you get inside the nightclub, you see big TV monitors that show the entrance room.

A: So everyone just saw what I did!

B: Exactly. They all clap and cheer when you come in.

C: Or they 'boo' if they didn't like your dance.

B: And when you're inside, there are lots of spy gadgets. It has two-way mirrors and secret windows and doors. It's lots of fun.

3
A = Man, **B** = Woman

A: How did this place remain secret?

B: That's an interesting question. We think it dates back to fourteen fifty but nobody knew about it for centuries.

A: What happened to the people who lived here?

B: They got ill – smallpox. At least fifty per cent of the population died.

A: Oh, that's terrible.

B: Do you like history?

A: I love it.

B: Then you'll love this place. The building work is very interesting.

A: It looks very advanced and well planned.

B: Yes, Inca society was highly developed and very well organized. But they didn't have a writing system.

A: There was no alphabet?

B: No, but they probably used diagrams and pictures.

A: And mathematics?

B: Well, that was interesting, too. They developed a system with coloured pieces of string and knots that they used for accounting.

11A, Page 88, Exercises 3 and 5

A management consultant went on holiday to a beautiful tropical island. One day he saw a local fisherman getting off his boat. The fisherman had some fresh fish and they looked very good.

'How long did it take you to catch those fish?' the consultant asked.

'Oh, not very long,' said the fisherman.

'Then why didn't you work longer and catch more?'

'Because I have enough fish here to feed me and my family.'

'But what do you do with the rest of your time?' asked the consultant.

'Well, I usually sleep late in the mornings. I spend time with my wife and I play with my children. And in the evenings I relax – I usually go out and have fun with my friends.'

The consultant thought for a moment and said, 'I have an MBA from the London School of Business and I can help you. You should work longer each day.'

'Really?' said the fisherman. 'Tell me more.'

'If you work longer, you'll catch more fish and then you can sell them. If you have more money, you can buy another boat. You'll double the number of fish you catch if you have another boat.'

'And what then?' asked the fisherman.

'Well, you can buy more boats, and then you can move into town, open a factory and run a fish business. And that's when it gets really interesting. If your business gets big, you can sell your company's shares on the stock market. You'll make millions.'

'How long will this take?' asked the fisherman.

'Maybe ten or fifteen years.'

'But is it worth it?' the fisherman asked.

'Yes, because then you can retire and live on a tropical island. You can sleep late, do a little fishing, spend time with your family and relax in the evenings …'

The consultant stopped talking when he saw the smile on the fisherman's face. It got wider and wider.

'Thanks, but no thanks,' said the fisherman as he walked away.

11B, Page 90, Exercises 6 and 7

A = Woman, **B** = Man 1, **C** = Man 2

A: Have you only just arrived?

B: Yes.

A: We don't have long. Where is everyone? Are you the only ones here?

C: Yes.

A: But there are only you two of you.

B: The others are coming later.

A: Where's Jasper?

C: At the office.

A: Still at the office?

C: Yeah.

A: If he hasn't left yet, he won't be here for at least half an hour.

C: Yeah.

A: But we start in an hour. When will Gary get here?

B: We're not sure.

A: Have you rung him?

B: His mobile's switched off.

A: Well, tell him to hurry up if he calls … Where's Anna?

C: I'll be surprised if she comes today.

B: Yes, she wasn't very well yesterday.

A: So there's just the two of you?

C: Uh huh.

B: Afraid so.

A: This is terrible. If you're going to set up in time, you need help. OK, what can I do?

B: Well … if you help Pete with the cables, I can set up the cameras.

C: What about the microphones?

B: Jasper can do them when he arrives.

6

A: Oh, this is crazy. Why didn't you come yesterday and do this?

B: We work very fast.

C: Very fast …

11C, Page 92, Exercises 6 and 7

A = Man, B = Woman, C = Woman, D = Man

A: What about electronic tags?

B: And alarms that go off when they leave the store?

A: That's right.

C: We've talked about this before.

D: Yes, I really don't like the idea. The tags look ugly.

C: And they're not cheap.

B: We could just put them on expensive items.

D: Yes, but they don't always work. Professional shoplifters know how to remove them.

C: Yes, that's a problem …

…

D: What about our security cameras? Do we have enough?

A: I think so, but do we want to upgrade?

D: To a digital system?

A: Yes.

B: The problem with that is the cables.

C: Yes. The cameras aren't expensive but installing the cables is.

D: A digital system's better.

A: You can store more data.

D: And the pictures are clearer.

B: We can't afford it. It's the cables.

C: Yes, it's too expensive.

D: How much does it cost?

…

C: Another idea – we could search our employees' bags and belongings.

B: When?

C: Not every day. But random searches at different times.

A: Is that legal?

C: Yes, if we put it in their employment contract.

B: They won't agree to that.

A: No, they won't like it.

C: We'll find out who's stealing.

D: I see a different problem with that. It's like saying, 'We don't trust you.'

C: Well, we don't.

D: Yes, but not all employees are dishonest.

11D, Page 95, Exercises 7 and 8

I'm Adam Saunders and I'm the owner of a marketing consulting firm. I love jogging, cycling and I go swimming five times a week. So I'm not worried about my health. But I am worried about the health of my staff. Some of them smoke, some are overweight and they don't move around enough. There hasn't been a very good atmosphere in the office recently and I think it's because of stress. Everyone spends too much time at their desks. I want to encourage them to lead a healthier lifestyle so I'm planning to make some changes.

I'm launching operation fitness – it's a plan that will make everyone healthier and fitter. The employees might not like the changes I'm going to make but they're for their own good. It'll be worth it.

12B, Page 98, Exercises 4 and 5

1

A = Woman 1, B = Man, C = Woman 2

A: Our kids always like this place.

B: They sell nice desserts – that's why.

C: Well, the place looks fun.

A: Yes, and every thirty minutes there's a thunderstorm.

C: How do they do that?

B: With water sprinklers and flashing lights.

A: And you hear the sound of thunder and rain.

C: Will we get wet?

B: No, no, it's just a show.

A: But the kids will like it.

2

A = Man, B = Woman

A: Where's the kitchen?

B: It's upstairs.

A: And where's the waiter?

B: We don't need one. We order the food with this computer.

A: Oh, I see.

B: Here's the fish menu … and the meat …

A: Oh, they have organic beef with onions. I'll have that.

B: OK.

A: So, no waiters, eh?

B: No.

A: Well, that's good news.

B: Why's that?

A: We don't need to tip anyone.

3

A = Woman 1, B = Man, C = Woman 2

A: So, what's this restaurant like?

B: It's dark and there are lots of different rooms. It's a little bit scary.

C: And the waiters and waitresses entertain everyone.

A: How?

C: They do magic tricks.

B: And they try to frighten you.

C: Yes, they all wear black clothes and they jump out suddenly and shout at you.

A: Is it scary?

C: Not really.

B: Well, it scares me.

4

A = Man, B = Woman

A: Where's my knife and fork?

B: They don't give us a knife and fork.

A: Why not?

B: People didn't have them in the eleventh century.

A: So, how do I eat my food?

B: Use your fingers.

A: My fingers?

B: Yes.

A: I need a napkin.

B: Shhhhh! The horses are coming back.

12C, Page 101, Exercise 6

A = Woman, **B** = Man

A: Great match last night!

B: … Yes.

A: I thought Pato played well … Alexander Pato?

B: … Yes.

A: Did you see the match?

B: … Yes.

A: So, what did you think of it?

B: It was good.

A: Do you think Milan deserved that second goal?

B: … I don't know.

A: Well, anyway, I must go. See you later.

12C, Page 101, Exercises 7 and 8

A = Woman, **B** = Man

A: Great match last night.

B: Yes, terrific.

A: I thought Pato played well.

B: Yes, he was brilliant. Definitely their best player.

A: But do you think Milan deserved that second goal?

B: No, I think it was a mistake. What do you think?

A: Yeah. It was a bad decision by the referee.

B: I'm looking forward to the Barcelona match tonight.

A: Do you think they'll win?

12D, Page 103, Exercises 3, 4 and 5

1

I = Interviewer, **J** = Leslie Sharp

I: Well, I'm here at the top of Cooper's Hill, a very steep hill in the south west of England and today's a special day. It's the day of the cheese-rolling festival. I have with me Leslie Sharp, one of last year's winners. Leslie, so this event happens every year, right?

L: Every year, yes, at the end of May.

I: I have to say it seems pretty crazy. What happens?

L: Well, everyone meets here at the top of the hill. Then we roll a big round of cheese down the hill and everyone runs after it.

I: And the winner is the person who gets to the bottom of the hill first?

L: That's right, they get the cheese as a prize.

I: And you also have to try to catch the cheese?

L: Try to yes, but usually nobody does. The cheese rolls too fast.

I: The hill's very steep. Isn't it a bit dangerous?

L: Well, yes, there are usually a few accidents, yes. But we have a team from the local hospital waiting at the bottom of the hill.

I: Oh, yes, I can see an ambulance there.

L: That's right. They'll look after any people who are injured.

I: There are lots of people here today. Is this a big tourist attraction?

L: Oh, it's a great attraction. We get people from all over the world – South America, Japan, China … It's becoming really international.

I: It's a shame that the weather is bad today. I hope it stops raining before the races begin.

L: Yes, it's not very nice, but that won't stop the races. It was pretty wet when I won last year.

I: And you're hoping to win again?

L: Of course.

2

I = Interviewer, **B** = Barry Hooper

I: Well, it's a beautiful day here in Port Lincoln. There are lots of people here enjoying the sunshine and also enjoying this year's Port Lincoln festival. I'm talking to Barry Hooper, one of the organizers.

B: Hi.

I: So this is your summer festival?

B: Yes, we have this festival every summer at the end of January.

I: I can see there's lots happening, but I want to ask you about one of the competitions.

B: Ah, I think I know which one. It's the tuna throwing competition, right?

I: Yes. Is it true that you're going to be throwing fish?

B: Absolutely. Yes. Port Lincoln's famous as a fishing port …

I: A big centre for the tuna fishing industry …

B: That's right. So it shows how important tuna fishing is for the town.

I: So, what exactly happens?

B: Well, you have a big frozen tuna fish and you tie a rope to it. Then you have to see how far you can throw it.

I: And how far do people throw it?

B: Well the world record is thirty-seven point two three metres. That was back in nineteen ninety-eight and no one has thrown it further than that yet.

I: Wow! So, are you hoping for a new world record this year?

B: Who knows? Maybe someone here can break it …

I: Well, there are lots of people here.

B: Oh, yeah, we get over twenty thousand people coming in from all over South Australia. There're lots of things happening – music, shows, lots of local art and craft you can buy …

I: So, for people who don't want to throw a fish, there's lots of other things you can do.

B: Right.

13B, Page 108, Exercises 2 and 3

A = Woman, **B** = Man

A: I often visit our offices in Boston and New York.

B: Oh, I often go to Boston, too. I really like it.

A: Yes, me, too.

B: Americans are so friendly.

A: Do people there ever invite you to their homes for meals?

B: Yes, it's happened many times.

7

A: One of the things I find surprising is Americans often give me a tour of their house – show me all the rooms.

B: That's happened to me, too.

A: I didn't know what to say at first. It seemed strange to look round another person's home.

B: You don't do that in Germany?

A: No, and I found it embarrassing. I had to say lots of nice things and admire everything.

B: I think it's just how Americans make us welcome.

A: Yes, that's right. At first I thought they were conceited about their houses.

B: Perhaps Germans are more modest?

A: No, I don't think it's that. I think it's just a custom.

B: Yes, that's right.

A: And then after a while, I stopped feeling embarrassed and I started to enjoy seeing their homes.

B: They're interesting. Everything's very big in America compared with Britain – the furniture, beds, washing machines.

A: And the refrigerators are enormous.

B: Oh, that was something that interested me. I once went to a party in Boston where the guests took drinks from the refrigerator. They didn't ask the host first.

A: They just helped themselves?

B: Yes. I found that strange. If they wanted a cold drink, they opened the fridge and took one.

A: That is strange.

B: I guess it's just the American way.

13C, Page 111, Exercises 4 and 5

J = Jeremy, **L** = Louise, **M** = Maria

J: Hi, Louise

L: Jeremy, hello!

J: It's nice to see you again.

L: You too. You look very well.

J: And you. Let me take your coat.

L: Thanks.

J: Did you have any trouble getting through security?

L: No, it was fine. I really love this meeting room. What a wonderful view.

J: Yes, it's great, isn't it? You can see the London Eye from here. Look.

L: Oh, yes.

J: Maria will be here in a minute. Make yourself comfortable. Have a seat.

L: Can I plug in my laptop?

J: Yes, of course … Ah, here's Maria.

M: Louise! Lovely to see you!

L: You, too.

M: You look wonderful. I love your new haircut.

L: My hairdresser persuaded me to try a new style.

M: It looks really nice. It really suits you.

L: Oh, thank you.

J: Coffee?

L: Yes, thank you.

J: Black or white?

L: Black's fine, thanks. I just told Jeremy. We have such a nice meeting room today.

M: Ah, well, I can't take credit for that. Jeremy booked it.

L: Thank you, Jeremy.

J: Is that a new laptop?

L: Yes.

J: The screen's really nice.

L: It's OK but it's not very fast. It takes a long time to boot up.

J: Coffee, Maria?

M: Yes, please.

13C, Page 111, Exercise 8

J = Jeremy, **L** = Louise, **M** = Maria

1

J: OK. Let's start work on the document.

L: Fine.

M: We want to tell you, we really like your work on this project so far.

L: Thank you very much. That's very kind of you.

J: We'd like to go through your document today and look for ways to improve it.

L: Fine.

2

J: Your market research is very good and well presented.

L: I had a lot of help. It was a team effort.

M: We have some questions and also some suggestions.

L: OK.

3

L: So, that's a problem?

M: Yes. Do you understand what's wrong?

L: Yes. Don't worry. I'll change it.

M: Thank you. You're so helpful and flexible.

L: No, it's easy to change. It won't take long.

4

J: There are some very interesting suggestions here.

M: Yes, they're excellent. Well done.

L: The suggestions came from customer feedback. We did a survey.

M: Well, they're very interesting.

5

J: We'd like more information on the market. It could really take us forward.

L: No problem. We'll do another survey and get some more feedback.

J: That's great. You're always so helpful – it's really nice working with you.

L: Well, I always enjoy working with you, too.

13D, Page 112, Exercises 4 and 5

A = Angie, **E** = Elaine, **M** = Max, **S** = Steve

A: Hello.

E: Hi.

M: Hello.

A: Lovely to see you.

S: Come in, come in.

A: So glad you could come.

E: These are for you.

A: Oh, they're beautiful. Thank you so much.

S: Let me take your coats.

M: Thanks.

E: What a beautiful house!

M: Yes, it's terrific.

S: We bought it last year. I'm afraid we still have some work to do on it.

A: Do come through to the living room …

13D, Page 112, Exercises 6 and 7

A = Angie, E = Elaine, M = Max, S = Steve

M: Well, I think we'll have to get going soon.

A: Really? How about another coffee first?

M: No, thanks. It's getting late and Elaine has a long day tomorrow.

E: Yes, I'm giving a paper in Manchester so I'm going up there tomorrow morning.

A: Oh, great. What's the paper on?

E: Eco-housing. It's one I've given before.

S: Oh, I know that paper. You gave it in Cardiff.

E: That's right.

S: I came to your talk. It was excellent.

E: Really? I didn't know you were there.

S: Well, you had a big audience.

M: Anyway, I think we'll have to get moving now.

S: OK, I'll get your coats …

M: Thanks.

13D, Page 112, Exercise 8

A = Angie, E = Elaine, M = Max, S = Steve

A: It's been so nice to see you. Thank you for coming.

E: Thanks for having us. We really enjoyed it.

M: And thanks for the great meal.

S: Glad you enjoyed it.

A: It's always lovely to see you.

E: Good to see you, too.

M: And remember it's our turn next.

E: Yes, you have to come to our house next time.

A: We'd love to.

E: Take care.

S: Bye.

A: Drive carefully.

S: Who's driving?

M: Elaine. Don't worry. Elaine's a very good driver.

E: Yes, I'm the world's safest driver …

14B, Page 116, Exercises 2 and 3

J = Janet, D = Daniel

J: Daniel?

D: Oh, Janet! Wow! I haven't seen you for ages.

J: I thought it was you. You haven't changed at all.

D: Oh, I think I have some grey hairs.

J: Nonsense. You look just the same.

D: It's lovely to see you again.

J: And you. I haven't seen you since we left university. What's happened to you?

D: Well, I became a software engineer and then I got a job with Microsoft.

J: Really?

D: Yes, I've been there for six years.

J: Well, you were always really good with computers.

D: What's happened to you?

J: Oh, lots of things. When I left university I got a job with a holiday company. I was a tour guide in Sardinia.

D: In Italy?

J: Yes, and that's when I met Carlo, my husband. We've been married for five years.

D: But now you're back in London?

J: Yes, we wanted to be nearer my parents. We've had a travel agency for a couple of years.

D: Specializing in holidays in Sardinia?

J: Of course. Have you ever been to Sardinia?

D: No, but I've always wanted to go there. Have you heard from Ethel?

J: Ethel Fry?

D: Yes.

J: Haven't you heard? She's become a singer. She's very famous.

D: Really?

J: Have you ever seen Selima Sanchez on TV?

D: Yes.

J: Well, that's her.

D: Ethel is Selima Sanchez?

J: Yes, she's changed her name.

D: You're kidding me!

J: Didn't you realize that was Ethel?

D: No. I've watched her show lots of times and never realized. That's amazing!

14C, Page 119, Exercise 7

Today I'm going to tell you about web conferencing and the different technologies we use. I've divided my presentation into three parts. First, I'll talk about telephone conferences. Then I'll talk about the use of video. And finally I'll give you a breakdown of costs. OK, so let's start with telephone conferences …

14C, Page 119, Exercise 9

1

One Saturday morning last April, Gloria Johnson left her house and she didn't come home for five days. Nobody knows where she went or what happened to her in that time. Gloria doesn't know and her family don't know.

2

You're walking along the street when a homeless person asks you for money. You've got twenty dollars in your pocket and you won't miss it. Should you give them the money? Or should you keep walking?

3

A famous writer once said, 'Getting fired is nature's way of telling us we're in the wrong job.' Well, I've been fired three times since I left school and every time I was in the wrong job. But I've found the right job now and I can help you find the right job, too.

8

4

Babies are often born on Tuesdays. Yes, Tuesdays. In fact sixteen per cent more babies are born on Tuesdays than any other day of the week. It's strange if you think about it. A lot of babies don't decide when to arrive any more. Hospitals decide instead.

14C, Page 119, Exercise 11

1

One Saturday morning last April, Gloria Johnson left her house and she didn't come home for five days. Nobody knows where she went or what happened to her in that time. Gloria doesn't know and her family don't know. Ladies and gentlemen, today I'd like to talk about memory loss and Alzheimer's disease.

2

You're walking along the street when a homeless person asks you for money. You've got twenty dollars in your pocket and you won't miss it. Should you give them the money? Or should you keep walking? Today I'd like to answer that question and tell you about some charities that work with homeless people.

3

A famous writer once said, 'Getting fired is nature's way of telling us we're in the wrong job.' Well, I've been fired three times since I left school and every time I was in the wrong job. But I've found the right job now and I can help you find the right job, too. Today I'm going to tell you about the services we offer at my employment agency.

4

Babies are often born on Tuesdays. Yes, Tuesdays. In fact sixteen per cent more babies are born on Tuesdays than any other day of the week. It's strange if you think about it. A lot of babies don't decide when to arrive any more. Hospitals decide instead. And that's what I'd like to talk about today: how hospitals schedule their work.

15A, Page 123, Exercises 5 and 6

A = Man 1, **B** = Man 2

A: So this is the birthplace of Silicon Valley?

B: Yes, it all began here – a garage in a backyard.

A: How did Bill and Dave meet?

B: They were both students at Stanford University. It's just up the road.

A: What were they studying?

B: Electrical engineering. They weren't studying computer science because the subject didn't exist back then. It was the nineteen thirties.

A: The nineteen thirties? There was a great depression at that time.

B: Yes. It was a very difficult time. A lot of companies were failing.

A: How did they survive?

B: Well, they were both good businessmen. Bill Hewlett was a great inventor and Dave Packard was good at marketing.

15B, Page 124, Exercises 3 and 4

T = Toby, **K** = Keith

T: Keith?

K: Toby, where have you been?

T: Nowhere. Why?

K: Why didn't you answer the phone?

T: Were you trying to reach me?

K: Yes, I rang at about ten.

T: Oh, I was probably in the basement.

K: I called your mobile, too.

T: Ah yes, there's no signal down there.

K: What were you doing in the basement?

T: I was looking for some old files.

K: When I'm out, you need to stay in the office to answer the phones.

T: Yes, Keith.

K: Then I called again about an hour later …

T: Oh. There was a fire alarm and everyone had to leave the building.

K: Is everything OK?

T: Yes, don't worry. It wasn't a real fire. I think someone was smoking and they set off the alarm by accident.

K: Was it you?

T: Me? No, no, I wasn't smoking. I was working when the alarm went off.

K: Oh, well, I've got you now. Listen, I'm on my way back to the office so …

15C, Page 126, Exercise 2

On my way to the meeting, there was an accident and the car in front of me was hit by a truck. Everyone was OK but there was a long delay so I was very late. It was impossible to turn the clock back half an hour but I had to try to do my best. So I ran as fast as I could and I apologized when I arrived. Of course the accident wasn't my fault but I didn't mention it because I didn't want to make excuses. I felt I should accept responsibility.

15C, Page 127, Exercises 7, 8 and 9

1

A = Man, **B** = Woman

A: Did you remember to lock the garage door?

B: Oh, I forgot.

A: Oh.

B: I'm sorry. The phone was ringing so I was rushing to answer it.

A: It's OK.

B: I usually remember. I'll go and lock it now.

A: No, don't worry. I'll do it.

B: Thanks, darling.

2

A = Woman, **B** = Man

A: That email I sent you was private.

B: Yes, I'm so sorry.

A: But you sent it to the rest of the team.

B: I wasn't thinking clearly.

A: I felt embarrassed.

B: I'm really sorry. I'm usually so careful about things like that.

A: Well, it's too late now.

B: It won't happen again, I promise.

3

A = Woman, **B** = Man

A: Coming … coming … Oh, it's you.

B: I've been knocking for ages.

A: Really?

B: Yes, what took you so long?

A: I'm sorry. The radio was on and I didn't hear you.

B: Oh, I see.

A: I didn't mean to ignore you.

B: It's all right. Forget it.

15D, Page 128, Exercises 4 and 5

I heard a funny story the other day. It was about a nice old lady. She was walking along the street when she saw two young boys at the front door of a house. She thought perhaps they were locked out. They were trying to ring the doorbell but it was too high up. The boys were very small and they couldn't reach it. 'Here, let me help you,' the old lady said. So she pressed the bell and gave it a long ring. 'Thanks, now run!' shouted the boys. When she turned round she saw them running away down the street. So it just goes to show that …

15D, Page 129, Exercises 7 and 8

A funny thing happened to me a few years ago. I was giving a training course on some project planning software. There were six people in the class and five of them were working hard. But the sixth one was looking really bored. So at lunchtime I spoke privately with her and asked if the course was useful for her. 'Well, actually,' she said, 'this is the fourth time I've done this course.' I was surprised. 'Why does your boss keep sending you on the same course?' I asked. 'Do you find it difficult to learn?' 'Oh, no,' she said. 'I know how to plan projects, but I hate doing it. So I always tell my boss I can't.' So it just goes to show that …

16A, Page 130, Exercises 2 and 4

A

I = Interviewer, **H** = Heike Keller

I: With us today on 'Dream jobs', is Heike Keller. Welcome Heike.

H: Thank you.

I: Heike, I'm sure everyone would love your job. Can you tell us what you do for a living?

H: Yes, I'm a chocolate taster.

I: So someone pays you money to taste chocolate?

H: Yes.

I: Who?

H: Well, I work for a large department store in London and my job is to travel and find the best chocolate – in this country and abroad. So I buy chocolate for the store and I have to taste a lot of really top quality chocolate.

I: How did you find this job?

H: My friends saw it advertised and they told me about it. They knew I'd love it.

I: And do you?

H: Oh, yes.

I: Is there anything you don't like about it?

H: Well, I'd prefer to travel less and stay home a little more – but I get to see some wonderful places. So this is the perfect job for me. I'd hate to lose it.

I: Could you ever get tired of eating it?

H: Tired of eating chocolate?

I: Yes.

H: Oh no, that'd be impossible.

B

I = Interviewer, **P** = Pilar Benitez

I: With me today is Pilar Benitez.

P: Hi.

I: Pilar is a personal shopper for a department store in London. Pilar, what exactly does a personal shopper do?

P: Well, a client rings the store and books an appointment with me. Then we meet and we have a chat about what they want.

I: Uhuh.

P: Then I take them on to the shop floor and help them choose the right clothes.

I: So you spend your days shopping?

P: Exactly.

I: My teenage daughter would love your job.

P: I love shopping and choosing clothes, so it's the ideal job for me.

I: Do you have any famous clients?

P: Oh yes. I have several singers and I also have one very famous politician who's a regular client.

I: Who?

P: I'd rather not say their name.

I: Oohhh!

P: Sorry, but I don't think he'd want people to know.

I: What would you like to change about your job?

P: Well, sometimes I'd like a little more free time, but no, really … it's so satisfying when my clients look great. I wouldn't want to do anything else.

C

I = Interviewer, **M** = Malcolm White

I: Hi. I'm at the Arcadium Hotel today and with me is Malcolm White. Malcolm, can you tell everyone your job title?

M: Yes, I'm the sleep director.

I: That's a very strange job title. What exactly does a sleep director do?

M: Well it's my job to stay in all our different hotels around the country and check that we provide the best possible conditions for a good night's sleep.

I: So you're the quality control manager?

M: That's right. We're a hotel chain, so our product's a good night's sleep. We wouldn't want to sell a product that wasn't tested.

I: So it's your job to sleep well.

M: That's right. I also speak to other guests and find out how they slept. And I meet sales representatives and collect information on new beds and bedroom furniture.

I: Is there anything you don't like about your job?

M: Oh, no. I wouldn't want to change a thing. Can you think of another job where you're paid to have the most relaxing time possible?

I: And nobody can fire you for sleeping on the job.

M: Exactly!

16B, Page 132, Exercises 2 and 3

A = Woman, **B** = Man

9

A: It's a difficult question. What would you say?

B: I think I'd tell the truth.

A: So you'd say your friend was travelling at thirty-five miles an hour?

B: Yeah, I wouldn't want to lie. It wouldn't be right. What about you?

A: It'd depend. What would happen to my friend if I told the truth?

B: Well, we don't know how serious the accident was. But if the pedestrian died, perhaps he'd go to prison.

A: In that case, it's easy. I'd lie.

B: You'd lie?

A: Yes.

B: But if the accident was serious, it'd be more important to tell the truth.

A: I don't see it like that. If the accident was serious, my friend would really need my help.

16C, Page 134, Exercises 4 and 5

A =Woman, **B** = Man

A: We're running a lot of courses for Chathams next month.

B: They're a very good customer.

A: I'm worried because they've booked five different courses on the same day and we only have four trainers.

B: I know. We're overbooked.

A: I'd like to talk to them and explain. We could try to reschedule one of the courses … OK?

B: Well, erm …

A: What's the problem?

B: Do we want to tell them that we can't handle five courses on one day?

A: I'm afraid they need to know.

B: I thought we might wait a little while.

A: No, I think we'd better tell them now. They need to reorganize their schedules.

B: What I'm saying is we don't want them to think we can't handle their business.

A: I'm only going to reschedule one course.

B: They might think we're too small and find another training supplier.

A: But we have no choice.

B: They sometimes cancel courses at the last minute.

A: Yes, but what if they don't?

B: I think we should wait and see if they cancel first.

A: It's too risky. We have to ask them to reschedule now.

16D, Page 137, Exercises 2 and 3

1
If risking your life is wrong, then why do we have coastguards? Rules are important, but in a life and death situation you have to throw the rulebook out of the window.

2
If a member of the public climbed down a cliff and rescued someone, they would be a hero. Why was Paul Waugh reprimanded? It's not fair.

3
Perhaps we don't know the full story. It makes no sense. Why did they reprimand Paul when he brought so much positive publicity to the coastguards?

4
I think the Coastguard Organization was right. Paul was lucky to survive. If other coastguards behaved like him, more people would die.

5
I think Paul Waugh just wanted publicity. Why did he go on a radio show? Why couldn't he resign quietly?

6
Paul's managers are crazy. What would they do if their child was hanging from a cliff? Go and get their rulebooks?

Present tenses

Present simple

Use

We use the present simple to talk about regular activities, long-term situations and things that are always true.

> I **play** football every Saturday.
>
> She **works** for a software company.
>
> Customers **want** low prices

Form

Affirmative sentences Use the base form of the verb. Add *s* to third person forms.	I/You/We/They **work**. He/She/It **works**.
Negative sentences Use *don't* (*do not*). Use *doesn't* (*does not*) with third person forms.	You **don't work**. He **doesn't work**.
Questions Use *do* or *does*.	**Do** I/you/we/they **work**? **Does** he/she/it **work**? Where **do** you **work**?
Short answers Use *do* or *does*.	Do you work in a garage? **Yes**, I **do**. Does he pay cash? **No**, he **doesn't**.

Spelling of third person forms

1 Regular verbs	+ *s*	*speak* → *speaks*
2 *do* and *go*	+ *es*	*do* → *does* *go* → *goes*
3 Verbs ending with *ss*, *ch*, *sh* or *x* sounds	+ *es*	*miss* → *misses* *watch* → *watches* *wash* → *washes* *fix* → *fixes*
4 Verbs ending in consonant +*y*	– *y* + *ies*	*try* → *tries*

Pronunciation

The pronunciation of the third person *s* depends how the verb ends. Some English consonants are voiced and some are unvoiced. Place two fingers on your throat. Say 'sssssss'. Then say 'zzzzzz'. You should feel no vibration when you say 's' and vibration when you say 'z'. The vibration comes from voicing.

Some voiced sounds are: *l, n, v, m*

Some unvoiced sounds are: *p, k, f, t*

Verbs ending with voiced sounds: Pronounce the *s* as /z/	*calls, learns, receives, comes, plays, goes*
Verbs ending with an unvoiced sound: Pronounce the *s* as /s/	*stops, talks, laughs, supports, looks*
Special cases: Verbs ending with a 'hissing' sound: Add an extra syllable: /ɪz/	*passes, advises, fixes, changes, watches*

Frequency adverbs

We usually place frequency adverbs before the main verb.

*I **sometimes carry** business cards.*

*He **usually remembers** my name.*

Frequency adverbs usually come after the verb *be*.

*I **am often** out of the office.*

*Life **is generally** more interesting if we have lots of friends.*

Present continuous

Use

We use the present continuous to talk about current activities or short-term activities.

*I**'m checking** my email at the moment.*

*She**'s training** for the New York marathon.*

> ⚠ There are some verbs that we do not usually use in their continuous form because they describe states, not activities. Examples are *want*, *need*, *know* and *have* (in the sense of *own* or *possess*).

Form

Affirmative sentences Use the verb *be* + the *-ing* form of the verb.	*I am working.* *You/We/They are working.* *He/She/It is working.*
Negative sentences Use the negative form of the verb *be*.	*You aren't working.* *He isn't working.*
Questions Change the word order.	*Am I working?* *Are you/we/they working?* *Is he/she/it working?*
Short answers Use the verb *be*.	*Are you looking for me?* **Yes, I am. / No, I'm not.** *Is he waiting in my office?* **Yes, he is. / No, he isn't.**

Spelling

1 Verbs ending in *e*	Drop the *e* before *-ing*.	*write → writing*
2 Verbs ending in a single vowel + a single consonant	Double the consonant after stressed syllables. Don't double the consonant after unstressed syllables	*get → getting* *be<u>gin</u> → beginning* *<u>hap</u>pen → happening*
3 *lie* and *die*	Change *ie* to *y*.	*lie → lying*

Present perfect

Use

We use the present perfect to speak about the past and the present together. We use it to talk about:

1 Present results – past actions with results that are important in the present:

*We**'ve improved** the design. (It's better now.)*

*I**'ve finished** the report. (You can have it now.)*

We often use the present perfect to give news:

*He**'s** just **bought** a new house.*

*They**'ve updated** their website.*

2 Unfinished actions – actions or states that began in the past and are still continuing now:

*We**'ve known** each another for ten years.*

*I**'ve had** a cold since Tuesday.*

In these sentences, we use *for* with a point in time and *since* with a period of time:

*She**'s worked** here since 2008.*

*He**'s lived** here for five years.*

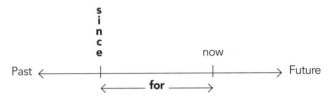

3 Experience – finished actions that happened at an indefinite time in the past:

*I love that film. I**'ve seen** it three times. (three times in my life before now)*

*She**'s worked** in four different countries. (it's part of her life's experience)*

***Have** you ever **been** to Paris? (at any time up to now)*

*I**'ve** never **seen** that before. (not at any time in my life)*

For information on when we use the present perfect and the past simple, see page 167.

Form

Affirmative sentences Use *have/has* + past participle. Irregular verbs sometimes have a special past participle form. For a list of irregular verbs, see page 176.	*I/You/We/They have finished the report. He/She/It has finished the report. I/You/We/They have been to Italy. He/She/It has been to Italy.*
Negative sentences Use *has/hasn't* + past participle.	*I/You/We/They haven't done this before. He/She/It hasn't done this before.*
Questions Change the word order.	***Have** I/you/we/they ever **done** this before? **Has** he/she/it ever **been** to Helsinki? **Where have** you **been**?*
Short answers Use *has/have* or *hasn't/haven't*.	*Has she written to you yet?* **Yes**, she **has**. *Have you seen Peter?* **No**, I **haven't**.

Past tenses

Past simple

Use

We use the past simple to talk about finished actions and situations in the past. One common use is to tell stories.

*I **went** to a birthday party last weekend and **met** an old friend.*

*One day, she **decided** to set up her own business.*

*A funny thing **happened** to me last month.*

Form

Affirmative sentences Add –ed to the base form of the verb. There is no special third person form.	work → **worked** I/You/He/She/It/We/They **worked**.
Irregular verbs have a special past form. See page 176 for a list of irregular verbs.	*The train **left** at ten.* *We **drove** to the station.*
The past form of *be* is *was* and *were*.	*He/She/It **was** in Paris.* *We/You/They **were** in Cairo.*
Negative sentences Use *didn't (did not)* + the base form of the verb.	*It **didn't** work.* *The train **didn't** leave on time.*
With the verb *be*, use *wasn't (was not)* and *weren't (were not)*.	*He **wasn't** at the meeting.* *We **weren't** late.*
Questions Use *did* + the base form of the verb.	**Did** it **work**? *What time **did** the train **leave**?*
With the verb *be*, change the word order.	***Was he** at the meeting?* ***Were you** late?*
Short answers Use *did/didn't*. With the verb *be*, use *was/were* or *were/weren't*.	*Did they win?* **Yes**, they **did**. / **No**, they **didn't**. *Was he successful?* **Yes** he **was**. / **No**, he **wasn't**. *Were you late?* **Yes**, I **was**. / **No**, I **wasn't**.

Spelling of regular verbs

1 Verbs ending in *e*	Add *d*	*live → lived*
2 Verbs ending in a single vowel + a single consonant	Double the consonant after stressed syllables. Don't double the consonant after unstressed syllables.	*stop → stopped* *prefer → preferred* *happen → happened*
3 Verbs ending in a consonant + *y*	Change *y* to *ied*.	*try → tried*

Pronunciation of regular verbs

The pronunciation of regular verbs depends on whether the verb ending is voiced or unvoiced.

Some voiced sounds are: *b, d, g, j, l, m, n, r, v, z*

Some unvoiced sounds are: *c, f, p, s, t, x*

For more information on voiced and unvoiced consonants, see page 164.

Verbs ending in voiced sounds: end with a /d/ sound, e.g. *cleaned*	*cleaned, retired, planned, earned, received, changed, discovered, happened, trained, opened*
Verbs ending in unvoiced sounds: end with a /t/ sound, e.g. *washed*	*washed, asked, focused, talked, worked, based, placed, looked, stopped, missed, promised*
Verbs ending with a /d/ or /t/ sound: add an extra syllable: /ɪd/, e.g. *wanted*	*wanted, needed, created, speeded up, exceeded, depended, contacted, decided, visited, mended*

> ⚠️ Make sure you pronounce the extra syllable with verbs ending with a /t/ or /d/ sound. The extra syllable is pronounced /ɪd/, not /ed/.
>
> *want* (one syllable) *wanted* (two syllables)
> *need* (one syllable) *needed* (two syllables)

Past simple vs present perfect

Use

We use both these tenses to describe actions that started or ended in the past. Which tense we select depends on whether:

a we're referring to a definite or indefinite time.

b the action is finished or unfinished.

We often use time expressions like *recently, already, yet, since, ever, never* and *just* with the present perfect.

We often use time expressions like *yesterday, ago, last night/week/month,* etc. with the past tense.

Indefinite time	Definite time
Have you **seen** John **recently**?	**Did** you **see** John **yesterday**?
We**'ve already met**.	We **met when** we **were at university**.
Has the meeting **finished yet**?	The meeting **finished an hour ago**.
We **haven't spoken since** Friday.	We **saw** each other **last Friday**.
Have you **ever been** to Tokyo?	I **visited** the Tokyo office **in 2008**.
I**'ve never been** to Greece.	We **didn't visit** Athens **last year**.
The show **has just started**.	The show **started at 7:30**.

Unfinished actions	Finished actions
She**'s worked** here **since** 2008. (She still works here.)	She **worked** here **in 2008**.
I**'ve had** this cell phone **for three months**. (I still have it.)	I **had** the phone **for three months** but then I lost it. (I don't have it any more.)

 British speakers use the present perfect slightly more in conversation than American speakers. American speakers sometimes use a past tense where only a present perfect is possible in British English.

British and American speakers both use *yet, already* and *just* with the present perfect.

***Have** you **done** it **yet**?*

*I**'ve already done** it.*

*I**'ve just finished**. (BrE and AmE)*

American speakers might also use a past tense with *yet* and *already*.

***Did** you **do** it **yet**?*

*I **already did** it. (AmE)*

British and American speakers both use *just* with the past tense to describe something that happened a moment ago.

***Did** you **just** call me?*

British speakers generally use *just* with the present perfect to give news.

*I**'ve just passed** my driving test!*

American speakers might say this, too, but they also use the past tense to give news.

*I **just passed** my driving test.*

Past continuous

Use

We use the past continuous to talk about the background situation in a story.

> We **were living** in Paris at the time.

> It **was raining** so I offered him a lift.

> They **were working** on the top floor when the fire alarm went off.

Form

Affirmative sentences Use *was/were* + the *-ing* form of the verb.	He **was studying**. We **were wearing** security badges.
Negative sentences Use *wasn't* (was not) and *weren't* (were not).	He **wasn't studying**. They **weren't wearing** security badges.
Questions Change the word order.	**Was** he **studying**? What **were** you **doing**?
Short answers Use *was/were* or *wasn't/weren't*.	Was he studying? **Yes**, he **was**. Were they wearing security badges? **No,** they **weren't**.

Obligation and permission modals

Use

1 *can* and *can't*

We can use *can* and *can't* to talk about things that are or aren't allowed or permitted.

NO PARKING
8 a.m. – 6 p.m.

You **can't** park here during the daytime.

You **can** park here after six o'clock at night.

2 *must*, *have to*, and *need to*

We use *must*, *have to* and *need to* to describe things that are necessary or obligatory.

We **must / have to / need to** turn left here.

Must is the strongest verb. We rarely use *must* to give orders to other people but we might use *must* to give orders to ourselves.

I **must** lose weight.

We **must** go on a diet.

Have to and *need to* are more common.

I **have to** log on to the computer system.

You **need** to give me a password.

In spoken English, people also use *want to* when they're giving instructions.

Don't tell anyone your password. You **want to** keep it secret.

3 *mustn't*, *don't have to* and *don't need to*

The positive forms of *must*, *have to* and *need to* have similar meanings. But the negative forms are different.

You **don't have to** drive at 70 miles per hour but you **mustn't** drive more than 70 miles per hour.

Mustn't describes things that are forbidden or not allowed.

Employees **must not** accept valuable gifts from clients.

Hurry up! We **mustn't** be late.

Don't have to and *don't need to* describe things that are not necessary.

We have plenty of time. You **don't have to** hurry.

It's only a small gift. You **don't need to** report it.

We can also say *needn't* instead of *don't need to*. The meanings are same.

It's OK. You **needn't** tell anyone.

4 *should* and *shouldn't*

Should and *shouldn't* are weaker forms of *must* and *mustn't*.

You **must** read the documents. (It's necessary.)

You **should** read the documents. (It's a good idea – the correct thing to do.)

You **mustn't** tell anyone your password. (It's forbidden.)

You **shouldn't** tell anyone your password. (It's not a good idea.)

We often use *should* with *think* to exchange opinions.

I **think** we **should** stick to the agenda in meetings.

I don't **think** people **should** take mobile phone calls in meetings.

Do you **think** we **should** hold meetings standing up? Yes, I **do**. / No, I **don't**.

> ⚠ American speakers use *must* less frequently than British speakers and they do not use the contraction *mustn't*. Instead of *must*, they might say *have to* or *required to*. Instead of *mustn't* they might say *not allowed to*.
>
> We **have to** meet the targets.
>
> We're **required to** meet the targets.
>
> We're **not allowed to** tell anyone our password.

Form

Modal verbs: *can, must, should*	
Affirmative sentences Use *can/must/should* + the base form of the verb. There is no special third person form.	You **can park** here for as long as you want. I **must remember** to switch off the lights. She **shouldn't agree** to that.
Negative sentences Add *not*	We **can't agree** to that. I **mustn't forget**. We **shouldn't worry** about it.
Questions Change the word order.	**Can I wear** jeans? **Must I report** this? **Should I wear** a suit and tie?

Semi-modals: *have to, need to*	
Affirmative sentences Add *s* to third person forms.	He **has to tell** his customers about it right away. She **needs to ask** her boss if it's OK.
Negative sentences Use *don't (do not)/doesn't (does not)*.	You **don't have to report** it. He **doesn't need to report** it.
Questions Change the word order.	**Do I have to attend** the meeting? **Does** the meeting **have to be** on Monday?

> ⚠ Do not use *to* after full modal verbs.
> You **should** report this.
> NOT ~~You should to report this.~~

4

Conditional sentences

Conditional sentences have two or more clauses joined with *if*. We use them in two kinds of situations.

1 Normal situations where we use normal verb forms.

*If we **charge** for parking, more employees **will cycle** to work.*

*Life **is** more interesting **if** you **have** a lot of friends.*

*If it's **not** the right size, **bring** it back.*

*If you're **going to keep staring** at me and I'm **going to keep staring** back, we should introduce ourselves.*

See the notes below on first conditionals for more examples.

2 Imaginary or unreal situations where we don't use normal verb forms.

*If I **had** a problem, my friend **would support** me. (= imaginary because I don't have a problem)*

*If I **were** you, **I'd tell** the truth. (= unreal because I'm not you)*

See the notes on the right on second conditionals for more examples.

Punctuation

The *if*-clause can be the first or the second part of the sentence. When it comes at the beginning, we usually put a comma between the two clauses.

You'll feel better if you do some exercise.

If you do some exercise, you'll feel better.

I'd feel terrible if the girl fell.

If the girl fell, I'd feel terrible.

The first conditional and similar forms

Use

We use the first conditional to talk about a possibility in the future. The *if*-clause contains the condition and the other clause contains the result.

If you take more exercise, you'll feel fitter.

You'll double the number of fish you catch if you buy another boat.

Form

First conditional	
Use *if* + present simple, *will/wont* (do).	*If we only **have** one income, it'**ll be** hard to survive.* *If the price **is** too high, she **won't buy** it.*
Similar conditionals	
Use *if* + verb forms that are normal for the situation.	*If you **work** harder, you **can earn** more money.* *If you **mix** blue with yellow, you **get** green.* *If it's too expensive, we **shouldn't buy** it.* *If employees **haven't upgraded** their skills, they **have to go**.*

⚠️ We cannot usually use *will* in the *if*-clause. Instead we use a present tense to express a future idea.

*If I **see** Peter, I'll tell him to call you.*

NOT ~~If I will see Peter, I'll tell him to call you.~~

The second conditional

Use

We use the second conditional to talk about imaginary or unreal situations.

*If I **had** six months paid holiday, I **would travel** round the world. (I don't have six months paid holiday.)*

Form

Second conditional	
Use *if* + past simple, *would/wouldn't* (do).	*If we **didn't have** friends we could trust, the world **would be** a worse place.* *If I **was** rich, I **wouldn't carry on working**.*

1 In spoken English, *would* often contracts to '*d*.

2 In formal English, we use *were* instead of *was* in all persons in the second conditional.

*If I **were** in your situation, I **would resign**.*

3 We can also use other modal verbs like *could* and *might* in second conditional sentences.

*If I **had** my boss's job, I **could make** some big changes.*

*If I **was** in that situation, I **might lie** to my boss.*

The passive

Use

We use the passive when we are more interested in the action than in the person who does it.

*Forty per cent of the budget **is spent** on marketing. (We are interested in how much is spent, not the person who spends it.)*

*The movie **was dubbed**. (We are interested in the movie, not who dubbed it.)*

We often use the passive when we don't know who did an action.

*My wallet **was stolen**. (I don't know who took it.)*

When we want to say who did an action, we use the preposition *by*.

*The Laff Box **was invented by** Charlie Douglass.*

Passives are more common in written than spoken English. They are also more common when we are writing or speaking in a formal style.

Form

The passive	
Affirmative sentences Use *be* + past participle.	*Prizes **are given** to the most entertaining couple.* *The book **was written** by Jhumpa Lahiri.*
Negative sentences Use *be* + *not* + past participle.	*It **isn't made** of gold.* *The goods **weren't delivered** on time.*
Questions Change the word order.	***Are** everybody's seat belts **fastened**?* *Where **was** the movie **shot**?*
Short answers Use *was/were* or *were/weren't*.	*Was it made in China?* ***Yes**, it **was**. / **No**, it **wasn't**.* *Were you offered the job?* ***Yes**, I **was**. / **No**, I **wasn't**.*

Grammar reference

Nouns and adjectives

Countable and uncountable nouns

Countable and uncountable nouns	
Countable nouns ...	Uncountable nouns ...
can be singular or plural. dollar → dollars bag → bags	cannot be plural. money → ~~monies~~ luggage → ~~luggages~~
are used with singular or plural verb forms. **A dollar doesn't** buy much these days. **Dollars aren't** a good investment at this time.	are only used with singular verb forms. **Money doesn't** grow on trees.

1 *much*

We use *much* with uncountable nouns, mainly in negative sentences, questions and with *too*.

>   We don't have **much information** about the market.

>   How **much money** do you have?

>   I've got **too much luggage**. I can't carry it all.

2 *many*

We use *many* with countable nouns, mainly in negatives sentences, questions and with *too*.

>   There aren't **many people** here today.

>   How **many dollars** are there to the euro?

>   I've got **too many bags**. I can't carry them all.

3 *a lot of / lots of*

We use *a lot of* and *lots of* with countable and uncountable nouns.

>   We have lots of jobs to do today.

>   We don't have a lot of time.

A lot of is a very common expression in informal spoken English. In more formal English we prefer other expressions like *a great deal of* + uncountable noun and *a great many* + countable noun.

4 We use *enough* with countable and uncountable nouns. We place *enough* before a noun and after an adjective.

>   My apartment isn't **big enough**. I don't have **enough space**.

-ing forms

Use

1 We use *-ing* to form part of continuous tenses.

>   I'**m flying** to Manchester tomorrow.

>   What **were** you **doing** when I called?

2 *-ing* forms can also be used as nouns. We can use them when an activity is the subject of a sentence.

>   **Taking** phone calls in a restaurant is bad manners.

3 We also use *-ing* forms after some verbs. This includes most of the verbs we use to talk about liking or disliking something.

>   I **like playing** games on my mobile.

>   I **hate** people **dropping** litter in the street.

>   I **don't mind waiting**.

4 Some adjectives also end in *-ing*.

>   It's **interesting** to look around other people's houses.

>   He has a very **annoying** habit.

5 In some cases there is a related adjective which ends in *-ed*. We use the adjective ending *-ed* to talk about how the person feels. We use the adjective ending *-ing* to describe the person or thing that causes the feeling.

>   **I was interested** to hear his talk. (Interested describes the reaction to the talk.)

>   He gave a very **interesting talk**. (Interesting describes the talk.)

Comparative and superlative adjectives

	Moscow	Mexico City	Beijing
Population	10.4 million	19.2 million	17.4 million
Cost of living	$$$$$	$$$	$$$$

Use

1 We use comparative adjectives to compare two things.

*Beijing is **larger than** Moscow.*

*Beijing is **more expensive than** Mexico City.*

*Mexico City is **less expensive than** Beijing.*

2 We use superlative adjectives to compare three or more things.

*Mexico City is **the largest** city in the world.*

*Mexico City is **the least expensive** of the three cities and Moscow is **the most expensive**.*

Form

Comparative and superlative adjectives	
Short adjectives Add *-er /-est*	*Beijing is **cheaper** than Moscow but Mexico City is **the cheapest**.*
Long adjectives Use *more/most* or *less/least*	*Beijing is **more expensive** than Mexico City but Moscow's **the most expensive**.* *Mexico City is **less expensive** than Moscow, but Beijing is **the least expensive**.*

Irregular adjectives *good better best*	*The weather in Beijing is **better** than the weather in Moscow but Mexico City has **the best** weather.*
bad worse worst	*The traffic in Beijing is **worse** than in Moscow but Mexico City probably has **the worst** traffic in the world.*
much/many more most	*Moscow has **many** traffic jams but Beijing has **more**. Mexico City has **the most** traffic jams.*
Other cases With many two-syllable adjectives, we use *more/most*. Examples: *modern, recent, famous, correct, normal, frequent* With some two-syllable adjectives, we use either *-er/-est* or *more/most*. Examples: *clever, simple, tired, stupid, polite, narrow, quiet* It's correct to say: *cleverer* or *more clever; the cleverest* or *the most clever*. If you're not sure whether to use *-er/est* or *more/most*, check in a good dictionary.	

Spelling of short adjectives

Most short adjectives: *high, cheap*	Add *-er/-est*	*higher/highest* *cheaper/cheapest*
Adjectives ending in e: *large, nice*	Add *-r/-st*	*larger/largest* *nicer/nicest*
Adjectives ending in one vowel + consonant: *big, hot*	Double the consonant but don't double *w*	*bigger/biggest* *hotter/hottest* *low/lowest,* *slower/slowest*

Numbers

Cardinal and ordinal numbers

Cardinals		Ordinals	
1	one	1st	first
2	two	2nd	second
3	three	3rd	third
4	four	4th	fourth
5	five	5th	fifth
6	six	6th	sixth
7	seven	7th	seventh
8	eight	8th	eighth
9	nine	9th	ninth
10	ten	10th	tenth
11	eleven	11th	eleventh
12	twelve	12th	twelfth
13	thirteen	13th	thirteenth
14	fourteen	14th	fourteenth
15	fifteen	15th	fifteenth
16	sixteen	16th	sixteenth
17	seventeen	17th	seventeenth
18	eighteen	18th	eighteenth
19	nineteen	19th	nineteenth
20	twenty	20th	twentieth
21	twenty-one	21st	twenty-first
22	twenty-two	22nd	twenty-second
23	twenty-three	23rd	twenty-third
24	twenty-four	24th	twenty-fourth

 We write *–th* with most ordinals, but not 1st, 2nd and 3rd

Pronunciation

We stress numbers ending *-teen* and *-ty* differently.	16 → six**teen** oO 60 → **six**ty Oo 18 → eigh**teen** oO 80 → **eigh**ty Oo
The stress is the same when we say them in front of other words	**six**teen people Oo **six**ty people Oo **eigh**teen years old Oo **eigh**ty years old Oo

Other common expressions

A dozen	= 12	We're expecting about a dozen people to attend.
A couple of	= 2	A couple of customers asked that question.
A pair of	= 2	A pair of shoes. (two that go together)

1
a quarter,
¼

2
a half,
½

3
a third,
⅓

4
two thirds,
⅔

5
three quarters,
¾

6
seven eighths,
⅞

Decimals

In English, write decimal points as a point, not a comma.	2.4 (NOT *2,4*)	
After the point, say numbers separately.	65.65	Sixty five point six five
After the point, 0 is *zero* or *oh*.	9.06	Nine point oh six Nine point zero six
Before the point, 0 is *nought* or *zero*. Sometimes we don't pronounce the 0.	0.45	Nought point four five Zero point four five Point four five

Larger numbers

Tens			Large numbers	
10	ten		100	A/one hundred
20	twenty		1,000	A/one thousand
30	thirty		1,000,000 (1m)	A/one million
40	forty		1,000,000,000 (1b/1bn)	A/one billion
50	fifty		365	Three hundred (and) sixty-five
60	sixty		202	Two hundred and two
70	seventy			Two oh two (AmE)
80	eighty		1,800	One thousand eight hundred
90	ninety			Eighteen hundred

British speakers generally say *and* before tens. American speakers generally don't.	2,355	Two thousand, three hundred **and** fifty-five (BrE) Two thousand, three hundred fifty-five (AmE)
We sometimes use fractions and decimals with large numbers.	3,500 3.5bn	Three and a half thousand Three point five billion
Between every three numbers, we write a comma (not a point).	Three million	3,000,000

We don't put plural *s* on words like *hundred, thousand, million* after a number. We say:

Three million (NOT ~~Three millions~~)

Long numbers

We generally say numbers separately in telephone, credit card and other long reference numbers. We often group them in threes or fours.	0671 824 9753 *Oh six seven one … eight two four … nine seven five three*
British English speakers often say 'double' or 'triple' with repeated numbers. American speakers don't.	488 577 3888 *Four double eight, five double seven, three triple eight (BrE)* *Four eight eight, five seven seven, three eight eight eight (AmE)*

Measurements and dimensions

1 m 60	*One metre sixty*
92 kg	*Ninety-two kilograms*
2 cm x 3 cm	*Two centimetres by three centimetres*
90°	*Ninety degrees*
32° F	*Thirty-two degrees Fahrenheit*
-3° C	*Minus three degrees Celsius*
60 km/h	*Sixty kilometers per/an hour*
50 mph	*Fifty miles per/an hour*

Prices

We write the money symbol before the number but say it after.	£79.99 → *Seventy-nine* **pounds**, *ninety-nine pence*
Sometimes we don't say the money symbol.	£79.99 → *Seventy-nine, ninety-nine*

Years and dates

We say years before 2000 in two parts	1998	*Nineteen ninety-eight*
We say the years 2000–2009 as one number	2008	*Two thousand and eight*
From 2010 onwards, we can say them in two parts.	2010	*Twenty ten*
British people say *the* and *of* with dates, but they do not write them.	8th May, 2012	**The** *eighth* **of** *May, twenty twelve*
In American English, dates are written differently. The month comes first.	5.8.2012	*May eighth, twenty twelve*

⚠ 5/8/2012 is a date in May for American speakers, not August.

Telling the time

We often say the time by saying the numbers.	7:45 9:20 3:00	*Seven forty-five* *Nine twenty* *Three/Three o'clock*
British speakers sometimes use the twenty-four hour clock, especially to talk about schedules. American speakers don't.	18:30	*The flight leaves at eighteen thirty. (BrE)* *The flight leaves at six thirty. (AmE)*
When American speakers want to be specific, they name a part of the day and write a.m. or p.m. British speakers can do this, too.	6:30 p.m.	*The flight leaves at six thirty in the evening. (AmE)*

⚠ We can say *six o'clock* or *six thirty* but we don't say ~~six thirty o'clock~~.

Here are some other ways to say the time:

1 *Three o'clock*
Three a.m./p.m.

2 *Five past seven*
Five after seven (AmE)

3 *Half past eight*
Eight thirty

4 *A quarter past six*
A quarter after six (AmE)

5 *Twenty to two*
Twenty of two (AmE)

Irregular verb list

Verb	Past simple	Past participle
be	was/were	been
beat	beat	beaten
become	became	become
begin	began	begun
bend	bent	bent
break	broke	broken
bring	brought	brought
build	built	built
buy	bought	bought
burn	burnt/burned	burnt/burned
burst	burst	burst
catch	caught	caught
choose	chose	chosen
come	came	come
cost	cost	cost
cut	cut	cut
deal	dealt	dealt
do	did	done
draw	drew	drawn
dream	dreamt/dreamed	dreamt/dreamed
drink	drank	drunk
drive	drove	driven
eat	ate	eaten
fall	fell	fallen
feel	felt	felt
fight	fought	fought
find	found	found
fly	flew	flown
forget	forgot	forgotten
freeze	froze	frozen
get	got	got (BrE) / gotten (AmE)
give	gave	given
go	went	gone/been
grow	grew	grown
have	had	had
hear (hɪər)	heard (hɜːrd)	heard (hɜːrd)
hide	hid	hidden
hit	hit	hit
hold	held	hold
hurt	hurt	hurt
keep	kept	kept
know	knew	known
lay	laid	laid
lead	led	led
learn	learnt/learned	learnt/learned
leave	left	left

Verb	Past simple	Past participle
lend	lent	lent
let	let	let
lie	lay	lain
light	lit	lit
lose	lost	lost
make	made	made
mean	meant	meant
meet	met	met
pay	paid	paid
put	put	put
quit	quit	quit
read (riːd)	read (red)	read (red)
ride	rode	ridden
ring	rang	rung
rise	rose	risen
run	ran	run
say	said	said
see	saw	seen
sell	sold	sold
send	sent	sent
set	set	set
shoot	shot	shot
show	showed	shown
shut	shut	shut
sit	sat	sat
sink	sank	sunk
sleep	slept	slept
speak	spoke	spoken
spend	spent	spent
spill	spilt/spilled	spilt/spilled
spoil	spoilt	spoilt
spread	spread	spread
stand	stood	stood
steal	stole	stolen
stick	stuck	stuck
swim	swam	swum
take	took	taken
teach	taught	taught
tell	told	told
think	thought	thought
throw	threw	thrown
understand	understood	understood
wake	woke	woken
wear	wore	worn
win	won	won
write	wrote	written